## ALSO BY DAVID ROBERTS

# THE
# PUEBLO
# REVOLT

### The Secret Rebellion
### That Drove the Spaniards
### Out of the Southwest

# David Roberts

Simon & Schuster Paperbacks
New York   London   Toronto   Sydney

SIMON & SCHUSTER PAPERBACKS
Rockefeller Center
1230 Avenue of the Americas
New York, NY 10020

First Simon & Schuster paperback edition 2005

Simon & Schuster Paperbacks and colophon are registered trademarks of
Simon & Schuster, Inc.

For information about special discounts for bulk purchases, please contact
Simon & Schuster Special Sales at 1-800-456-6798 or business@simonandschuster.com

*Designed by Nancy Singer Olaguera*

Manufactured in the United States of America

10   9   8   7

The Library of Congress has cataloged the hardcover edition as follows:
Roberts, David, date.
The Pueblo Revolt : the secret rebellion that drove the Spaniards out of the
Southwest / David Roberts.
p.     cm.
Includes bibliographical references and index.
1. Pueblo Revolt, 1680. 2. Pueblo Indians—Government relations. 3. Pueblo Indians
—Colonization. 4. New Mexico—History—To 1848. 5. Mexico—History—Spanish
colony, 1540–1810. I. Title.
E99.P9R538 2004
978.9'01—dc22                    2004048706
ISBN-13: 978-0-7432-5516-5
ISBN-10: 0-7432-5516-X
ISBN-13: 978-0-7432-5517-2 (Pbk)
ISBN-10: 0-7432-5517-8 (Pbk)

In memory of my sister,

Jennifer Roberts Nobles,

who loved a New Mexico I never knew

1946–2004

# CONTENTS

# CONTENTS

by the Puebloans during the Revolt. And who knows how many pueblos today still hoard, in secret repositories, long-lost chronicles seized from the oppressor in 1680? What would a scholar not give to be able to peruse the documents Bill Whatley told me about that October morning at Jemez!

Watching the men strike flakes of chert free from their cores, I mused further—about just what value those hoarded documents must possess for the Jemez. As I would come to see, in struggling to fathom photocopies of records from the archives in Mexico City, the orthography of handwritten Spanish in the seventeenth century is so arcane that only experts in a field called paleography ("old writing") can read it. It seemed doubtful that anyone at Jemez could decipher the records seized in 1680 and guarded so zealously ever since. In Ladakh, I had seen Buddhist monks reverently curating ancient scrolls that they had no idea how to read. But that veneration could be explained by faith: the scrolls had the power of holy relics. Perhaps for the Jemez, the three-century-old scribblings that they kept hidden away from the eyes of prying scholars were relics in a reverse sense: talismans of the tyrannic power the Puebloans had wrested from the Spanish in 1680, charms against the oppression they had borne ever returning in full force.

In any event, all kinds of knowledge of what scholar France V. Scholes called "troublous times in New Mexico" vanished in the bonfires and seizures of 1680. Santa Fe, for instance, was founded in 1610, yet the earliest surviving map of the town was drawn only in 1767. Of course there were earlier maps, but they have disappeared. As a consequence, we do not know precisely where the climactic battle in August 1680 between the Puebloans and Spanish, culminating in the siege of Santa Fe, took place.

In another respect, the Spanish record is fundamentally unreliable. So sure were the officers and settlers in New Mexico that they carried a superior civilization into the midst of benighted savages, so arrogant were the friars in wielding the absolute truth of their Catholic faith to wipe out the "hideous apostasies" of the native religion, that it is fre-

twelve years of freedom. Yet about how the Revolt had been organized and pulled off, about the eighty-two years of tribulation under the Spanish yoke that had preceded it, about how after 1680 Puebloan unity had fallen apart and allowed the reconquest, and above all about what had happened in New Mexico during those twelve years without the Spanish, I knew next to nothing.

Two years ago, I scratched the old itch and returned to the Pueblo Revolt, as I began work on this present book. The mild sense of guilt I felt about my ignorance was shared, as I soon learned, by many a Southwest savant. Archaeologists and anthropologists who had toiled in New Mexico for two or three decades confessed to me a kindred ignorance of the details of the great uprising of 1680. A handful of books purported to cover the Revolt, but to my mind they did so in an unsatisfying fashion, leaving the central questions unanswered. All kinds of myths had attached themselves to that stunning interlude in New Mexico history, but it seemed impossible to test the truths that lay at their core. Most surprisingly of all, I began to suspect that even among today's Puebloans, the living memory of the Revolt was dim.

This struck me as a strange state of affairs. As one historian justly observes, the Pueblo Revolt remains "the point of highest drama in New Mexico's long history." From the Indian point of view, the Revolt, in its complete eradication of the European oppressor from the people's homeland for more than a decade, far outmatches in terms of lasting impact the famous massacre of Custer's army by the Sioux and Cheyenne at Little Big Horn in 1876. In its tragic dimension, the Revolt and reconquest took a toll among the Puebloans every bit as dolorous as the better-known campaigns of the Cherokee Trail of Tears or the Navajo Long Walk to Bosque Redondo.

As I immersed myself in research on the Pueblo Revolt, I discovered that the Spanish record of that conflagration was voluminous and vivid. Yet the documents preserved in archives in Seville and Mexico City represent but a portion of the testimony recorded at the time by friars and governors, for great piles of those documents were burned

less lumps of chert and obsidian into sleek points that—hafted to straight sticks that were fletched with bird feathers, sent winging from a well-flexed bow—could bring down a deer in the forest or an enemy on the trail. Gradually, however, during the decades after the Spanish conquest of New Mexico in 1598, under Don Juan de Oñate, the Puebloans lost the art of arrowhead making. There was no reason to keep that craft alive, once the men had learned how to use harquebuses (the small-caliber muskets of the day) and, later, rifles.

Through twenty years of trial and error, Bradley had taught himself to flint-knap so well that he could turn a core of creamy chert into any kind of projectile point he wished, from the long, fluted Clovis point favored by Paleo-Indians 9,000 years ago to the tiny triangular arrowheads Puebloans reserved, in the years just before the Spanish came, for killing rabbits. On that chilly October morning, the Zia and Jemez men had assembled under Bradley's tutelage not out of some atavistic yearning for a golden age before the Europeans had come and changed everything, but simply because they had formed an archery club.

Beside me sat another Anglo, Bill Whatley, who was serving as official archaeologist for Jemez Pueblo. It was Whatley who had arranged my visit. Evidently the paradox before our eyes had set him musing, just as it had me, for now, out of the blue, he leaned close and whispered in my ear, "Do you know that these guys still have Spanish documents they seized during the Pueblo Revolt, which no Anglos have ever seen?"

Electrified in that moment by Whatley's revelation, I have been haunted by it through the ten years since that October morning in front of the visitor center. In 1994, despite all the research I had done for my Anasazi book, I possessed only a vague understanding of the Pueblo Revolt. In 1680, I knew, the various pueblos scattered along the Rio Grande and to the west had united, for the first and only time in their history, to make a lightning strike that drove all the Spaniards out of New Mexico. Inevitably, I knew, the Spaniards had returned and accomplished the reconquest, but not before the pueblos had enjoyed

# PROLOGUE

At dawn, frost silvered the yellow cottonwood leaves strewn in the dirt in front of the visitor center. The men had built a bonfire to warm their morning's play. A fusillade of sharp reports—stone knocking upon stone—rang echoless in the cold, clear air. I sat just outside the circle of men, witnessing a cultural paradox whose roots stretched more than five centuries into the past.

It was October 1994. Near the end of three years of research for a book about those prehistoric geniuses of the Southwest, the Anasazi, I had come to Jemez Pueblo in northern New Mexico. Nine of the ten men laboring before my eyes were from Jemez and its neighbor pueblo, Zia, ten miles to the south. As Puebloans, they were direct descendants of the Anasazi who had built such wondrous villages as Cliff Palace at Mesa Verde, Pueblo Bonito in Chaco Canyon. The tenth man was an Anglo archaeologist named Bruce Bradley, who lives in Cortez, Colorado. The paradox lay in the fact that, at the moment, Bradley was teaching his protégés how to make arrowheads.

At the time of Coronado's landmark *entrada* into the Southwest, in A.D. 1540, every Zia and Jemez man knew how to flake and chip form-

quently impossible to read between the lines of Spanish dogma to fig-ure out just what was going on at Taos or Jemez or Acoma.

As for the Pueblo record of the Revolt, it looms for the Anglo scholar of today as a yawning void. An old truism of the Southwest has it that Spanish persecution in New Mexico was so severe that it drove the Pueblo religion (and indeed, the very culture) underground. Underground, it remains today. Yet the secrecy that lies at the heart of Puebloan life goes far deeper than a response to the Spanish. In basic ways, it long predates European contact, forming an intrinsic feature of the culture. In 2004, moreover, it has become harder for an outsider to learn anything new about the Pueblo belief system or Pueblo his-tory than at any time since the 1870s, when Anglo ethnographers began working in the Southwest.

At the time of Coronado's *entrada* in 1540, Spain was at the height of its glory, the most powerful nation in Europe and perhaps in the world. Its monarch, Charles I, had been elected Holy Roman Emperor in 1519; as the Hapsburg Charles V, by 1540 he presided over a domain that stretched from the Netherlands to North Africa, from Austria to Mexico and Peru. Charles's reign provided the seedbed for an unprece-dented florescence of Spanish culture, bringing forth in subsequent generations such writers as Cervantes and Lope de Vega, such painters as El Greco and Velázquez.

In contrast, by the 1670s, on the eve of the Pueblo Revolt, Spain had become a distinctly second-rate power. She had suffered not only the crushing decimation of her Armada by the British fleet in 1588, but had lost one war after another, in France, in Holland, in Italy, and elsewhere. Catalonia and Portugal had successfully revolted against Castilian rule. Under the feckless Charles II, Spain suffered an irre-versible decline. The Venetian ambassador to Spain characterized Charles's reign as "an uninterrupted series of calamities." Thanks to warfare and the exodus of Spaniards to the colonies, the population of Castile itself declined from 6.5 million in 1600 to 5 million in 1680. Beginning in 1677, earthquakes, plague, and crop failures dealt further blows to the mother country. In cultural terms, the vaunted "Golden Century" had come to its close.

The decline of Spain had a bitter relevance for New Mexico. No part of the sprawling colonial empire of New Spain lay farther from its capital in Mexico City than the northern hinterland called Nùevo México. By horse and cart, it was a journey of six months and 2,000 miles from Santa Fe to Mexico City. For a governor to send a message to the capital and receive his answer thus routinely took at least a year. To communicate with the king in Madrid took considerably longer.

As Castile preoccupied itself with threats and troubles nearer home, the remote colony luxuriated in an anarchic autonomy that spawned grotesque abuses. Settlers routinely ignored Spanish laws promulgated since the 1570s to protect natives from the excesses of the first conquistadors. More than one governor of New Mexico set himself up as an absolute despot, growing rich off the labor of Indians reduced to virtual slavery. More than one friar in the colony arrogated to himself the right to punish native "heresies" with torture and execution. Sexual exploitation of Puebloan women, including rape, was commonplace, even on the part of priests sworn to celibacy. As if all this were not burden enough for the Pueblos, for eighty-two years after the conquest church and state in New Mexico waged a relentless struggle against each other. There was no possible way for a "good Indian" to serve both masters.

It is not, perhaps, going too far to see New Mexico in the 1670s as a colony gone collectively mad. Freed by Spain's troubles at home from the corrective hand of humanizing civilization, the leading figures of Nuevo México lived and ruled as they pleased. A stunning symptom of that madness is that the Spaniards never saw the Revolt coming. As the colony's governor complained in an official dispatch, written less than a month after he had lost Santa Fe, as he straggled south down the Rio Grande with his fellow survivors, the uprising was "wholly contrary to the existing peace and tranquility" of the colony. The "cunning and cleverness of the rebels," the governor ruefully confessed, was abetted

The meeting broke up. The runners returned to the trail to set off for another pueblo farther south. As they watched the lean young men retreat into the distance, the leaders of San Marcos felt the first stirrings of a purifying rage. It tasted like joy—the bursting of a dam that held in check a reservoir of resentment that had been brimming for decades.

All the leaders except one: the *cacique* himself. Inside the *opi*'s chamber, the others had noticed their headman's discomfort. They knew that the *cacique* had certain ties to the despised Spanish governor of New Mexico, Don Antonio de Otermín. Now, to their dismay, the San Marceseños watched the headman prepare for a journey of his own. Within an hour, he had left the pueblo, headed in the opposite direction from that of Catua and Omtua—north, toward Santa Fe, fifteen miles away.

No matter: let him go. But now, on the edge of the San Marcos plaza, only a few dozen yards away from the *opi*'s room, Father Manuel Tinoco, the Franciscan friar who for the last six years had ministered to the ignorant children whose souls God had appointed him to save, emerged from his mission church. Perhaps the *cacique* had whispered some warning in his ear, for it was clear that the priest realized that something terrible was about to happen. In a panic, he gathered up the skirts of his brown robe, mounted a horse, and rode for his life toward Galisteo, another pueblo eleven miles to the east.

This man, the San Marceseños were not willing to let go. On foot, several warriors took to the trail that led to Galisteo. At a certain point—some say halfway to the neighboring village, some say in a field within sight of Galisteo—the pursuers overtook Fray Tinoco. They pulled him from his horse, then bludgeoned and stabbed him to death where he lay in the dirt.

Two days later, scores of San Marcos men gathered on a hill with their allies from Pecos, San Lázaro, Galisteo, and La Ciénega. They prepared for their march to Santa Fe, where already the addled Spaniards under Otermín had taken refuge inside a stockade at the center of the

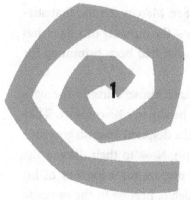

# 1

# THE KNOTTED CORD

Nearly naked, their skin glistening with sweat and dust, the pair of young men halted in the main plaza of San Marcos Pueblo. It was August 9, 1680. The youths, whose names were Catua and Omtua, had run that day all the way from Tesuque, twenty-five miles to the north, to deliver a message. Now they asked for the *opi*, or war chief, of San Marcos.

Inside a small room made of adobe walls, with a mud-covered grid of wooden beams and sticks for a ceiling, the *opi*, along with the *cacique* or headman of San Marcos and several other village leaders and shamans, waited for Catua and Omtua to speak. In the dim light, the San Marcos men watched as the youths produced a knotted cord made of yucca fiber. The San Marcoseños stared at the cord, awed by the gravity of the moment. Now the runners explained. Untie one knot each day, they said softly. When no knots remain, attack. The command was not to be taken lightly, for it came from Popé himself. And Popé had further decreed that if San Marcos failed to join in the assault, a horde of Puebloans would descend from the north and kill every villager, women and children included.

of oral tradition, a clear-eyed appreciation of the ravages that acculturation has wrought upon today's inhabitants of Acoma or Hopi or Jemez. But I began and ended my effort in admiration of the culture of the pueblos, as of that of their Anasazi ancestors.

About the sixteenth- and seventeenth-century Spaniards, I am far more ambivalent. For every Bartolomé de las Casas, the Dominican friar who became the eloquent champion of the Indians in the New World, there were a dozen Pedro de Alvarados (the genocidal conqueror of highland Guatemala).

The central mystery of the Pueblo Revolt remains what happened between 1680 and 1692, during the years the Spanish were absent from New Mexico. Even for today's Puebloans, I suspect, those twelve years linger as something of a lacuna in the middle of their long past in the Southwest.

Yet of the scores of tantalizing hints as to what transpired during that Puebloan interregnum, I would hope that I have made a partial synthesis, one that previous commentators have not attempted. The ambiguities of that period do not prevent our forming an understanding of what is still one of the most astonishing chapters in North American history.

And I hope that my readers, as they accompany me on my rambles through New Mexico, can taste some of the joy I felt in lonely canyons and on lordly mesa tops, some of the curiosity that tantalized me as I talked with Puebloans who told me only what they thought it was safe for me to hear, some of the fussy pleasure I found in squeezing latent meanings out of old texts. This book is meant as a passionate personal journey into the heart of a mystery. I do not presume to have emerged, on the last page, with anything more than a key to the puzzle. But that key, if I have succeeded, at least fits into the lock. And a lock can be opened with a turn of the hand, or a twist of the mind. . . .

by "a certain degree of negligence" on his own part, for he simply did not believe the first rumors of rebellion that reached his ears.

Pursuing my research on the Pueblo Revolt, I read everything I could get my hands on, from the eyewitness Spanish accounts to modern histories of New Mexico to archaeological site reports to the many scholarly articles about the Revolt, as well as a novel based upon it, published in 1973 under the by now very un-PC title, *Red Power on the Rio Grande*. I also visited today's pueblos, and spoke to as many Puebloans as I could—not very many, as I was hardly surprised to discover—who were willing to share their thoughts about the Revolt with an outsider.

From the start, however, I did not intend to write another quasi-objective history of the uprising, in the vein of Robert Silverberg's *The Pueblo Revolt* (1970) or Andrew L. Knaut's *The Pueblo Revolt of 1680* (1995). I wanted instead to undertake a journey through the landscape where the Revolt had unfurled. Just as I had found while researching my previous book about the Anasazi, hiking into the wilderness gave me at least as much insight into my subject as hours of interviewing or burrowing through stacks and archives. A petroglyph carved on an obscure basalt boulder sometime after 1540 captured the shock of first contact better than any number of firsthand accounts. A day spent contemplating the ruins of an ancestral village, all but lost in the forest on top of a high plateau, conveyed to me the integrity of Pueblo life before the Spanish came better than some dry ethnographic report.

Some readers may find my take on the Revolt one-sided—too sympathetic to the Puebloans, too hard on the Spanish. If so, so be it. My book, to repeat, is not meant to be an "objective" history, but rather a bearing of empathic witness to one of the great triumphs and tragedies of American history—not a disinterested recitation of events, but an *engagé* account of what I found in New Mexico.

The easiest trap in such a work, of course, is to romanticize Native Americans, à la *Dances with Wolves*. I hope that I have retained a healthy skepticism about the pueblos, an awareness of the limitations

town. Ecstatic with the fever of millenarian vengeance, the Puebloans prepared to undo eighty-two years of oppression, poverty, and illness, by wiping every last one of the hated invaders from the face of the earth.

Three hundred and twenty-three years later, on a bitterly cold day in late March, with snow whipping on a thirty-mile-an-hour wind, I strolled across an undulating shelf of land beside a dry arroyo—the ruins of San Marcos. The shelf was barren of trees but strewn with weeds and cholla cactus. The ground was littered with broken bits of pottery, white, gray, and occasionally black-on-orange, as well as with chert flakes of all colors.

Each undulation, I knew, hid a long row of back-to-back cubicles, twenty-two rows in all, buried beneath the drifted sand and soil of the centuries. One of the largest villages ever built in the prehistoric Southwest, San Marcos once comprised as many as 3,000 rooms. In the square depression before me, during the centuries before the Spanish had come, mystic dances in the plaza had marked the seasonal round, and men and women had coiled the pots and flaked the scrapers and arrowheads whose debris I found scattered in the dirt.

It was here that Catua and Omtua had arrived on August 9, 1680. Between the plaza and the mission, whose grid of earth ridges stood atop a bench of land on the northwestern corner of the village, some sixty or seventy yards away, the events of that fateful day had unfolded.

A five-year-long excavation of one small portion of the San Marcos site, undertaken in the late 1990s by the American Museum of Natural History in New York, had uncovered the mission from which Fray Tinoco had fled on the last day of his life.*

---

*A combination of AMNH work with archival Spanish records allows me to invent the imaginative reconstruction of the messengers' arrival that opens this chapter. Something very like that drama played itself out at San Marcos between August 9 and 11, 1680.

Now I wandered down to the arroyo that runs just south of the pueblo. Only here, where the streambed had cut into several roomblocks, could I see the bare, 500-year-old walls of the original village. Even these looked ephemeral, for, unlike most pueblos in the Southwest, made of stones and mortar, this one had been built of coursed adobe—slabs of gooey mud laid one on top of another like squat loaves of bread. I pushed on up the arroyo's sinuous bed, coming to a thicket of cattails. Still seeping from beneath the earth, the water of one of the village's three perennial springs flowed clear and cool— the pueblo's raison d'être, in this landscape watered by less than ten inches of rain per year.

What struck me most forcibly about the ruins of San Marcos was that they lay open to the surrounding plains on all sides. There was no trace of any defensive fortifications, natural or man-made. Although nomadic tribes had begun to threaten Pueblo life even before the advent of the conquistadors, San Marcos seemed to breathe an air of supreme confidence in its people's right to claim the land.

San Marcos had been a flourishing village at the time of Coronado, who probably saw the pueblo from a distance, if he did not actually visit it. (Scholars have spent more than a century trying to figure out just which pueblos Coronado and other early conquistadors stopped at. The problem is made all the knottier by the arbitrary names the Spaniards bestowed on the villages they visited. San Marcos, of course, was not so called by its inhabitants, but its Puebloan name has been lost to history.)

That March day, as I leaned against the wind and meandered aimlessly across the site, I gained a slow but vivid appreciation of the sheer magnitude of the village, whose roomblocks sprawl across sixty acres of cholla-covered earth. The very beginnings of San Marcos reach back as far as the twelfth century A.D. In its heyday, perhaps in the fifteenth or early sixteenth century, with its 3,000 rooms, San Marcos would have been one of the grandest villages not only in the Southwest, but in the whole pre-Columbian sweep of what is now the United States.

By 1680, however, the pueblo was in decline. Most of the rooms had fallen into disrepair, or were filled with trash. Only some 600 villagers still dwelt at San Marcos. Whatever vicissitudes had turned this once lordly village into a marginal place, they were not reversed by the Pueblo Revolt. After 1680, except for brief occupations by bands of squatters who may have subdivided the ruined mission into cubicles from which they eked out a scrabbling existence, San Marcos was never again inhabited.

Still, despite the bitter wind that lashed my face, as I strolled from ridged mound to flat depression, conjuring up in my mind's eye the three-story apartments that had looked in on busy plazas, it was not hard to see that San Marcos must once have been a blithe place to live. The springs would always flow, it must have seemed, the corn grow ripe in the adjoining fields, the deer flit shyly through the junipers to the west, where a crouching hunter drew his bowstring. And for quite a while, there was no enemy within hundreds of miles powerful enough to trouble the sleep of the children who nightly curled around small fires laid in the hearths of the snug adobe rooms.

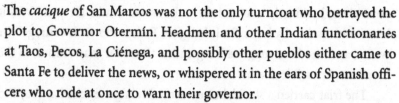

The *cacique* of San Marcos was not the only turncoat who betrayed the plot to Governor Otermín. Headmen and other Indian functionaries at Taos, Pecos, La Ciénega, and possibly other pueblos either came to Santa Fe to deliver the news, or whispered it in the ears of Spanish officers who rode at once to warn their governor.

Popé had shrewdly planned the Revolt for August 11, the night of the new moon, only days before the triennial resupply caravan from Mexico City was scheduled to arrive. As soon as Otermín had been prematurely alerted by the loyalists, he had the runners, Catua and Omtua, seized and tortured. Under duress, the young men revealed the meaning of the knotted cords, yet they claimed to know nothing of the causes of the Revolt, for they had not been admitted to the councils of the elders where the uprising had been hatched. It is possible that even as they were being tortured, the runners bought the pueblos extra time, for Otermín emerged from his grilling of the prisoners convinced that the Revolt had been planned for August 13, not August 11.

In any event, with the secret plot now leaked, the various pueblos launched their attacks at once, on August 10. So unprepared were the Spaniards, who had grown complacent in the "peace and tranquility" of their colony, that the forewarning hardly mattered.

At Tesuque, the pueblo from which Catua and Omtua had set out running with their knotted cords, Father Juan Pío had arrived from Santa Fe on the morning of August 10 to celebrate Mass. He was accompanied by a single soldier, one Pedro Hidalgo. The two men rode into Tesuque, only to find the pueblo deserted; even the few cows the Puebloans owned were absent from the fields. Fray Pío and Hidalgo set out to search for the friar's parishioners. They found them less than a mile from the village, the men armed with bows, arrows, lances, and shields, their faces daubed with war paint.

"What is this children; are you mad?" said the friar, as he rode fearlessly toward the warriors, still intent on gathering them inside the mission church to observe the Mass. But then, discerning the Tesuque men's intentions, he added (according to Hidalgo), "Do not disturb yourselves; I will help you and die a thousand deaths for you." Was it blind faith in his Catholic God that gave Father Pío such courage? Or was it, as some have suggested, a genuine thirst for martyrdom, as the loveliest of possible deaths?

The friar carried a shield, but no arms. Hidalgo watched as Fray Pío descended into a ravine with several Tesuque men. A few minutes later, one Puebloan emerged from the ravine carrying the priest's shield, another beside him "painted with clay and spattered with blood." Hidalgo wheeled to ride pell-mell back to Santa Fe, as several warriors seized his horse's reins. In the struggle, the soldier lost his sword and hat, but held on to his harquebus. He forced his horse down a hill, dragging his would-be murderers with him. At last the horse broke free. Hidalgo galloped south for all his worth, as arrows cut the air around him.

With Hidalgo's arrival back in Santa Fe, Governor Otermín learned for the first time that the impending plot had already begun to be carried out. At once he sent soldiers to the various pueblos, and to the wayside *estancias* where prosperous Spanish families lived off the land and the toil of their Indian servants, to warn them about the rebellion; but it was already too late. Otermín gathered the rest of Santa Fe's thousand-odd settlers into the *casas reales* (literally, "royal houses") at the center of the seventy-year-old capital of New Mexico, "so that," as he wrote in a dispatch penned that very day, "we can defend ourselves and oppose the enemy if the occasion shall arise." Every harquebus, sword, dagger, and shield in Santa Fe was gathered up; every man and teenage boy was given arms; and guards were posted at the corners of the stockade in which the settlers cowered.

Meanwhile, all over northern New Mexico—and even as far west as the Hopi mesas in what is now Arizona, 250 miles from Tesuque—Puebloans were beginning to carry out Popé's apocalyptic vision. No one in New Mexico was hated more bitterly than its thirty-three Franciscan friars, and so the cruelest executions were reserved for them. At Jemez, which had suffered over the preceding years more egregious punishments than perhaps any other pueblo, the Indians seized Fray Juan de Jesús, a small, aged man who had served for three years as the resident priest. His captors stripped the friar naked, tied him to a pig's back, then rode him through the village as they taunted him with catcalls and blows. Then they untied him and forced him to crawl, still naked, on his hands and knees, while one warrior after another rode him like a puny horse, digging their heels into his thighs to urge him forward.

Yet as the Jemez men prepared to kill Father Juan, dissension broke out. An old legend has it that the friar pleaded, "Children, I am a poor old man, do not fight, do not kill each other in order to protect me; do what God permits." At that, one of the warriors stabbed the priest through the heart with a sword, while others pummeled his corpse with further blows.

We do not know why Father Manuel Tinoco, as he fled San Marcos on August 9, thought he might find safety at neighboring Galisteo Pueblo, but in that hope he was deluded. Another friar, hastening from Pecos, thirteen miles away, hoped to alert Fray Juan Bernal, who was custodian of all the Franciscan friars in New Mexico, but he never reached Galisteo: some say he was killed in a field within sight of the village. Either just before or just after that deed, the Galisteo warriors executed Fray Bernal and his assistant; the manner of their deaths remains unknown.

At Santo Domingo, chosen by Juan de Oñate during his first months in New Mexico in 1598 to serve as headquarters for the church in the new colony, three friars were slain in the mission convent on August 10. Their bodies were then dragged to the church and piled in a heap before the altar. Their putrefying corpses were discovered two weeks later, as Otermín's caravan of survivors stumbled down the Rio Grande. Writes Charles Wilson Hackett, the great early-twentieth-century scholar who first assembled the Spanish documents pertaining to the Revolt, "Doubtless by thus piling the dead bodies of the missionaries before the Christian altars, which for eighty years had symbolized the hated domination of an unknown religion, the Indian idea of vengeance found its fullest expression."

All told, in a single day—August 10, 1680—the Puebloans killed twenty-one of the thirty-three Franciscan friars in New Mexico (or, more precisely, nineteen friars and two assistants). The carnage did not end with the priests. From Taos all the way to Hopi, the Indians killed 380 settlers, sparing neither women nor children, virtually all of them on August 10. In an official letter written three weeks later, from the safety of El Paso, a shell-shocked Governor Otermín would characterize that fateful day as a "lamentable tragedy, such as has never before happened in the world."

As Otermín's hyperbolic outcry indicates, the Spaniards holed up in Santa Fe, awaiting an all-out assault that would mean life or death, had no idea what had hit them. They had never heard of Popé. It is likely that Otermín did not even learn Popé's name for another sixteen months, until, in the midst of a failed attempt to reconquer New Mexico, the governor questioned a captive Tesuque man named Juan, who at last named and characterized the shadowy shaman from San Juan Pueblo who had masterminded the Revolt. Almost surely, the Spanish leaders in 1680 never knew that Popé had been one of forty-seven "sorcerers" arrested by Otermín's predecessor, Governor Juan Francisco Treviño, in 1675. For obstinately continuing to practice their "idolatry" (i.e., the kachina religion, instead of the Catholicism that had bathed their souls in Christ's mercy), the medicine men were imprisoned in Santa Fe and severely flogged. Treviño hanged three shamans as an example to the others; a fourth committed suicide by hanging. Only when a de facto army of Indians from the northern pueblos descended on Santa Fe and demanded the release of the forty-three surviving shamans did Treviño capitulate and set free his prisoners. It would take another sixteen months after August 1680 for Otermín to learn that Popé had been one of the forty-three captives, and that as he had returned to San Juan, the shaman's heart smoldered with the first flames of the Pueblo Revolt.

By August 1680, of the roughly 2,900 Spaniards in New Mexico, fully three-fifths lived in the Río Abajo country, south of present-day Albuquerque. Uncertain of the loyalties of the more southern (and more acculturated) pueblos, the leaders of the Revolt excluded all pueblos south of Isleta from the plot. The military officer in charge of this sector of Nuevo México, Lieutenant Governor Alonso García, got news of the massacres to the north on August 11. García made a halfhearted attempt to ride to the rescue of the Spaniards trapped in Santa Fe, but on finding ranches burnt to the ground and settlers dead in the fields, he hesitated. Then word came to García (how, we do not know) that all the refugees to the north had already been killed. The heartsick lieutenant governor turned tail and launched a mass retreat of all the Spaniards in Río Abajo toward El Paso. Upon reuniting with García a month later, at a pueblo just north of present-day Socorro, New Mexico, Otermín would fly into a rage and order his second-in-command arrested.

By August 13, Otermín and his thousand-odd fellow survivors were keeping their vigil inside the stockade in the center of Santa Fe, awaiting the attack that seemed inevitable. Of those thousand, scarcely a hundred were men and boys capable of bearing arms. We have today no clear description of that makeshift fortress, no good idea how effective its ramparts were against Indian assault. Still uncertain just how widespread the Revolt was proving to be, Otermín sent out a pair of "Christian Indians" whom he deemed loyal on a daring mission to gather intelligence. A day and a half later, these spies returned with the worst possible news: more than 500 warriors from pueblos ranging from Pecos to San Marcos had amassed less than three miles away. They were awaiting reinforcement by yet more warriors from Taos, Picuris, and other northern pueblos. Once the whole fighting force had gathered, the Puebloans would attack the stockade, level it to the ground, and kill every Spaniard they found inside. "They were saying," Otermín cited the Indian spies as reporting, "that now God and Santa María were dead . . . and that their own God whom they obeyed [had] never died."

A mass attack on a fortified stockade, however, with bows and arrows against harquebuses and swords, was not the Puebloan style of warfare. Instead the "rebels" surrounded the fortress and began to wait out the demoralized refugees. On August 15, the siege of Santa Fe began. It would last five days.

On a warm, cloudless afternoon in October, I alighted in Santa Fe's central plaza, hoping to conjure up, in the course of an hour's haphazard stroll, the ghost of the stockade of 1680 among the trendy shops and restaurants of today's little city. Slanting autumnal sunlight made every red chile pepper hanging in bunches from shop lintels, every leaf turning from green to yellow on the drooping willow branches, stand out with a crystalline clarity.

The usual convocation of Indian merchants, their bracelets and earrings and seed jars and rugs spread out before them, sat elbow-to-elbow on the porch of the Palace of the Governors, soaking up the restorative sun as tourists browsed among their offerings. I heard Dutch, French, and Swedish spoken, as well as English and Spanish. I caught one Puebloan vendor trading a bemused glance with her neighbor as a German harridan tried to bargain her down to half her asking price for a liquid-silver necklace. Behind the shoppers, an elderly tour group stood at attention around a woman who, in the fervid tones of the self-educated expert, was expatiating on the excellent qualities of Governor Pedro de Peralta, who had founded Santa Fe in 1610. Nearby, a circle of appropriately scruffy latter-day hippies kicked a hacky-sack, while two or three homeless men slept off their last-night drunks on wrought iron benches. From curbsides on the other side of the plaza, I heard the crashing thuds of neophyte skateboarders wiping out.

At the center of the one-block-square plaza stands a modest obelisk erected as a monument shortly after the Civil War, commemorating such New Mexico battles as Glorieta and Valverde (the first a Union, the second a Confederate victory). I copied down the inscription on the north side of the monument, which I had first read more than thirty years before:

TO THE HEROES

WHO HAVE FALLEN IN THE

VARIOUS BATTLES WITH _____

INDIANS IN THE TERRITORY

OF NEW MEXICO.

In the space between "WITH" and "INDIANS," a word had been neatly chiseled out of the marble, leaving a lacuna that might have gladdened a classical scholar. I knew, however, just what epithet had been expunged in some PC spasm of revisionism in 1974: the word was "SAVAGE."

A few days before, State of New Mexico archaeologist Cordelia Snow, who had worked on several digs in the plaza area, had cautioned me: "We don't know where Otermín's stronghold was. It was probably near today's Palace of the Governors, but we don't even know where that building stood in the seventeenth century—only in the eighteenth. We do know the plaza was twice as big in 1680 as it is today.

"I'd put my money on the vicinity of today's plaza. The *casas reales* that Otermín speaks of surrounded the original plaza.

"In any case, the whole area was a swamp. Santa Fe was a stupid place to lay out a community. A document from 1692 speaks of the stronghold as 'shaded morning and afternoon,' because of the profusion of trees growing out of the boggy ground. The swamp itself, according to that document, 'contained mists of known and evident detriment.' As early as 1620, there was a plan afoot to move the *casas reales*."

I walked east on Palace Avenue, leaving the Indian vendors behind. Within a single block, I passed under shingles touting Tribal Reflections Jewelry; Shibui: Fine Asian Wares; Miss Maybe: An Exceptionally Whimsical Boutique; Diva Hair Design; Knitworks: Creative European Apparel; Paris Flea: Antiques and Interior Design; and several other cutesy shops. No, it seemed impossible to imagine the siege of Santa Fe taking place in this neighborhood. But then I paused before a tiny plaque, affixed to the wall between a pair of boutiques, that read: "A building stood here before 1680. It was wrecked in the great Indian uprising. This house incorporates what remained."

I wandered to the north and east. The names of the streets gave off a historical whiff: Otero and Marcy streets, Washington Avenue—the first commemorating a nineteenth-century Hispanic legislator and railroad merchant, the second the author of the Gadsden Purchase of 1853 (which added a handsome chunk of Mexico to southern Arizona and New Mexico), and the third, of course, the father of our country. Yet only Cienega Street hinted at Santa Fe's origins—*ciénega* being Spanish for "swamp."

A small ditch that ran through Otermín's stronghold—presumably diverted from the Santa Fe River, which today runs three blocks south of the plaza—served as the only source of drinking water for the besieged Spaniards. Early on, the Puebloans cut off the ditch, leaving only the jars and pitchers previously filled inside the *casas reales* to slake the thirst of the thousand prisoners of the rebellion. On my stroll, I found no trace of old waterways near the plaza, unless one counts the storm sewer grates that unobtrusively mark the corners where each pair of streets intersects.

I ambled south to the so-called cathedral that stands a block east of the plaza. Dedicated to the same Saint Francis from whose order all the priests in seventeenth-century New Mexico came, the church, built of warm brown sandstone blocks, dates only from 1869. With its neo-Romanesque windows, its neo-Gothic rosette, this much admired church has always struck me as a bit grandiose. In 1680, another church stood near the center of Santa Fe, perhaps on the very spot where Archbishop Jean Baptiste Lamy erected today's cathedral. That earlier church must have lain close to the walls of Otermín's stockade. According to archaeologist Cordelia Snow, "We know that in the 1620s the friars were irate because a *fuerte* [fort] was constructed in such a way that the cannons stood in the very shadow of the church."

Finally I hiked up to the top of the small hill that overlooks downtown from the northeast. Here lies Old Fort Marcy Park, commanding the finest view in central Santa Fe—a greensward that ought to be idyllic, but that seems a bit dingy, strewn as it is with broken glass and dog turds. On the edge of the park, a group called the American Revolution Bicentennial Council, joined by the Santa Fe Fiesta Council, erected the Cross of the Martyrs in 1977. A truly ugly monument, the twenty-foot-tall cross is made of metal I-beams painted white. In front of the cross, a small brass plaque names the twenty-one Franciscans from the various pueblos who lost their lives on August 10, 1680. Locals, however, must find the monument inspiring, for scores of them had made donations that won each the privilege of having his or her name inscribed on one of the bricks that pave the platform from which the martyrs' crucifix soars toward the martyrs' heaven. I lingered here as the sun sank low

in the west, musing on the mute and ambiguous testimony with which
landscape so often confounds history.

On the morning of August 15, the first day of the siege, Otermín's men
saw an army of 500 Puebloans approaching from the south, burning
the cornfields and villas on the other side of the Santa Fe River. According to the pair of "Christian Indian" spies the governor had sent out to
gather information, these were the Pecos and Tano warriors, the latter
term designating the pueblos on the northern edge of the Galisteo
Basin: San Marcos, San Lázaro, San Cristóbal, and Galisteo itself. Otermín sent a small contingent of soldiers out to "reconnoiter" this invading force. They found a Tano man named Juan riding at the head of the
army. His very appearance bespoke the devastation these Puebloans
had already wreaked south of Santa Fe, for he was not only on horseback, but armed to the teeth with harquebus, sword, and dagger, and he
wore not only a Spanish leather jacket but a sash of red taffeta that some
of the soldiers recognized as belonging to the convent of the Galisteo
mission. (Under Spanish rule up to August 1680, even as allies against
the "heathen" nomads—Apaches, Navajos, perhaps Comanches—who
occasionally raided their villages, Puebloans had never been allowed to
ride horses, nor to carry Spanish firearms or swords.)

With "fair words," Juan was persuaded to enter the stronghold to
parley with Otermín. The two men knew each other well, it seems. Yet
a sense of the absurd hangs over this initial conference, even as
reported by the governor himself, for his account reveals just how out
of touch the Spaniards were with the true wrath of the natives they
had subjugated for the previous eighty-two years. How was it, Otermín
demanded without preamble, that Juan had gone crazy? He was, after
all, an Indian who was intelligent enough to have learned Spanish, had
lived his whole life in Santa Fe, and had become a promising young
leader in whom Otermín placed a great deal of confidence.

Juan deflected the governor's entreaties. The "rebels," he replied, had elected him captain. At that very moment, they were bringing to the stronghold a pair of crosses, one white, the other red. It was up to the governor to choose his cross. In Otermín's own words, "If we wished to choose the white it must be upon our agreeing to leave the country, and if we chose the red, we must perish, because the rebels were numerous and we were very few."

Somehow, Otermín still didn't get it. "I spoke to [Juan] very persuasively," he would later record. The Indian leader and his followers, the governor reminded him, were Catholics, having been baptized in the church. How could they expect to live without the spiritual protection of the friars? Yet even though the Indians had already committed numerous "atrocities," Otermín would pardon Juan and his followers if only they "would return to obedience to his Majesty."

Instead, Juan demanded the delivery of Puebloan hostages he believed Otermín had taken captive, including his own wife and children. Eventually, the governor would conclude that this counterstroke was a mere ruse, a way of buying time until the warriors from the northern pueblos could arrive. The parley ended in utter impasse. As Juan left the stronghold, by Otermín's own admission, his people saluted him "with peals of bells and trumpets, giving loud shouts in sign of war."

Thus rebuffed, Otermín now had to watch as, "with shamelessness and mockery," the Pecos and Tanos crept closer and closer to the stockade, burning houses as they came. As a preemptive strike, the governor sent out all his soldiers to engage these Puebloans in battle. The struggle was short but brutal. Otermín claimed that his men killed "many of the rebels," turning the tables on some by setting fire to the very houses in which they had taken up defensive positions. Spanish losses amounted to only one soldier and the *maestre de campo*, Francisco Gómez, with fourteen or fifteen soldiers wounded. In the midst of this strike, however, Otermín got news of the arrival of warriors from the northern pueblos, so he had to recall his troops to safeguard the 900-odd women, children, and old men huddled inside the *casas reales*.

The siege persisted for two more days. The Spaniards "suffered greatly from thirst because of the scarcity of water," Otermín would report. Horses, sheep, goats, and cattle lodged inside the fortress began to die from thirst. By August 17, the governor estimated that his people were surrounded by 2,500 Indians. If this number counts only warriors, then the Spanish soldiers were outnumbered twenty-five to one; if not, still at least three or four to one.

That day, at dawn, the attack intensified, as Puebloans rained gunshots, arrows, and stones over the walls of the stockade. By that evening, the refugees were reduced to a numb terror: "the entire night," Otermín swore, "was the most horrible that could be thought of or imagined, because the whole villa [i.e., the town] was a torch and everywhere were war chants and shouts. What grieved us most were the dreadful flames from the church and the scoffing and ridicule which the wretched and miserable Indian rebels made of the sacred things, intoning the alabado [a hymn of praise] and the other prayers of the church with jeers."

The scene inside the stockade must have been infernal, as dead animals began to rot, its denizens were "perishing from thirst," and a nonstop "wailing of women and children" filled the air, while flames and "war whoops" testified to the devastation being carried out beyond its walls. On the evening of August 19, Otermín resolved on a desperate measure—to go out in the morning "to fight with the enemy until dying or conquering." A measure of the governor's faith in his God is that he sincerely believed "that the best strength and armor were prayers to appease the divine wrath." Though the women inside the stockade had been fervently praying day and night, Otermín now implored them to redouble their efforts. At dawn, the three Franciscans sequestered with the refugees celebrated Mass, and every man, woman, and child was exhorted to repent their sins, to accede to the divine will, and to beg absolution "from guilt and punishment."

Then, "in the best order possible," with Otermín at their head, the force of 100 soldiers, some on horseback but most on foot, burst out of the stockade's gates. The thrust took the Puebloans by surprise. "They were attacked in force," the governor later recorded, "and though they resisted the first charge bravely, finally they were put to flight, many of them being overtaken and killed." Surging through the ruined streets of Santa Fe, the soldiers set fire to houses inside which their enemy hid. Otermín himself received two arrow wounds in the face and a "remarkable" shot from a harquebus in the chest, and nearly died from loss of blood.

The desperate escape saved the settlers their lives. By the end of the day's battle, Otermín claimed that his men had slain more than 300 Indians, suffering the loss of only five soldiers. The governor's reckoning should perhaps be taken with a grain of salt. It would not have been easy to pause amidst the carnage and count the bodies of the enemy. And even as he wrote his official dispatches, Otermín knew that sooner or later he would come under the severest scrutiny for so ignominiously losing New Mexico. A heroic counterattack, under the miraculous protection of the "most serene Virgin," might put the best possible face on what must otherwise be construed as a complete debacle.

On the other hand, the casualty toll may indeed be accurate. Surprise worked entirely in the Spaniards' favor. As would be proved again and again in the Southwest, bows and arrows were no match for guns and swords. Otermín's soldiers had trained most of their lives to wield the harquebus and the sword; the Puebloans who had seized such weapons from settlers they had killed may have been using them for the first time. Finally, even with the loss of some 300 dead, the Indians, in driving the Spanish out of New Mexico, had achieved the ultimate aim of the Pueblo Revolt.

Otermín's men also took forty-seven Puebloans prisoner. These unfortunates were tortured to reveal what they knew of the plot, then executed on the spot. In that inquisition, Otermín gained a tantalizing glimpse of the shadow of its mastermind, Popé. Some of the captives revealed that the Revolt had been "planned a long time before by the Teguas [Tewa] Indians of the pueblo of Tesuque, and that now, in order to carry it out, they had the mandate of an Indian who lives a very long way from this kingdom, toward the north, from which region Montezuma came, and who is the lieutenant of Po he yemu." Ever since 1680, scholars have struggled to untangle this cryptic formula.

On August 21, the 1,000 exhausted survivors of the siege of Santa Fe began their straggling retreat down the Rio Grande. Otermín still had no word of the fate of the 1,500 inhabitants of Río Abajo, under Lieutenant Governor Alonso García: for all he knew, they had been massacred to the last woman and child. From the outskirts of Santa Fe, wrote Otermín later, "I left without a crust of bread or a grain of wheat or maize."

As the bedraggled caravan crawled south, plucking the odd ear of corn from the odd half-fallow field, it found evidence everywhere of the wreckage of the Revolt. At the church in the pueblo of Sandía, just north of present-day Albuquerque, one eyewitness reported, "We went inside and found the convent deserted and destroyed, the cells without doors, and the whole place sacked. . . . On the main altar there was a carved full-length figure of Saint Francis with the arms hacked off by an axe. The church had been filled with wheat straw for the purpose of burning it, and the fire had started in the choir and in the choir stalls. Everything was broken to pieces and destroyed."

According to another Sandía witness, the Puebloans' "hatred and barbarous ferocity went to such extremes that . . . images of saints were found among excrement, two chalices were found concealed in a bucket of manure, and there was a carved crucifix with the paint and varnish taken off by lashes. There was also excrement at the place of the holy communion table."

On reaching the pueblo of La Alameda, near present-day Albuquerque, Otermín learned from an old Indian standing in a cornfield that fourteen or fifteen days earlier, García and the settlers of Río Abajo had passed by on their way to El Paso. It was not until September 6 that the governor caught up with his lieutenant. After imprisoning García in an impetuous rage, Otermín calmed down long enough to listen to his story. At last he freed the man, and the caravan resumed its plod toward El Paso.

Even as he retreated in disgrace, Otermín was obsessed with the idea of avenging his great defeat. The question of "whether or not this miserable kingdom can be recovered" preoccupied his every waking hour. "For this purpose," he wrote on September 8, "I shall not spare any means in the service of God and of his Majesty, losing a thousand lives if I had them, as I have lost my estate and part of my health, and shedding my blood for God."

His was a vain avowal. It would fall not to Otermín to taste the fruits of reconquest, but to a more efficient governor and better general a dozen years hence. In a more contrite and private moment, Otermín took on the full blame for the loss of New Mexico. In his unquestioning faith, the governor concluded that God must have "permitted [the Revolt] because of my grievous sins." In 1683, he was stripped of his in absentia governorship of New Mexico.

The Pueblo Revolt had cost its perpetrators many lives. But it had succeeded as no other rebellion by natives in North America against a European oppressor ever had, or ever would in the centuries to come. By September 1680, New Mexico was rid of Spaniards. After eighty-two years of vassalage, the Puebloans were free to worship the gods that had never failed them, to live in the peace and prosperity their ancestors had known.

Those twelve years of independence, however, would prove fragile and precarious, and during that span, the Puebloans could not for a single day afford the luxury of dreaming that the Spanish would never return.

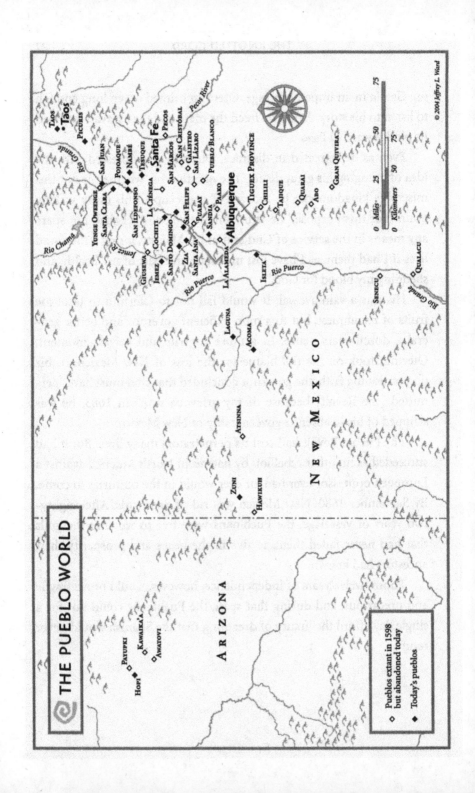

THE PUEBLO WORLD

© 2004 Jeffrey L. Ward

Taos
PICURÍS
Taos
Pecos River
Rio Grande
SAN JUAN
POJOAQUE
NAMBÉ
Santa Fe
PECOS
TESUQUE
SAN CRISTÓBAL
YUNGE OWENGE
SANTA CLARA
SAN ILDEFONSO
LA CIÉNEGA
SAN MARCOS
GALISTEO
SAN LÁZARO
PUEBLO BLANCO
Rio Chama
GIUSEWA
JEMEZ
COCHITI
SANTO DOMINGO
ZIA
SANTA ANA
SAN FELIPE
PUARAY
PAAKO
SANDÍA
Albuquerque
TIGUEX PROVINCE
Jemez R.
Rio Puerco
LA ALAMEDA
Rio Puerco
ISLETA
Rio Grande
CHILILI
TAJIQUE
QUARAI
ABÓ
GRAN QUIVIRA
SENECÚ
QUALACU

LAGUNA
ACOMA
ATSINNA

N E W   M E X I C O

ZUNI
HAWIKUH

PAYUPKI
KAWAIKA'A
AWATOVI
HOPI

A R I Z O N A

0    25    50    75  Miles
0   25   50   75  Kilometers

◇ Pueblos extant in 1598
  but abandoned today
◆ Today's pueblos

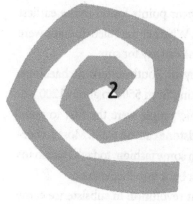

# THE COMING OF
# THE KACHINAS

At the time of Coronado's far-ranging foray through the Southwest, from 1540 to 1542, at least 110 separate pueblos flourished in the region. By 1680, on the eve of the Pueblo Revolt, that number had dwindled to a little over forty. Today, a mere twenty pueblos survive (if one counts the several villages on the three Hopi mesas as a single pueblo). Fourteen of them are situated on or near the Rio Grande: from north to south, Taos, Picuris, San Juan, Santa Clara, San Ildefonso, Pojoaque, Nambé, Tesuque, Cochiti, Santo Domingo, San Felipe, Santa Ana, Sandía, and Isleta. Five range across New Mexico west of the great river: Zia, Jemez, Laguna, Acoma, and Zuni. The Hopi mesas are situated in northeastern Arizona.

The dolorous toll that the coming of the Spanish took on the Puebloan way of life emerges vividly in the fact that in 1598, when Oñate established the colony of Nuevo México, the native population was an estimated 80,000. By 1680, Puebloan numbers had fallen to a mere 17,000.

The origins of the Pueblo people are lost in prehistory. Paleo-Indians, who roamed the Southwest between their arrival from across the Bering

Strait (perhaps as early as 10,000 B.C.) to about 5,500 B.C., were nomadic gatherers and hunters of such big game as the mammoth. Their culture phases are named after the distinctive spear points found in the earliest sites: Folsom, Clovis, Sandía, and the like. Whether the Paleo-Indians were the ancestors of today's Puebloans, no one can say for sure.

After Paleo-Indian, in the taxonomy of Southwestern archaeology, comes the Archaic, loosely defined as lasting from 5500 to about 1200 B.C. Among their other achievements, Archaic people were the first to paint pictographs and etch petroglyphs on sandstone canyon walls. Most archaeologists would venture the opinion that in some fashion, today's Puebloans can trace their residence in the Southwest back into the Archaic.

In this severely arid region, the great revolution in subsistence came with the discovery of how to plant and harvest corn—an innovation that slowly crept its way north from Mexico over several millennia. An intense scholarly debate exists over the moment when corn first reached New Mexico and Arizona, with most experts placing the date between 1500 and 2000 B.C. In any event, corn was responsible for launching the momentous shift from a nomadic to a sedentary way of life.

However deep stretch the roots of Pueblo origins in the Southwest, we know one thing for sure: the ancestors of today's Hopi, Zuni, Acoma, and Santa Clara Indians (along with those of the other sixteen pueblos) were living in the region for a very long time before the arrival of such relative latecomers as the Navajo, Apache, Ute, Comanche, and Paiute.

In a sense, it was the first Spanish explorers in the Southwest who "invented" the Pueblo Indians. Struck by the evident difference between tribes who, on the one hand, owned few possessions, traveled constantly, and lived in temporary shelters such as wickiups or teepees, and, on the other hand, natives who grew corn, beans, squash, and sometimes cotton and lived in solid adobe-and-stone villages up to three or even four stories tall, the conquistadors lumped the latter under the all-purpose term "Pueblo" (Spanish for "town"). As virtually all European explorers did, the first Spaniards assumed that the Indians who dwelt in more-or-less permanent pueblos represented a far more advanced stage of civilization than did the nomadic *indios bárbaros* who surrounded them.

Over breakfast one morning in a Santa Fe café, I discussed Puebloan origins with one of the leading experts in the field, Museum of New Mexico archaeologist Eric Blinman. "You know," he said, "we do a real disservice to those peoples simply by calling them Puebloans. Sure, when the Spanish came, they all lived in mud-and-stone roomblocks, they all grew corn, but the differences between one pueblo and the next are enormous. Typically, they have completely different social structures. Two adjoining pueblos will have different clans and societies. And when you look at the language problem . . ."

I did not need Blinman to elucidate this last point. I knew that among the twenty pueblos extant today, a great variety of languages and dialects is spoken, springing from four completely distinct language groups. Tiwa is the tongue spoken at the two most northern

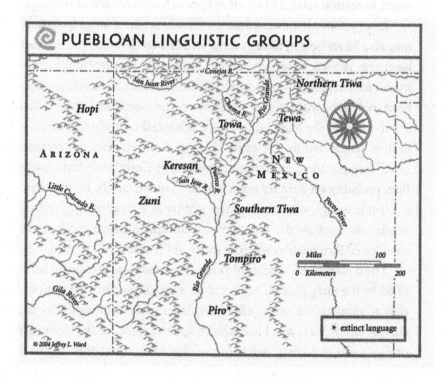

pueblos, Taos and Picuris, but also at the two southernmost Rio Grande villages, Sandía and Isleta. In between, six pueblos (San Juan, Santa Clara, San Ildefonso, Pojoaque, Nambé, and Tesuque) speak Tewa. (It was Tewas who were, for the most part, responsible for initiating the Pueblo Revolt.) Towa is spoken today only at Jemez, though at the time the Spanish came, it was also the language of Pecos, sixty-five miles away, with many other pueblos in between. When Pecos was finally abandoned in 1838, its last inhabitants moved to Jemez to join their linguistic kin.

Though mutually unintelligible, Tiwa, Tewa, and Towa are related, three branches of a language group called Tanoan. A completely different linguistic stock, known as Keresan, furnishes the tongues spoken today at Acoma, Laguna, Zia, Santa Ana, San Felipe, Santo Domingo, and Cochiti. Thus the Keresan block of pueblos drives a wedge between the Tanoan-speaking pueblos along the Rio Grande. What is more, Keresan is related to no other known Native American language.

Zuni, yet another distinct tongue from a separate language group, may also be an isolate, though some scholars see affinities to Penutian languages spoken in certain parts of California. Finally, Hopi springs from a fourth group, Uto-Aztecan, which thus hints at ancient connections not only with Numic speakers to the north and west (Utes, Shoshone, and the like), but with the advanced central Mexican civilization conquered by Cortés in 1521. As if all this were not complicated enough, the southernmost pueblos in Coronado's time spoke Piro, probably yet another branch of the Tanoan family. By now, Piro is a lost language, whose only traces survive in a smattering of archaic words still used by the thoroughly acculturated descendants of the abandoned Piro pueblos who live today in the vicinity of El Paso.

The conundrum, then, is obvious. If the *indios de los pueblos* identified by the early Spanish explorers are a single people, what can possibly account for the crazy quilt of languages spoken among the twenty villages today? Years ago, I had asked Stephen Lekson, of the University of Colorado, a leading generalist in the field, about this linguistic diversity. "It's one of the most intractable problems in all of Southwestern prehistory," he answered.

If it does nothing else, however, the patchwork of languages underscores just how remarkable an event it was that in 1680 most of the pueblos united in a common cause, and executed Popé's plan on a single day. At Acoma, I discussed the Keresan language with Brian Vallo, a former lieutenant governor of the pueblo. "The difference in dialects today is considerable," he explained. "When I go to Zia, I have some trouble understanding what they're saying. At Cochiti and Santo Domingo, I can't understand at all."

Some scholars argue, however, that the mutual intelligibility of the Pueblo languages must have been far greater in 1680 than it is today—or at least that there was an abundance of Puebloans who could speak several different languages. As another expert in the field, freelance archaeologist Kurt Anschuetz, told me, "By the fifteenth and sixteenth centuries, there must have been multiple language speakers all over the Pueblo world."

Archaeologists who have analyzed the thousands of prehistoric sites that have been excavated in the Southwest now identify three distinct cultural groups, well in place by A.D. 1000, that occupied most of present-day Arizona and New Mexico, as well as southern Utah and southwestern Colorado. They are called Hohokam, Mogollon, and Anasazi (see map, page 34). The Hohokam, who cremated their dead and made great use of irrigation canals, ranged across a 200-mile-wide swath roughly centered around today's cities of Phoenix and Tucson. To their east and southeast flourished the Mogollon. Some skeptics feel that Mogollon is a kind of catch-all designation, but the common denominator of all prehistoric people so labeled is a pottery called brownware. The third group, the Anasazi, who occupied a vast heartland stretching from today's Las Vegas, Nevada, to Las Vegas, New Mexico, are the ones who get all the headlines, for it was they who built the spectacular cliff dwellings found in Mesa Verde, in the Tsegi Canyon system, at Canyon de Chelly, at Chaco Canyon, and in hundreds of other sandstone defiles. By A.D. 1000, the Anasazi were mak-

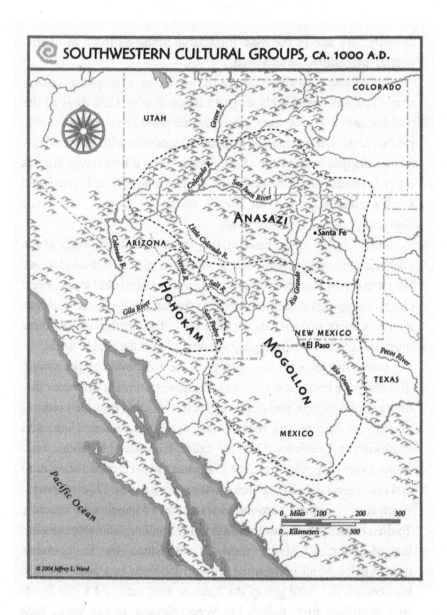

SOUTHWESTERN CULTURAL GROUPS, CA. 1000 A.D.

COLORADO

UTAH

*Green R.*

*Colorado R.*

*San Juan River*

ANASAZI

• Santa Fe

ARIZONA

*Little Colorado R.*

*Colorado R.*

*Verde R.*

*Salt R.*

HOHOKAM

*Gila River*

*San Pedro R.*

*Rio Grande*

NEW MEXICO
• El Paso

*Pecos River*

MOGOLLON

*Rio Grande*

TEXAS

MEXICO

*Pacific Ocean*

0   Miles   100          200          300

0   Kilometers          300

© 2004 Jeffrey L. Ward

ing, for the most part, black-on-white pottery, quite different from Mogollon brownware.

All of today's twenty pueblos lie within the prehistoric realm of the Anasazi. And we know beyond the shadow of a doubt that the Anasazi became Puebloans. That simplistic formula, however, no longer suffices to bridge the gap between prehistory and history. The descendants of the Hohokam, we can say with assurance, are today's Tohono O'odham (formerly known as the Papago), whose reservation claims a vast desert region west of Tucson. What happened to the Mogollon is a genuine puzzle. No living peoples in either the United States or Mexico have been conclusively identified as their descendants, though some experts are convinced that the Mogollon became assimilated among today's western pueblos (particularly Hopi and Zuni).

The single greatest upheaval in Southwestern prehistory—as well as, arguably, the most celebrated mystery in American archaeology—is the sudden, complete, and irrevocable abandonment of the Four Corners area in the last two or three decades of the thirteenth century. By A.D. 1300, in a huge, once fertile tract of land stretching from today's Moab, Utah, to just north of the Hopi mesas, from Pagosa Springs, Colorado, to Gallup, New Mexico, not a single person dwelt in a region that had once teemed with Anasazi. Only the occasional far-ranging jaunt of a seasoned hunter, the journey of a mystic seeking a half-forgotten shrine, disturbed the silence of that former heartland.

Much to the disgust of living Puebloans, the abandonment of the Four Corners area is often misconstrued (especially by the popular media) as the "disappearance" of the Anasazi. In 1991, Leigh Kuwanwisiwma, cultural preservation officer for the Hopi, told me about a research conference that had recently convened to discuss the problem. "They invited me at the last minute," said Kuwanwisiwma. "All these professional archaeologists debating the question, 'What happened to the Anasazi? Where did they go?' I said, 'They didn't go anywhere. They're still around. I can tell you exactly where.'"

Kuwanwisiwma's sardonic jab notwithstanding, the exodus at the end of the thirteenth century remains poorly understood. It used to be thought that the Anasazi simply moved south and east and became today's Puebloans. Virtually all the pueblos have migration stories that locate them once in regions north and west of where they currently live. Along the Rio Grande, the remarkable similarity between a black-on-white pottery first produced in the fourteenth century and Mesa Verde black-on-white (crafted in the twelfth and thirteenth centuries) seemed proof of that formulaic migration. Yet in recent years, a number of New Mexico scholars (including Eric Blinman) have argued persuasively that a sizable population of pueblo dwellers was already in place along the Rio Grande by A.D. 1300.

The whole question of the abandonment, which has spawned many a fat volume of research papers, is too complex to go into here. But whatever was happening in the Pueblo world on the eve of the Spanish invasion cannot be understood without a good look at another major cultural upheaval, which may or may not be all tied up with the abandonment. That is the coming of the kachinas.

To the casual traveler in the Southwest today, "kachina" conjures up chiefly the elaborately costumed dolls sold as tourist knickknacks at some of the pueblos, particularly Hopi. (The best-wrought kachina dolls have transcended the gift shop to become museum pieces.) The dolls may have had their origins as instructional toys for young girls, who by playing with them might learn to recognize the identities of the semi-supernatural beings they represent—no mean feat, since as many as 400 different kachinas exist.

Dolls, however, symbolize only the most limited and concrete aspect of a complicated religious phenomenon. As archaeologist E. Charles Adams, author of a landmark 1991 study called *The Origin and Development of the Pueblo Katsina Cult*, succinctly defines them, "Katsinas are not gods, they are spirits. They are ancestors who act as messengers between the people and their gods. They are also rainmakers, coming as clouds to the villages to which they are annually summoned." (The alternate spelling "katsina" more closely adheres to the pronunciation of the term at Hopi.)

Typically, the kachinas live half the year (from December through

June) in a given pueblo, the other half away from the pueblo. At Hopi, it is believed that shortly after the summer solstice, the kachinas return to the underworld from which all humans sprang before creation, via a ladder at the top of the San Francisco peaks, just north of present-day Flagstaff, Arizona. If the people's prayers and dances are efficacious, the kachinas will regularly emerge from the mountaintops as clouds, bringing rain to the pueblos.

In terms of ceremonies, the kachinas are embodied in a trove of masks, some quite ancient, that are stored in secret niches inside kivas. During the kachina dances, men don the masks. But in the act of dancing, they believe they *become* the kachinas. It is, moreover, essential to keep the children unaware of this magical transformation. It would cause grievous injury to a young boy to learn that the masked, painted dancer in the smoke-filled gloom of the kiva is actually his father or uncle in costume.

The centrality of the kachina phenomenon to the people's religion today varies greatly from pueblo to pueblo. At Hopi and Zuni, the kachinas are all-important; at Taos and Picuris, virtually nonexistent. Yet there is abundant archaeological evidence that a kachina-based religion prevailed among all the pueblos in the Southwest at the time of Spanish contact.

One of the hottest areas of research today is the attempt to trace the origins of the kachina phenomenon. So murky is the question that one influential early ethnographer, Elsie Clews Parsons, postulated that the kachinas were introduced from Mexico by the Spanish. We now know that the kachinas long predate Coronado. Archaeologists have found traces of these supernatural beings dating back to about A.D. 1325, but what kind of religion the kachinas replaced, and why, remain unsolved questions. The debate over where the phenomenon first appears focuses on two early loci—the villages along the Little Colorado River north of present-day Winslow, Arizona, and the middle Rio Grande south of Santa Fe. Whether the kachina religion was an indigenous creation or was imported from Mexico anchors another contentious debate among today's scholars.

That 1325 date, however, pinpoints the significance of the coming of the kachinas. The great upheaval in Puebloan life at the end of the thirteenth century is not limited to the abandonment of the Four Corners region. Two other profound transformations occur at the same time. One is, of course, the appearance of the kachina religion. The other is a radical change in the shape and size of the pueblos.

Before A.D. 1250, the Anasazi typically lived in small villages that seem to have been virtually autonomous from one another. The characteristic social and ceremonial center that brought different families together was the great kiva (the best known example is Casa Rinconada at Chaco Canyon, a magnificent circular underground chamber sixty-three feet in diameter). After 1250, however, the Anasazi begin to aggregate in villages of unprecedented size, with multistory blocks of upward of 2,000 rooms. The great kiva seems to be replaced by the plaza, upon which the roomblocks focus their windows and doorways.

Virtually no experts today doubt that the kachina religion and the huge, aggregated pueblos are inextricably tied up with each other. Among its other benefits, the kachina phenomenon, by cutting across kinship and clan lines, serves to integrate a large village's social life. But here a chicken-and-egg controversy erupts. Does the kachina religion create a need for large, inward-looking pueblos? Or does the new style of pueblo create a demand for a religion to serve as its social glue? As E. Charles Adams puts it, "The need to develop social systems capable of integrating newly large and diverse populations seems clearly to be the stimulus for the development of the katsina ritual."

In either case, are these major social transformations provoked by a massive influx of refugees from the Four Corners at the end of the thirteenth century, or is that influx coincidental to a reorganization of pueblo life already well under way? About ten years ago, as research into the origins of the kachina phenomenon was gathering steam, it became fashionable to view the new religion as the "pull" triggering the great abandonment. The "push" had long been known: severe drought at the end of the thirteenth century, the depletion of big game, possible deforestation as forests were pillaged for firewood, and a disastrous drop in the water table caused by a geological anomaly called arroyo-cutting. If by A.D. 1250 life had grown really hard around the Four Corners, it was argued, and the Anasazi got wind of a new religion taking hold to the south and east, the push of failed crops would combine with the pull of a new belief in new demigods to launch the wholesale exodus. Archaeologist Bruce Bradley had characterized this theory to me in 1994, as we stood among the ruins of a pueblo in southwest Colorado that had been abandoned in the 1280s: "Down there, the Anasazi found an answer about how to live together. They didn't find one up here. Surprise, surprise—up here they're all gone."

Since 1994, however, this theory has slowly gone out of vogue. The problem is the researchers' failure, despite assiduous efforts, to find solid evidence of the kachina phenomenon before 1325. If the new religion really dates from the first quarter of the fourteenth century, it can hardly have been the pull that launched the massive migration beginning in the 1270s.

The whole question goes far beyond mere scholarly nit-picking— it is vital to understanding the pueblos today. A religion introduced or invented some 700 years ago still by and large organizes Puebloan life today. And it was the suppression of the kachina rituals by Franciscan priests in the seventeenth century that blew the smoldering embers of a conquered people into the conflagration of the Pueblo Revolt.

How does one look for archaeological signs of the coming of the kachinas? It is not an easy matter. Kachina masks are so fragile, they tend to disintegrate in the soil. Only a handful of masks confidently dated to before Coronado's time has ever been excavated.

Failing such firsthand proof, archaeologists have ransacked the Southwest for a secondhand reflection of the great religious transformation. This takes the form of images of kachinas and of kachina masks. These have cropped up on broken bits of pottery, and on a very small number of kiva murals—scenes painted on the fragile plaster walls inside the subterranean chambers—that have been rescued from oblivion by responsible excavation. But above all, the kachinas proliferate in rock art etched and painted all over certain sectors of the Southwest, in obscure canyons and ridges where the people first celebrated the ancestral spirits who brought them rain and health.

The Galisteo Basin, which ranges from twenty to forty miles directly south of Santa Fe, is a grassy plain bordered by low sandstone mesas and bisected by basalt dikes. It is virtually treeless except on the mesa tops, which are swathed with stands of piñon and juniper. A pair of lonely highways (U.S. 285 and New Mexico 41) traverses the basin from north to south. Only two settlements, Stanley and Galisteo— each almost too small and sleepy to call a genuine town—huddle against the emptiness. Otherwise, a mere several dozen ranchers inhabit this sweeping plain. None of the basin's five or six shallow, sandy streams, most of which flow into Galisteo Creek, runs today except after heavy downpours.

Yet thanks to windmill-driven wells planted at intervals across the grasslands, this is prime cattle country. Virtually the whole of the basin is occupied by a few sprawling spreads, whose taut barbed wire fences are spangled with no-trespassing signs promising dire punishments to foot-loose intruders. (Rumors persist that on certain Galisteo tracts, hikers in search of ruins or rock art are routinely shot at—or at least near.)

There are, however, a number of springs in the region that flow today just as reliably as they flowed five centuries ago. These, and a subtly but crucially different climactic regimen that obtained in the past, made the Galisteo Basin probably the most densely populated area in all the Southwest in the fifteenth century. During that heyday, no fewer than eight major aggregated pueblos flourished here, the largest of which was San Marcos, across whose adobe ruins I had strolled that bitter, windy day in March. Prehistoric population estimates are notoriously unreliable, but it is not unreasonable to speculate that at some point in the fifteenth century, as many as 10,000 Puebloans lived in the Galisteo Basin.

During seven or eight seasons stretched over the last five years, I have spent many a blissful day wandering among the accessible canyons, ridges, and mesas of this serenely beautiful semiwilderness. Only two of the eight pueblos, alas, lie on public land: San Marcos, recently purchased from private owners by the Archaeological Conservancy; and Pueblo Blanco, which occupies a small square of state land surrounded by working ranches.

Pueblo Blanco is the southwesternmost of the eight Galisteo ruins. On each of five or six visits to the place, I made a leisurely perambulation across the site, absorbing through my boot soles the shape of the roomblocks and plazas covered by centuries' worth of wind-blown earth. And during the last two visits, I carried with me photocopies of the pages of Nels Nelson's 1914 report of the sample excavation he had performed at Pueblo Blanco two years earlier.

Nelson's summer fieldwork was part of a grandly ambitious program, sponsored by the American Museum of Natural History, to discover the prehistoric riches of the Galisteo Basin. In six months, he and his workers excavated a total of 430 rooms in seven of the eight major pueblos. It is inevitable that by today's standards, Nelson's digs seem a bit crude and hasty; but in his time, the man was among the finest archaeologists working in the Southwest, one of the very first to apply the powerful principle of stratigraphy to date the succession of layers his shovel penetrated.

At Pueblo Blanco, Nelson dug only forty-seven rooms. With my photocopy of the excellent map he had made of the ruin in hand, I could not only easily discern the boundaries of roomblocks that stand as broad, low ridges protruding from the ground, but I could find the slight depressions that still bespoke the spadework of ninety-one years before, marking each of the forty-seven excavated rooms, which lie scattered across a site fully 1,000 feet square.

Blanco is cut in half by an arroyo flowing from west to east. This stream must have been the water source for the pueblo, since no spring lies nearby, but on none of my five or six visits had I found even the shallowest puddle of recent rainfall in the sandy wash. As if to underscore the aridity of the place, its builders had erected an earthen dam across a feeble tributary of the arroyo's main channel, some 400 yards to the north, thereby creating a small reservoir. I had missed this feature on my previous visits, but with Nelson as my guide, I hiked north and located the dam.

Several times a year, flash floods still thunder down the arroyo. The most visible architecture at Pueblo Blanco is the roomblock being eaten away by the floods on the arroyo's south bank. Four-foot-high walls of still-mortared stones cling precariously to the hard mud of the bank, hanging half in air: a gentle push would collapse each one of them. On my last visit, I recognized that rooms I had seen four years before had vanished. Yet Nelson's 1912 photo of the same arroyo bank looks remarkably like what I now beheld. The ruin is not, of course, limitless, but it will take another millennium or so to erode it into oblivion.

Nelson estimated that 2,000 rooms had been built at Pueblo Blanco. Because among the 463 "specimens" he collected, he found "not a single scrap of evidence suggesting European contact," he concluded that the pueblo must have been abandoned by the time of Oñate's conquest in 1598, and probably by the time of Coronado's journey fifty-eight years earlier. The vast village had thus evidently flourished only during the fourteenth and fifteenth centuries.

Having walked the whole ruin, I returned to the small square depression Nelson had numbered Building X, Room 3, and stared at another photo from his report. Nine decades ago, seven feet below my boot soles, Nelson had found what he called "by far the most interesting discovery of the season." On the floor of an otherwise unremarkable room, in an equally unremarkable sector of the village, the archaeologist had uncovered an altar seventeen by twenty-five inches square, raised four to six inches above the rest of the floor. Atop the altar had been placed, in a deliberate array, thirty-two ceremonial objects. These included several miniature clay pots, two bone tools, arrow points of flint and obsidian, worked pebbles, pieces of petrified wood, and other less identifiable implements. The pièce de résistance of the assemblage, leaning upright against the back wall, was a beautifully shaped sandstone effigy, twenty-one inches tall, on which a stern, stylized human face had been carved, importing to the object an eerie anthropomorphic presence. Never in any museum, not even in another photograph, had I seen a Puebloan or Anasazi effigy anything like the one in Nelson's picture.

The excavator himself had been utterly baffled by his find. "For the present at least," Nelson wrote cautiously in his 1914 report, "the writer cannot attempt to discuss the nature and function of this discovery." At the time, scholars had not begun to speculate about the origins of the kachina religion. The term "kachina cult" had not yet been coined. As I stared at the photo, however, I could not help thinking that Nelson must have found in situ the paraphernalia of some kachina ritual from the fourteenth or fifteenth century. No doubt the thirty-two objects rest today in some obscure drawer in the archives of the American Museum of Natural History in New York, but I doubt that more than three or four savants (if that many) have bothered to look at them since Nelson deposited them there at the end of 1912.

I left Pueblo Blanco with reluctance, for on my second visit, five years before, the ruin had graced me with one of the most magical moments of all my wanderings in the Southwest. It was a hot, breezy day in early September. After walking the ruin, I had sat on the ground to eat lunch, then lain full-length with my day pack as a pillow and dozed off for ten or fifteen minutes. On awakening, I got up and walked north, crossing what I would later identify as Nelson's Building XI. As I crested the roomblock, I suddenly stood face-to-face with a mountain lion, only ten yards away. As startled as I, the magnificent animal turned and ran away in great leaping bounds, while I stared transfixed. That is still the only mountain lion I have ever seen in the wild.

Even the driest of field reports contain nuggets of observation that take on, in the light of subsequent history, the burnish of rueful irony. In 1912, archaeology was all about collecting artifacts. From his 430 excavated rooms, Nelson gathered up and carried back to New York the mind-boggling total of 4,957 "specimens." This number does not include "something like 23 bushels of potsherds." But Nelson assumed that his fieldwork in the summer of 1912 was only the beginning of a massive scholarly assault on the Galisteo Basin. "As there is every prospect that the investigations of the American Museum may continue for some time," Nelson wrote, "it is deemed advisable to reserve treatment of the artifacts . . . until such time as most, if not all, of the Tano ruins have been partially excavated. This may require two or three years."

Two or three years! More than ninety years on—thank God—the eight big pueblos of the Galisteo Basin remain virtually unprobed. Precious little fieldwork has followed on the heels of Nelson's energetic sampling digs, though some of it, such as the AMNH's excavation of the mission at San Marcos from 1998 to 2002, has been performed with a sophistication far beyond anything possible in 1912.

On the one hand, Nelson's fanatic collecting looms today as a minor tragedy: despite the excellent report he published in 1914, not much real insight has ever been wrung from those 4,957 artifacts. In 2004, what was going on in the Galisteo Basin in the fourteenth and fifteenth centuries remains largely a mystery. During all those decades since Nelson dug, the eight pueblos have been vulnerable to the depredations of illegal pothunters. Yet on my last visit to Pueblo Blanco, I was happy to see that well more than twenty-three bushels of potsherds still lay strewn across the surface of the site. (Not for the first time, I wondered how a people otherwise so apparently deft and handy could have managed to break so many pots in only 200 years.)

From the ruin I hiked to a low sandstone cliff that rims a mesa sheltering Pueblo Blanco on the north. Here I found, for the fifth or sixth time, a vivid gallery of petroglyphs. On the far-right-hand end of the cliff, a massive, beautifully carved bear (only a little smaller than life-sized) ambles casually toward the ruin. Alas, some early-twentieth-century rancher saw fit to carve his initials or his brand—an interlocked capital W and R—athwart the bear's midsection. Toward the center of the cliff, three huge plumed serpents, each more than twenty feet long, slither in sinuous zigzags from left to right. These are the largest representations I have ever seen of a fairly common image in the rock art of the Rio Grande. The plumed or horned serpent, also known as Avanyu or Awanyu, is thought to have affinities with Quetzalcóatl, the Aztec and Toltec serpent-god. That very association forms a powerful argument for a Mexican origin of the kachina cult.

Kachinas indeed abound on this cliff near Pueblo Blanco, several of them carved directly under the bodies of the serpents. Here the kachinas are rendered as circles with simplified facial features—round staring bug eyes, slits for mouths, square boxes for ears. A pair of adjoining kachina faces incorporates "puns" from the surface of the cliff, for the artist has appropriated two natural horizontal creases in the rock as mouths. The kachinas thus seem to be grinning at the onlooker with a macabre omniscience.

It is all but certain that this rock art was created by the same people who lived at Pueblo Blanco: there is no evidence for any sizable occupation of this corner of the Galisteo Basin during any period but the fourteenth and fifteenth (and possibly early-sixteenth) centuries. If so, the art on the cliff near the ruin must celebrate the new religion that tied together a village populous enough to require 2,000 rooms.

The kachina imagery, however, reaches its zenith not on the sandstone mesa cliffs of the basin, but on its basalt dikes. Over the last five years, I have spent many an hour seeking out these dazzling petroglyphs, some so fresh they look as though they had been etched just the previous week.

Many of these designs, some graven on boulders as small as filing cabinets, echo images found elsewhere and earlier in the Anasazi world. There are hundreds of depictions of animals and birds, the former ranging from badgers to deer to bears to mountain lions, the latter from storks to herons to eagles to quails (and quail tracks). Some mingle different animals in a single petroglyph, creating chimeras whose meanings must be buried in long-lost myths. One finely carved beast seems to have the body of a rodent, the tail of a beaver, and the pinwheel feet of a stylized mountain lion. Another hallucinatory panel depicts Kokopelli, the hunchbacked flute player, as a rabbit with gigantic ears and erect penis, piping what looks more like a bassoon than a flute at a small human dancing with ducks held aloft in each hand.

Abstract mazes may hint at maps of ancestral migrations; stepped pyramids allude perhaps to the thunderclouds that bring the life-sustaining rain. (Both interpretations are based on the readings of Hopi elders in the twentieth century.)

Along these dikes, I also found a dazzling profusion of kachinas. Most anthropomorphic images elsewhere in the Anasazi world depict the whole or at least a good part of the body, as well as the head. Here, however, the kachina is reduced to a straight-on, stylized head, at once a picture of the kachina mask and a conjuring up of the kachina itself.

These Galisteo images tend to look fierce, bordering on the monstrous. The mouth is rendered as a rigid rectangle with bared rows of sharp teeth. The eyes are blank diamonds, ovals, and squares. Horns and plumes sprout from crowned, pulsating heads; bizarre earrings, shaped like spinning tops, dangle like antennae from lobed ears. One mask renders both ears as the fletchings of an arrow, the nose as the arrow itself.

For me, the cumulative impact of this picture gallery is an ecstatic chill, akin to what I had felt in Romanesque churches in Spain and France, where hundreds of carved column capitals summon up mythical beasts and wild animals devouring human beings and each other. I had once spent three weeks alone in wintry Catalonia, during which I managed to visit and admire a mere sixty-nine of the 2,400 Romanesque churches built there in the eleventh and twelfth centuries. From that quest, I emerged with a bewildered awe that I found stunningly articulated in a quote by the French art scholar Henri Focillon: "What name can we give, what meaning assign to these fancies, which seem to emanate from the caprice or delirium of a solitary visionary and which yet recur throughout Romanesque art, like the images of some vast collective nightmare?"

The kachina petroglyphs in the Galisteo Basin strike me as every bit as baleful as Romanesque capitals, and even more haunting for being strewn across a trailless outback, rather than marshaled into formal chapels. Yet I have to remind myself that all these carved faces celebrate benevolent ancestral beings, the bringers of rain, the growers of corn.

The Galisteo rock art reaches an apocalyptic climax in one short section of basalt dike only three miles away from Pueblo Blanco. Here it is hard to tell where the kachina leaves off and Focillon's "delirium of a solitary visionary" may begin. One motif repeated again and again is the four-pointed star, sometimes with a kachina-like face at the center. Beasts and humanoids alike are carved with other figures inside their bodies. Is the meaning literally pregnancy, or—more likely—some kind of symbolic immanence, the outer figure invested with the supernatural power of the inner? On several boulders, kachina-headed humans carry a club in one hand, and what looks like a corn stalk in the other. There are plumed serpents, flute players, men dancing with snakes (as in historic times they did at many of the pueblos). A stepped rain cloud has a birdlike kachina head; a mountain lion sprouts a giant feather from the back of its skull.

The single finest panel of rock art in all the Galisteo Basin appears near the highest part of the crest of this volcanic dike. The anthropomorphic figures here are huge, almost life-sized. One female with outstretched arms, twin eagle feathers sprouting from her goggle-eyed head, carries a small horned warrior inside her trunk—an upright humanoid with club in left hand, pointed spear in right. Another warrior is seen in profile, a ruffled crown on his head, the man-sized spear planted butt on the ground, the point held in front of the figure's sneering face. The petroglyphic masterpiece in the center of the panel, however, is a pair of "shield-bearers"—humans with recognizable heads, arms, and legs, but whose torsos bulge as decorated disks that conjure up shields. The upper figure has short horns on his head and carries a war club in his right hand. His shield has two eyelike circles on the upper chest, and is fringed with triangular rays suggestive of the sun. The lower figure, also horned, wields a lethal-looking trapezoidal club or axe in his right hand; his shield is dominated by a pair of bear paws dangling like pectoral pendants. (See first photo in insert.)

What does all this frenzied imagery mean? And how does it tie into the eight Galisteo pueblos that flourished here between 700 and 400 years ago?

The leading expert on rock art in the Southwest is Polly Schaafsma, who lives south of Santa Fe, and who for almost forty years has assiduously sought out, characterized, and analyzed pictographs and petroglyphs across a region stretching from southern Texas to northern Utah and down into Baja California, Sonora, and Chihuahua. It was Schaafsma who first demonstrated that much of the Rio Grande rock art depicts kachinas, and it was she who dated the bulk of those images to the period from 1325 to 1600.

In 2000, Schaafsma published her most ambitious interpretive effort yet, a book called *Warrior, Shield, and Star: Imagery and Ideology of Pueblo Warfare.* By brilliantly synthesizing patterns in the rock art with turn-of-the-twentieth-century ethnography performed in the pueblos (especially in the relatively unacculturated pueblos of Hopi and Zuni), and fixing the art in time by association with well-dated nearby ruins, Schaafsma has wrung meanings from panels (a good number of them in the Galisteo) that had left all previous experts grasping at speculative straws.

Her arguments are too intricate to summarize here, but taken as a whole, they seem to me utterly convincing. For Schaafsma, then, the ubiquitous four-pointed star is at once a kachina, a representation of Venus (which in Pueblo mythology is a guardian warrior of the sun), and a symbol of ceremonies tied to the scalping of enemies. The "knife-wing," a semimythical bird that looks much like an eagle (and of which I saw many representations on the Galisteo dikes), is likewise linked to scalping and to beheading. The sun itself is at once a mask (some Puebloans believe that a disk-shield covers the true face of the sun) and "the supreme patron of war." Schaafsma quotes a pithy oral tradition collected at Hopi by ethnographer and linguist Ekkehart Malotki in the 1980s, to the effect that Masau, a supreme deity, explains to the people that "keeping the sun going will be possible only at the expense of human life. Only by flaming with human grease can the sun burn with such heat that it will produce enough light. For this reason people will have to die from now on." The winter solstice was always a perilous time for prehistoric Puebloans, whose sky-watchers pulled out all the stops to ensure the reversal of the southeasterly drift of the sun's point of rising on the horizon. According to tradition, the plumed serpent was a particularly dangerous enemy of the sun at the time of the winter solstice.

Schaafsma points out that nowhere in the Southwest is there such an abundance of shield imagery as in the Galisteo Basin. Real shields were produced by the Anasazi only relatively late, after about A.D. 1150. By 1325, shields were most likely made of elk or bison hide. But the decorations on the shields had a magical potency. The painting on the shield, writes Schaafsma, was "designed to blind and confuse the enemy as it strengthened the user with supernatural assistance."

The two superb shield-bearers on the Galisteo dike, Schaafsma argues, may well depict the War Twins. These are central Puebloan deities, sons of the sun himself. In some stories, they are responsible for carrying the sun across the sky. The bear paws on the lower figure's shield conjure up the bear as an animal patron of war. Among the Keres pueblos, the Twins are named Masewi and Oyoyewi; at Zuni, they are collectively designated as Ahayu:da. The War Twins play many roles for the Puebloans, including those of bringing rain, of slaying monsters, and of hunting big game through magic tricks; but their supreme importance is, in the words of one ethnographer, as "effective culture heroes who lead the people at the time of the emergence and protect them from outlandish and imaginary foes."

The masterly panel cresting the dike three miles from Pueblo

Blanco, Schaafsma concludes, is thus a war shrine. "Between ca. 1325 and 1525," she writes, "this topographic eminence was regarded as the residence of supernatural powers that could be appealed to in time of conflict. The numerous shield figures and the repetition of the war themes undoubtedly served to increase the power of the locality." And because of its proximity to the ruin, it was almost certainly the inhabitants of Pueblo Blanco who had worshiped at this shrine.

At San Marcos, walking the vast site that seemed defenseless against the plains stretching away on all sides, I had been seduced into imagining a people who, before the advent of the Spanish, had lived in peace, unthreatened by nearby enemies. A long and stubborn Anglo ethnographic tradition has fostered the myth of the Puebloans as essentially peaceful folk. Before the Pueblo Revolt, the Spanish themselves had cherished such an illusion: one friar and governor after another characterized the Puebloans as "meek," "well-mannered," and "tractable," as opposed to the "savage nomads" that marauded on their borders.

All the while, anthropologists and historians ignored abundant evidence to the contrary about Puebloan culture. Countless old stories, many collected at the end of the nineteenth century, tell of one pueblo making war upon another. The persistence well into the twentieth century—and, in some cases, up to the present—of war and scalp societies among the pueblos gives credence to the idea that armed conflict has always been a central feature of Puebloan life and thought.

I came away from all my Galisteo wanderings, then, with new inklings as to what might have gone on there in the fourteenth and fifteenth centuries. It is likely that the four southernmost of the eight aggregated pueblos were abandoned by Coronado's time—not only Pueblo Blanco, but Pueblos Largo, Colorado, and Shey. What caused their demise? Many scholars see raids by increasingly aggressive nomads from the south and east as triggering the abandonment, but it is also possible that the four northern pueblos—San Marcos, San Lázaro, Galisteo, and San Cristóbal, whose warriors would play such a pivotal role in the Pueblo Revolt—had vanquished their neighbors and driven them from their once prosperous villages.

The coming of the kachinas was only partly a matter of, in Bruce Bradley's phrase, "finding an answer about how to live together." The new religion was also all about war. In front of the great panel on the Galisteo dike, I had stood where Puebloans had once come (if Polly Schaafsma's theories are correct) to invoke their gods to help them annihilate an enemy. And in some instances, that enemy was almost certainly other Puebloans. If, sometime in the early sixteenth century, all the engraved knife-wings and four-pointed stars and the War Twins themselves had failed the people who sought their aid, those images and beings would not fail the Puebloans who once more prayed to them for divine vengeance in 1680.

The first Europeans in the Southwest were not Coronado's army of 1540. Those explorers were preceded, five years earlier, by as unlikely a quartet of vagabonds as the New World has ever seen. Their story has oft been told, and endlessly ruminated over, but it bears recounting one more time.

In 1528, a 600-man expedition under Pánfilo de Narváez sailed from Cuba to explore and plunder the coast of Florida. Narváez was, in the words of historian Carroll L. Riley, "a brutal and wildly incompetent commander." During his first months on the American coast (to quote Riley again), he "floundered around northern Florida, committing a number of atrocities but finding little treasure." Narváez eventually landed most of his party near present-day Apalachicola, Florida, while the ships sailed west to reconnoiter the coast. This was a fatal error, for the feckless pilot guiding the fleet quickly lost track of the land party. Eventually the ships returned to Cuba, having given up Narváez's men for dead.

Hoping to reach the rumored Spanish settlement of Pánuco, somewhere on the Gulf Coast, the men hiked westward. Swamps and hostile Indians soon stalled their progress. Out of animal hides, they crafted skin rafts and pushed onward. Many men died when these rafts swamped or were driven out to sea. At last two boats, with a mere ninety survivors, wrecked on the coast near Galveston Island, Texas. There, the men attempted to winter over, throwing themselves on the mercy of local Indians. By the spring of 1529, only about a dozen Spaniards were still alive.

One group of four survivors was led by Alvar Núñez Cabeza de Vaca, Narváez's second-in-command. Two others among this quartet, Andrés de Dorantes and Alonso de Castillo Maldonado, were also well-born Spaniards. The fourth, a man known only as Esteban or Estevánico, was a Moorish slave from Morocco belonging to Dorantes. Slave or no slave, Esteban was a gifted fellow—by far the best traveler among the four, and a born linguist, whose facility at learning Indian languages proved an immeasurable boon to the desperate men.

During the next six years, the group made its way slowly across Texas toward northern Mexico, insinuating itself within one Indian tribe after another. Cabeza de Vaca proved efficacious as a trader and, at times, as a shaman who cured patients not by blowing on the skin or laying on of hands, but by reciting the Ave Maria and the Pater Noster.

The *Relación* that Cabeza de Vaca ultimately published in 1542 is as enigmatic a book as it is an important one—a veritable hodgepodge of memoir, myth, observation, and rumor. (Chapters have such intriguing titles as "How We Departed After Eating the Dogs" and "How Some Indians Robbed the Others.") For centuries, scholars have tried to match the author's all too vague or fanciful descriptions of landscapes crossed and peoples encountered with actual geography and Indian tribes. One of the most assiduous students of the narrative has the vagabonds crossing southern New Mexico and perhaps a sector of southern Arizona, thus becoming the first Europeans known to have entered the Southwest.

At a certain point in 1535, near the Rio Grande, the four Spaniards spent considerable time among Indians whom they called "the People of the Cows." These bison hunters may have been Jumanos, Teyas, or Conchos. Whoever they were, they traded with another people to the north and west. The Spaniards were perplexed that these nomads had plentiful stores of corn, yet did not grow the plant themselves. "Where, we asked them, did they get the corn they had?" wrote Cabeza de Vaca later. "From where the sun goes down; in that country it grew all over; the quickest way there was the path . . . along the river northward." This passage almost surely records the first glimmering awareness by Europeans of the existence of the pueblos of present-day New Mexico and Arizona.

The bison hunters also possessed what Cabeza de Vaca called "emeralds made into arrow points" (possibly from a copper ore). To acquire these items from the northern people, they had traded macaw feathers and plumes acquired in turn from Mexico. The Spaniards' hosts further explained that "there were towns there with many people and very large houses." Cabeza de Vaca somehow ascertained that "the place where the permanent houses are is very warm, so much so that the weather is hot in January. . . . The Indians who live in the permanent houses, and those behind them, have no regard for gold or silver, nor do they believe that any use can be made of them."

Thus was sown the seed of the fabulous myth that came to be called the Seven Cities of Cíbola, or, alternatively, the Seven Cities of Gold. On April 1, 1536, the four wanderers finally reached the Spanish outpost of Culiacán, on the Pacific Coast, having walked and rafted, over a span of eight years, all the way from Florida—completing one of the most astounding journeys ever performed by Europeans in the New World. Long before the *Relación* was published, New Spain was aflame with gossip about the rich towns in the far north.

Such was the torpid bureaucracy of Mexico City, however, that it took almost three years for an exploring expedition to be launched. Finally, in the spring of 1539, a party led by the Franciscan friar Marcos de Niza set out from Culiacán. The bulk of the expedition was a large group of Mexican Indians. The guide and scout was Esteban, the Moorish slave who had been so useful to Cabeza de Vaca.

By now Esteban must have thought he had the Indians all figured

out. Cabeza de Vaca insists in his *Relación* that, on the four Spaniards'
long journey west from Texas, as one Indian tribe had handed them on
to the next, "among all these folk there was a firm conviction that we
had come from heaven." The chronicler also recounts how the four
men comported themselves on reaching a new tribe: "We behaved to
them with great authority and gravity and, to preserve this impression,
spoke little. The black [Esteban] talked with them constantly, found
out about the ways we wanted to go and what towns there were and
the things we wished to know."

Fray Marcos had been with Pizarro during the conquest of Peru
from 1531 to 1533. Rumors had it that the remote towns to the north
of New Spain were as rich in gold as the kingdom of the Incas had
been. On his exploratory journey in 1539, the friar was, to be sure, on
the lookout for gold, but he hoped also to reap a rich harvest in souls
by converting the heathens to the true faith.

From the very start, things went badly. The impetuous Esteban
could not bear to travel at the friar's poky pace. By the time they
approached the land of the pueblos, the scout, with a small party of
Indians, was several days ahead of the main body of the expedition.

The first contact between Europeans and Puebloans occurred
sometime in May 1539. Within hours, the encounter turned, at least
from the Spanish point of view, into a complete debacle.

On a warm day in late September, I drove into Zuni and stopped at the
visitor center. I was hoping to visit the ruins of Hawikuh, some fifteen
miles southwest of the current pueblo. In 1539, the Zuni lived in six
villages scattered around the flanks of Dowa Yalanne, or Corn Mountain, a high, dramatic butte that would become a sovereign refuge for
the people during and after the Pueblo Revolt. Ever since archaeologist
Frederick W. Hodge excavated Hawikuh in the 1910s and 1920s,
most experts have agreed that it was this pueblo that Esteban had
approached on that eventful day in 1539.

I was greeted at the visitor center by Lena Tsethlikia, a spunky woman apparently in her fifties, who had served for several years as a tour guide. She had bad news. "We got a new governor last January," she said. "He says we can't go to Hawikuh any more. It's 'culturally sensitive.'" There was no disguising the note of annoyance in Tsethlikia's voice. The governor's conservatism was costing her a part of her income.

We chatted on. I realized that Tsethlikia was discreetly checking me out. I must have passed some unwritten test, for all at once she decided that she could fit me in for one more tour, under a kind of grandfather clause she had negotiated with the governor.

We hopped into my rental car and drove through the pueblo, passing the handsome adobe mission, whose original walls date from 1629. An Arizona archaeologist had told me that if I did nothing else at Zuni, I should visit this church, inside which, during the last several decades, a Zuni artist had painted a series of remarkable murals covering the walls and ceiling, elaborating themes from the people's folklore. (One guidebook calls this interior "The Sistine Chapel of the Americas.") Now, however, Tsethlikia told me that the mission was permanently closed. For $25, the artist himself would unlock the door and let a visitor wander briefly inside.

We emerged from the pueblo on a back road. Musing on Hawikuh, Tsethlikia told me, "The name means 'bundle of grain.' They say there's spirits out there. They can feel them there. Even Anglos can feel them."

On dirt roads, we were able to drive straight to Hawikuh, though I would never have found the place on my own (nor, of course, would I have attempted to). We got out of the car and strolled across the site. The debris from scores of fallen walls—innumerable shaped blocks of purplish sandstone—sprawled from the crest of a low hill down to a grassy plain that stretched off into the southwest. It was obvious how Esteban and his Indian companions would have seen Hawikuh from afar, as they rode in from that direction.

There were polychrome potsherds scattered everywhere. Here and there, the upper surfaces of small boulders had been packed solid with the prettiest sherds. All over the Southwest, I had seen such "museum rocks," a fad of the last twenty or thirty years. Well-meaning visitors, who might once have pocketed these souvenirs, instead lay them out for others to see. Archaeologists, however, frown on these assemblages almost as sternly as they do on the act of pilfering, for museum rocks wreak havoc with the sherds' provenience (the exact places where they have lain in the dirt for centuries, from whose patterns scholars may someday wring new understandings). Museum rocks had always struck me as annoying on purely aesthetic grounds, as well. (I liked the term a New Mexico archaeologist used as, a month hence, we stumbled upon another such display in Bandelier National Monument. "Goody piles," he spat, as he swept the sherds off the boulder top.)

Tsethlikia, though, had no such qualms. Beside one museum rock, she knelt to add three or four especially handsome sherds she had found nearby. Not for the first time, I was struck with a humbling thought: *Who are we Anglos to tell Native Americans how to take care of their ancestral places?*

"What happened here with Esteban?" I asked.

Tsethlikia had the story as it had been passed down to her by her father. "At first the Zuni thought he was a great man," she said. "They liked the parrot feather plumes that he had. They thought he must be an important man.

"But Esteban came to look around and see what was here. He started demanding food and shelter. Then he started wanting our women. That's why the Zunis got mad and killed him."

The Spanish record of this first encounter gone wrong differs significantly from Tsethlikia's version. That we have a Spanish account at all depends on the fact that one of the Mexican Indians in Esteban's entourage escaped and ran back to tell what had happened to Fray Marcos, languishing several days behind. According to this exhausted informant, on approaching Hawikuh, Esteban had sent messengers ahead carrying a string of rattles and a red feather and a white feather. (Could these be the plumes to which Tsethlikia alluded?) This peace gesture had apparently worked well for the Moor on his long traverse with Cabeza de Vaca.

But at Hawikuh, the gambit only enraged the local headmen. They warned Esteban's party that if they persisted in approaching, they would all be killed. Esteban haughtily ignored the warning and marched on toward the pueblo, whereupon the Zuni seized the men, imprisoned them in a house, and denied them food and water.

Fray Marcos's informant managed to slip out of confinement and hide in the weeds. The last thing he saw was Esteban and his supporters running away, chased by Zuni men shooting arrows at them. Later two or three other survivors straggled in to Marcos's camp, confirming the story.

This version has to be regarded as seriously flawed. Marcos himself would emerge from his disastrous expedition to the pueblos with a reputation for unreliability. Modern scholars have characterized him as "the lying monk," "the mystery man . . . of the American Southwest," and "a monumental liar." Moreover, a pall of linguistic confusion must have hung over this fatal clash of cultures. Polyglot though he was, Esteban could hardly have spoken Zuni, nor, one suspects, could any of the Mexican Indians who accompanied him.

Several months after my visit to Hawikuh, I came upon the transcript of an informal lecture by Edmund J. Ladd, called "Zuni on the Day the Men in Metal Arrived." Ladd, who died in 1999, was that rarest of people, a Puebloan who became a professional archaeologist and ethnographer.

In his talk, Ladd muses with a sly irony on what might have happened that day in May 1539, informing his fantasia both with "book learning" and with the oral traditions he had imbued in a lifetime at his home pueblo. For Ladd, there is no doubt that the Zuni knew of the coming of the Spaniards to the New World long before the Spaniards heard the first rumors about the northern pueblos. Long-distance traders bearing macaw feathers, copper bells, and exotic seashells would have come to Zuni during the years after Cortés's conquest of Mexico. "They told of white men coming there and that they were very vicious, cruel. They had seen with their own eyes whole villages wiped out by . . . men on great animals using fire sticks that could blow a hole right through you."

According to Ladd's educated whimsy, the Zuni at first greeted Esteban in friendly fashion. But, beset by the mutual incomprehension that must have issued from the language barrier, the Spaniards mistook an offer of accommodation in "a large house outside the village" for an attempt to imprison them. Esteban began to make "demands for food, gifts, and I suppose women, as he had done with other people he came in contact with along the way." The proffering of the "medicine gourd" backfired. "The head war chief took the gourd," Ladd imagines, "and dashed it to the ground and said, 'This is not from our people.'"

Now the Moor was summoned to the tribal council, where he made his last and fatal mistake. "He declared he was the leader of white men who were following and who were more powerful than himself." The Zuni, Ladd thinks, had heard of Spanish slave raids among the Indians as far north as Sinaloa in western Mexico. "All of these elements were no doubt computed by the war priest. The only thing that came up was '*slave spy*.' So Estevan was killed. . . . He was killed not because he was black, not because of his demands, but because of his statement that he was 'leading white men more powerful than himself.'"

Almost a year before I read Ladd's transcribed talk, I had interviewed Joe Sando, a seventy-nine-year-old Jemez man who, like Ladd, had been university-educated and had written historical works about his home pueblo. Sando recited for me an oxymoron he had learned as a child: "The first white man we saw was a black man." Later I repeated this remark to a Santa Fe archaeologist, who promptly told me (though not for attribution) that the accident of Esteban's having had black skin had fostered a legacy of prejudice against African-Americans that could still be detected in the pueblos.

Alarmed by the news of Esteban's death, Fray Marcos rode (so he claimed in his report) only close enough to see Hawikuh from a great distance. Then, in Ladd's sardonic phrasing, the friar "lifted up his skirts again and ran as fast as he could back to Mexico." Somehow, Marcos deduced that the name of this place was "Cíbola," and that it consisted of six other villages besides Hawikuh (only a slight exaggeration of the five other villages that then existed at Zuni). *Ciwolo* is the Zuni word for bison. Ladd imagines Esteban's Indians wearing buffalo robes, pointing to them in hopes of trading for more such hides, only to hear the Zuni murmuring, "Cíbolo, cíbolo."

In his official report, Fray Marcos made no mention of gold. But it was gold the expedition was after, and within weeks of the friar's return, Mexico City was aflame with gossip that the priest had seen a massive city plated with gold—just as Cuzco had appeared to Pizarro. The dream of the Seven Cities of Gold had seized the imagination of New Spain.

At the ruin of Hawikuh, Lena Tsethlikia had ventured a curious confirmation of this rumor. "My father said," she told me, "that when the Zuni built their houses, they plastered them with mud and straw. When the sun was going down, the straw would glisten. That's why the Spanish thought it was gold."

Failure or not, Fray Marcos's timid foray served as the scouting expedition for one of the most ambitious *entradas* ever launched by Spaniards in the New World. In April 1540, Francisco Vázquez de Coronado rode out of Culiacán at the head of a veritable army consisting of 350 Spaniards, as many as 1,300 Indian allies from Mexico, and an unspecified number of slaves and servants, as well as four Franciscan friars, including Fray Marcos de Niza himself. The Spaniards possessed 559 horses and drove with them 1,500 head of livestock—sheep, cattle, and pigs to provision the men on their way.

Following Fray Marcos's directions, on July 7 Coronado's advance party came in sight of Hawikuh. When the conquistadors saw that the fabled Cíbola amounted to a rude pueblo made of stones and mud, they turned on the friar with such anger that Coronado feared for the man's life. Nevertheless, the soldiers marched toward the village.

Coronado had left Mexico under explicit orders to cause no harm to the Indian peoples he might meet in the Southwest. Yet his very first encounter with the Puebloans, at Hawikuh, turned into a pitched battle. It was clear that the Zuni were not going to allow the Spaniards to enter their village. According to the official chronicle of the expedition, Coronado announced (no doubt in Spanish) that he had come in peace "to protect these Indians as children of their great emperor across the sea." Whatever the Zuni made of this proclamation, they were not impressed. So Coronado made a show of laying down his guns and swords, entreating the Indians with sign language to lay down their bows and arrows. Instead the Zuni attacked, losing a dozen men to the Spaniards' superior firepower before they retreated to defend Hawikuh. Coronado counterattacked and took the pueblo, though not before he himself was badly wounded. The surviving Zuni fled, while the Spaniards ransacked the buildings for corn to feed the hungry soldiers.

Edmund Ladd imagines a very different scenario at Hawikuh, from the Zuni point of view. On July 7, the people would have been in the midst of a multiday celebration of the summer solstice that required a pilgrimage to a shrine at the junction of the Zuni and Little Colorado rivers. The attack on the Spaniards, then, was led by the bow priests charged with guarding the pilgrimage. "What the bow priests were saying," Ladd paraphrases, "was, 'Don't cross the trail.' . . . I don't think they tried to kill them. I think they just tried to scare them off."

When the Spaniards advanced anyway, Ladd speculates, the head bow priest laid a line of cornmeal across their path. This was a universal Puebloan practice, indicating the sternest possible interdiction. But the Spaniards did not understand its meaning, walked across the line, and warfare broke out.

Ladd further muses, "The Zunis had killed Estevan the year before as a spy and now here came another group of people with the same kind of dogs, riding on strange animals, waving flags. . . . There was no interpretation that the Zunis could make other than that this was a slave-raiding party. That may have been another cause for the battle."

Despite the sacking of Hawikuh, the pueblo fronting the empty plains to the southwest would survive for another 130 years. As we walked slowly across the ruin, Tsethlikia showed me where the Spaniards had built their mission after Oñate's conquest in 1598. "They built the church right on top of our kiva," she said. Such was indeed the Spanish practice, a vivid demonstration that the Catholic faith must supplant the "sorcery" of the kachinas. But now Tsethlikia added a piquant observation. "After that, the Zuni decided to make their kivas rectangular and aboveground, so they'd blend in with the houses." I knew that ever since ethnographers, toward the end of the nineteenth century, had concluded that the windowless, rectangular, aboveground ceremonial chambers that the Hopi called "kivas" were the modern equivalent of the circular underground chambers found archaeologically, they had been at a loss to explain the transformation in shape and location. But I had never before heard Tsethlikia's simple, commonsense explanation.

The demise of Hawikuh finally came, Tsethlikia told me, in 1676, only four years before the Pueblo Revolt. "That's when the Apaches raided this place," she said, as if remembering a family story. "The Zuni men were out in the fields, harvesting wheat for a pageant. They would come home in the evening. The Apaches came and killed all the women and children that were here."

My guide's fund of oral tradition even comprised Hodge's excavations in the early twentieth century. "There used to be a graveyard here," she said, as we paused on the eastern edge of the ruin. "The archaeologists took the bodies all out and took them to the Smithsonian. The Zuni didn't like that."

Just before we got back in my rental car, Tsethlikia stood on the brow of Hawikuh's hill and gazed over the site. "The spirits," she said softly. "It's just something by you, next to you. I don't feel uncomfortable when I come here. It seems like they're happy when I come."

Coronado's spectacular and tragic two-year odyssey in the Southwest is too grand an epic even to summarize here. Many books have been written about the *entrada*, including the official chronicle by a participant, Pedro de Castañeda. Yet an aura of mystery continues to hover over this monumental undertaking.

Were Coronado's journey to be regarded simply as a voyage of discovery, it ought to rank among the finest exploring expeditions in North American history. As a mere addendum to the main thrust of the *entrada*, in August 1540 Coronado sent a party westward under his lieutenant, García López de Cárdenas, to find a route to the Pacific Ocean. Cárdenas's men ran smack into the Grand Canyon, thus making the European discovery of that wonder. Rather than gaze in awe at the magnificent chasm, Cárdenas cursed the great ditch that blocked his way.

Yet exploration for its own sake was not Coronado's aim. He was after gold and silver, and as he passed month after month without locating any promising ore beds, the conquistador's mood grew dark. The Puebloans showed the Spaniards turquoise, the most precious substance in their world, but Coronado's men laughed and threw the worthless blue-green stones aside.

It seems astonishing, given the massive scale of the expedition, that modern scholars still have only the foggiest idea of where Coronado went. The Spaniards visited many pueblos, naming them as they went, but it is often next to impossible to correlate those arbitrary Spanish appellations with actual villages. A few, such as Hawikuh and Pecos, have been firmly fixed, but the dotted lines linking them up remain conjectural. One would think that the sheer material abundance of the gear Coronado's army lugged with them should have left plenty of evidence on the ground, but as recently as 1997 a scholar could publish a learned paper struggling with the question of whether or not some crossbow boltheads found at the now abandoned Santiago Pueblo were from the 1540–42 expedition. As Coronado experts Richard and Shirley Cushing Flint conclude, "It is all but impossible to say with certainty that any particular event recorded in the sixteenth-century

Coronado documents occurred at any specific place locatable on the ground on a modern map." Where, indeed, are Coronado's Coofor, the bridge across the Río de Cicúye, Chichilticale, the Querecho villages, and Quivira?

From the Puebloan point of view, the most devastating impact of the expedition occurred in what Coronado called the Province of Tiguex, which can be generally correlated with the Tiwa villages between modern-day Bernalillo and Albuquerque. As 1540 drew to a close, Coronado needed to establish a winter headquarters for his vast force. He chose a pueblo on the Rio Grande that the chronicles call Alcanfor or Coofor, summarily expelling the natives to make room for the Spaniards. (Archaeologists have yet to settle the question of precisely which site corresponds to Alcanfor.)

A resupply train from Mexico had turned back more than 500 miles short of Coronado's hungry soldiers. As the men settled in for the winter, they were woefully lacking in food, blankets, and clothing. With Castilian arrogance, they demanded that the Puebloans supply the deficit. When the Indians refused, the Spaniards attacked. During that first winter, most of the villages in Tiguex were depopulated and burned to the ground.

Out of these desperate times was born what historian Carroll Riley calls the Pecos plot. Of all the murky doings on the Coronado expedition, this is the murkiest. It hinges, moreover, on one of the most fascinating yet enigmatic figures to appear on the Southwestern stage in the sixteenth century. Nicknamed "Turk" by the soldiers, on account of his fancied resemblance to a figure out of the Ottoman Empire, he was apparently a Pawnee Indian from the plains who had been captured by the Puebloans. With a pair of leaders, possibly bow chiefs, from Pecos (the easternmost of the pueblos), Turk hatched his secret plan.

Turk told Coronado that in a region called Quivira, far to the east, he would find all the gold and silver he desired. In exchange for his freedom, moreover, Turk would guide the expedition to that storied land. Coronado swallowed the bait. In April 1541, he set out with

1,700 men (including Puebloans enslaved in the Tiguex war) to explore Quivira. Though he eventually sent back a large part of his force, the Pecos plot succeeded in ridding the Pueblo world of the oppressive conquistador for five months.

Turk's hidden agenda was to lead the Spaniards far out onto the disorienting plains, then lose them there. Where the straggling army traveled during those five months remains the least-well-documented segment of Coronado's two-year itinerary. Most scholars conclude that the Spaniards made a long loop through western Oklahoma and Kansas, returning along the Arkansas River.

Coronado, of course, found no gold. For his pains, Turk was tortured and executed rather than freed. But by the time the Spaniards settled back into Tiguex for a second winter, Coronado was heartily sick of the mythical Seven Cities of Cíbola. The Puebloans endured another winter of deprivation, but to their incalculable joy, in April 1542 the invading army packed up and headed back to Mexico.

Not long before, Coronado had fallen from his mount and been trampled by another horse. He suffered a serious head injury from which he would never fully recover. Upon his return to Mexico City, he was greeted not as a pathbreaking pioneer, but as an abject failure. An official investigation indicted the conquistador for his ruthless conduct among the northern pueblos, though he was eventually acquitted. At the time of his death in 1554, Coronado had no reason to think that he would ever be hailed as one of the great explorers of the New World, or made the hero of biographies with titles such as Hubert E. Bolton's *Coronado, Knight of Pueblos and Plains*.

There is a rueful footnote to Coronado's colossal *entrada*. Despite all the evidence they had seen of Puebloan resistance to Spanish demands, two of the friars, Juan de Padilla and Juan de Ubeda, elected to stay on alone in the Southwest to perform the noble work of bringing Christ into the hearts of the heathen. Perhaps here were exhibited the first signs of the Franciscan longing for martyrdom that some historians have postulated. If so, the priests achieved their goal: both were soon murdered, though how and by whom have escaped the record. To the Puebloans, these chanting men in their strange brown robes were the true sorcerers.

For thirty-nine years after Coronado marched south that April, no Spaniard (as far as we know) entered the Pueblo world. As the decades passed, the natives from Hopi to Pecos could begin to cherish the belief that the invaders on horseback had lost all interest in their northern villages. As Edmund Ladd imagined the residents of Zuni musing even before Esteban arrived, "We're lucky. We're too far north and all we have is the *ihílaqua,* the turquoise from the east. We don't have any of the shiny yellow stone that we can be afraid of."

The temperament of New Spain, however, was above all else restless. Despite Coronado's failure to find precious metals, the legend of the Seven Cities did not die. A point often made about the conquistadors as a whole bears repeating. Though some were well-born, others were regarded as little better than criminals back in Spain, the riffraff of a society in which birth and breeding meant everything. There was no better way to make one's fortune from scratch than in the New World. And in that quest, land was even more important than gold.

Yet the first Spanish *entrada* into the Pueblo world after Coronado's had saving souls as its rationale. By the late 1570s, a Franciscan convent had been established in what is today southern Chihuahua, near the silver mines of Santa Bárbara. Probably from the Jumano Indians whom he served, one Fray Augustín Rodríguez learned of the existence of thousands of other Indians to the north, languishing in pagan benightment. A military co-leader, Francisco Sánchez Chamuscado, was appointed to the expedition, which left Santa Bárbara on June 5, 1581. By the standards of Coronado's massive army, the Rodríguez-Chamuscado vanguard was modest in the extreme: nine soldiers, three friars, and nineteen Indian "servants." Incredibly, so low had Coronado's star fallen during the thirty-nine years since the conquistador had returned to Mexico that the leaders of this new expedition seem to have been completely unaware of the 1540–42 *entrada*. So far as Rodríguez and Chamuscado knew, *they* were the first Spaniards to explore the Pueblo world.

Their small force entered that world by a route far to the east of Coronado's, roughly following the Rio Grande north. In a pattern that would be repeated again and again, the inhabitants of the first pueblo the Spaniards approached fled to the hills. No doubt the memory of Coronado's laying waste of Tiguex was still strong among the natives, who may also have caught wind of illegal slaving raids farther south carried out by Spanish renegades in the decades after Coronado.

During the ten months the expedition was in the field, it covered a vast region, ranging apparently from Zuni to Cochiti and out onto the plains in search of bison. The party's chronicler made a list of some sixty pueblos visited, almost none of which can be correlated with present-day villages or known ruins. All in all, however, the Rodríguez-Chamuscado expedition accomplished little. It did, however, give this new land a Spanish name, San Felipe del Nuevo México, apparently in homage to King Philip of Spain. This was quickly shortened to Nuevo México.

The chronicler does not tell us how many Puebloans the friars were able to convert to Christianity. Very few, one suspects. A chapter titled "Evil Practices of These People" reads as a classic document in cross-cultural befuddlement: "We learned nothing of the rituals performed by the people of this settlement, except that when someone dies they dance and rejoice. . . . They bury the dead in cavelike cellars." The prose of the chronicler's description of the snake dance at one pueblo seems literally to crawl with horror and revulsion.

At some point, one of the friars, Juan de Santa María, decided to hasten back to Mexico to report on the strange doings he had witnessed among the pueblos. Despite the soldiers' attempts to dissuade him, he set off through the Galisteo Basin alone, and quickly became the third Franciscan martyr in Nuevo México—the first of whose demise we have any details.

A curious work published in 1893, called *The Martyrs of New Mexico*, by the Very Rev. James H. Defouri, gives (without specifying sources) an almost eyewitness account of Fray Juan's execution, which probably took place near the pueblo of Paako, just north of today's little town of San Antonito. "The Tanos of Galisteo did not care for him," writes Defouri; "they were openly hostile to him. Still he remained there for a time, and succeeded so well that he excited the ill-will of the medicine men. His death was resolved upon. He was apprised of it."

Defouri advances this death threat as the motive for the friar's hasty departure from New Mexico, not the urge to deliver news of the Pueblo world to Mexico City. "Much fatigued by crossing the mountains, the good Father laid down to take a little rest, soon he was asleep. The enemies were at hand. . . . Cautiously they went up the flank of the mountain, and detached a huge bowlder which, falling upon him, crushed him beneath its weight. And then they left him . . . heaping, besides, rocks upon him, to hide both the extremities of his body which protruded, and the bowlder itself, so that no trace of the crime could be found." Dropping a big stone on a sleeping man, ethnographers would later learn, was the prescribed Pueblo fashion for dispatching a witch.

Narrating the friar's bad ending, the expedition chronicler credulously comments, "From then on [the Indians] knew we were mortal; up to that time they had thought us immortal."

Despite this lesson in Pueblo "treachery," as the expedition prepared to return to Mexico, the other two friars, one of them Rodríguez himself, decided to stay behind to complete (or, more likely, begin) the work of bringing Christ to the Puebloans. Once more, the soldiers tried to talk them out of staying, to no avail. The priests took up residence in the pueblo of Puaray, smack in the middle of the Tiguez province that Coronado had devastated.

The singular accomplishment of the Rodríguez-Chamuscado expedition was once more to set New Spain abuzz with gossip about the northern pueblos. Now, however, it was not gold and silver that loomed as the primary lure, but the establishment of a new colony. The king himself, in Madrid, decreed that it was time to settle Nuevo México.

Between 1582 and 1593, no fewer than four colonizing expeditions set out from Chihuahua to "pacify" (in the euphemism of the day) the Pueblo world. But for the lasting and dolorous impact on the natives of these ragtag caravans of fortune seekers and otherworldly friars, it would be tempting to see their ventures as a decade-long comedy of errors. The first of these four *entradas* was entrusted to a cattle rancher, Antonio de Espejo, whose chief motivation for heading north was to avoid prosecution for the murder of another rancher in a brawl. Espejo's official mandate was to rescue the two friars that Chamuscado had left behind at Puaray.

Espejo's party covered a lot of ground during ten months, and left behind another list of pueblos visited that modern scholars puzzle over (though we do know that Espejo's men were the first to make a thorough investigation of the Hopi mesas). At Puaray, they learned that the Franciscans had been murdered. A poet and historian who passed by the same pueblo twenty years later would claim that Espejo found murals of the friars' executions painted on the inner walls of a kiva—a fanciful notion that contradicts what we now know of Puebloan art and religion.

The quasi-omniscient Very Rev. Defouri tells us how Fray Augustín Rodríguez met his end, as he prayed at the altar of a makeshift chapel: "His enemies surrounded the sanctuary, and with wild shouts entered and smashed his head with a wooden block. . . . Some authors say that in their frenzy his enemies took his body and cast it into the river then in a flood, to be food for the fishes." The body of Rodríguez's brother friar had already been pierced with arrows as he prayed at the same altar.

No matter what the nature of the friars' demise, Espejo's party settled the score. On entering Puaray, they found some thirty Indians standing on the rooftops, shouting insults down upon the Spaniards. The soldiers captured some of these men and imprisoned them in a kiva. Then, according to Espejo's chronicler, "We set fire to the big pueblo of Puala [Puaray], where we thought some were burned to death because of the cries they uttered. We at once took out the prisoners, two at a time, and lined them up against some cottonwoods close to the pueblo of Puala, where they were garroted and shot many times until they were dead." Adds the chronicler, with Castilian righteousness, "This was a remarkable deed for so few people in the midst of so many enemies."

The third *entrada* of the 1580s and 1590s was an unauthorized, illegal invasion by blatant treasure hunters. The fourth was sent to arrest the third and bring the interlopers back to Mexico in chains. The fifth ended dismally, somewhere out on the buffalo plains, when one of the two leaders stabbed the other to death. The Indians then wiped out the rest of the party.

This tragicomedy of errors came to a close, however, in 1598, under the command not of a Castilian, but of a Basque, a man whose ruthless efficiency would prove equal to the task of turning Nuevo México into a Spanish colony. One of his recent biographers styles him "the last conquistador." His name was Don Juan de Oñate y Salazar.

# 3

# OÑATE

Oñate's father, Cristóbal, had come to New Spain in 1524, where he soon became an entrepreneur on the northern frontier of Cortés's expanding empire. In 1548, he was one of four adventurous Basques who founded the town of Zacatecas, 300 miles northwest of Mexico City. The lure was a butte called La Bufa, made of green rock: here, two years before, the four men had gathered burro loads of promising ore that they carried south to be assayed. Zacatecas quickly became the richest silver mining center in New Spain, as well as its second most populous city.

Unfortunately for the miners, Zacatecas lay smack in the middle of the homeland of various aggressive Indian tribes whom the Spaniards lumped under the designation Chichimecas. These indigenes did not look favorably upon the European invasion. Oñate's biographer Marc Simmons sums up the Spanish terror of these "barbarians":

> The Chichimecas habitually tortured and scalped victims alive, then beheaded them and paraded the grisly trophies on wooden pikes. Captive children were forced to drink the blood and brains

of their murdered parents. And the tribesmen themselves were cannibals, for as one contemporary Spaniard testified, "Those whom they carry away alive are sacrificed. They are roasted on spits and eaten as one would do with cows."

In Zacatecas, either in 1550 or 1552, Juan de Oñate was born. To know that at an early age the conqueror of New Mexico had become an accomplished Indian fighter goes a long way toward explaining the severity with which Oñate would later deal with the Puebloans. (One Zacatecas contemporary who eventually rode north with Oñate claimed that he had first borne arms against the Chichimecas at the age of ten.)

Like his father, Juan de Oñate helped found a silver mining boomtown, called San Luis Potosí, about a hundred miles southeast of Zacatecas. It was here, as he served as mayor of the burgeoning community, that the restless miner, having recently turned forty, conceived of the ambition to colonize Nuevo México. It would take another six years, however, for Oñate to win governmental permission for that enterprise and to assemble an expedition to carry it out.

In his biography, *The Last Conquistador*, Marc Simmons makes what is probably the shrewdest assessment of Oñate's character to date. The constant vigilance and fierce combat against the Chichimecas that circumscribed his youth in Zacatecas may, Simmons suggests, "have contributed to an air of melancholy that seemed to mark his adult years. Certainly, there exists nothing in the written record to suggest that humor softened his speech or lightened his mood."

On the eve of setting out for New Mexico, Oñate was in the prime of his life and at the peak of his ambition. "All signs point to his being a visionary," writes Simmons, "but one endowed with a streak of tough practicality. . . . He also had a touch of romanticism in his nature and a good measure of idealism, which in Spaniards manifested itself in a lofty pride and an exaggerated sense of honor."

Though he would succeed in conquering and colonizing New Mexico, Oñate's twelve years in the northern province were so fraught with setbacks and intrigues that the romantic idealism turned into a darker outlook on life and fate. "His early difficulties," analyzes Simmons, "had the effect of souring his mood and pushing him along a path that eventually led to suspicion of underlings, showing of favoritism, and brutal retribution meted out to those who opposed him—in short, the behavior of a natural autocrat, or even a petty despot." That "brutal retribution" took its toll among once loyal comrades who fell out of Oñate's favor, but more importantly, it set the standard by which a conquered people came to know its conquerors. Oñate's treatment of the Puebloans sowed the field from which would spring the Revolt of 1680. And despite the passage of more than four centuries since Oñate's *entrada*, among the pueblos today a bitter sense of having been wronged serves as the conquistador's enduring legacy in New Mexico.

In any event, Oñate set out from the northern outpost of Santa Bárbara in early January 1598, at the head of the largest expedition since Coronado's to enter what is now the American Southwest. No complete roster of the party has survived, but scholars have deduced its general makeup. There were some 560 future colonists in Oñate's entourage, including at least 129 soldiers. Not only Indian "servants" swelled the throng, but a large number of women and children, though the latter remain virtually undocumented. (Oñate brought along his eight-year-old son, Cristóbal, officially commissioning him as a lieutenant. Cristóbal would eventually become an interim governor of New Mexico.)

Like Coronado, Oñate drove a herd of livestock north to provide food for his pilgrims, mounts to ride, and beasts of burden to carry supplies—all told, some 7,000 cattle, sheep, goats, oxen, donkeys, mules, and horses. Unlike Coronado, Oñate was burdened with a veritable warehouse of tools and goods with which the settlers might craft their future homesteads: from plowshares to saws, hammers to hoes, cotton bolts to medicine chests, and the tidy sum of 13,500 nails. There were enough harquebuses among the soldiers to require eighteen barrels of gunpowder, and for good measure, the party dragged along three bronze cannons. At the same time, bent on peaceful trading, Oñate hoarded 80,000 glass beads, as well as innumerable other trinkets. The eight Franciscan friars and two lay brothers among the party carried rosaries and sacred images made of tin to help facilitate conversions.

To transport all this truck, as well as the women and children, Oñate employed eighty wagons and carts, drawn usually by oxen. He was not the first Spaniard to bring wheeled vehicles to the Southwest: the illegal *entrada* of 1590 had used an unspecified number of wagons, which left ruts in the riverbanks that Oñate's party would find eight years later. But a caravan of this magnitude—one witness claimed that while under way, it stretched across two miles of desert—had never before been seen in the Southwest.

Encumbered by the sheer weight of all its baggage, Oñate's procession required five full months to advance from Santa Bárbara to Nuevo México. Along the way, the commander performed bold deeds to encourage his often fretful colonists, like plunging on horseback into the flooding Río Conchos, then engineering what must have been a mind-boggling ford with eighty heavy-laden wagons. Yet so aggravating were the expedition's setbacks and delays, that by the time Oñate had reached his promised land, his patience was stretched to the breaking point.

On April 30, though still south of present-day El Paso, Texas, Oñate paused to make a formal proclamation of his possession of Nuevo México. The archival copy of this declaration demonstrates Spanish rhetoric at its most bombastic: the first sentence alone, 296 words long, invokes God, Christ, the Virgin Mary, Saint Francis, King Philip II, and the ark of the covenant as the explorer lays claim not only to the territory, but to "every creature" therein, "spiritual and corporal, rational and irrational, from the highest cherub to the lowliest ant and tiniest butterfly."

In mid-May, Oñate sent a small scouting party ahead, under the command of Captain Pablo de Aguilar. Their orders were to proceed with utmost secrecy, not even to let themselves be seen by Indians (an impossible mandate, of course). Oñate hoped at all costs to avoid the

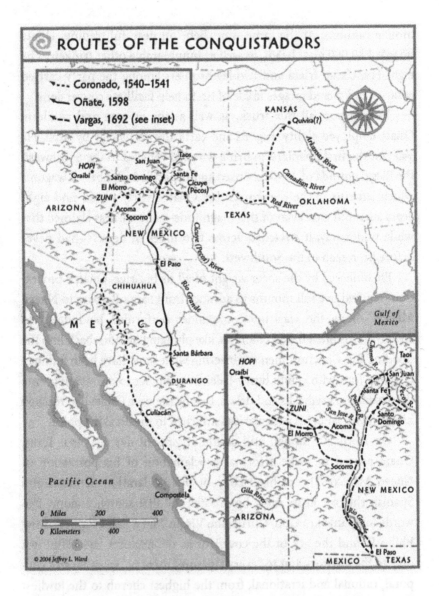

ROUTES OF THE CONQUISTADORS

▼··· Coronado, 1540–1541
▬ Oñate, 1598
▼·· Vargas, 1692 (see inset)

pattern of contact recorded by the five previous *entradas* since 1581:
Puebloans fleeing their villages to hide in the surrounding hills. When
Aguilar returned to confess that his scouts had not only met the inhabitants of the first pueblo they found, but had entered the village, Oñate
flew into a rage. He sentenced his captain to death by strangulation,

and might well have carried out the execution with his own hands had his other officers not pleaded for mercy.

On May 28, Oñate's advance party came in sight of its first pueblo, a Piro-speaking village called Qualacu, on the Rio Grande just south of today's town of Socorro. Just as he had feared, the Indians fled at first sight. Eventually, however, the glass beads worked their magic, as the wary Puebloans crept back to their dwellings and started to trade precious corn for baubles. Oñate camped for most of a month at Qualacu, as he brought the main body of his caravan north to settle in and recover from its arduous trek across the Jornada del Muerto ("the Journey of the Dead," a waterless shortcut east of the meandering course of the Rio Grande).

Through the end of June and into July, Oñate pushed his caravan slowly north along the great river, passing through the Tiwa villages Coronado had decimated more than half a century before, climbing the *bajada*—the "jump," or cliff, that separates the Río Arriba from the Río Abajo—and plunging into Tewa country. On July 11, he reached the pueblo of San Juan, where he had already decided to establish the first capital of Nuevo México.

In village after village, Oñate's men observed the same reception: Puebloans fleeing at first sight, only to trickle back under the sway of trade goods and curiosity. There was no need for firearms, no pitched battles to pacify the pueblos. Could the conquest really proceed so easily? Oñate flattered himself that the presence of so many women and children among his entourage assuaged Indian fears. At Santo Domingo, he hosted a grand convocation to explain to the natives from all around why he had come into their country.

The document recording the "Act of Obedience and Vassalage by the Indians of Santo Domingo" is a piece of work to marvel over. At this point in his journey, the only interpreters Oñate had were a pair of Mexican Indians left behind by some earlier expedition, who may have picked up a bit of Keresan in the interim. Undaunted, the conquistador bade these go-betweens to translate to the assembled "chieftains" of some thirty-three different pueblos (many no doubt non-Keresan speakers) such pronouncements as the following: "He told them that he had been sent by the most powerful king and ruler in the world, Don Philip, king of Spain, who desired especially to serve God our Lord and to bring about the salvation of their souls."

One can only imagine what the Puebloans must have made of this cryptic declaration. According to Oñate's own sworn statement, the Indians "replied to this through the interpreters, all in agreement and harmony and with great rejoicing. One could easily see and understand that they were very pleased with the coming of his lordship. After deliberation they spontaneously agreed to become vassals of the most Christian king, our lord." As earnest of this pledge, Oñate requested that the Puebloan headmen kneel on the ground before him. This they readily did. Oñate went on to explain that "if they were baptized and became good Christians, they would go to heaven to enjoy an eternal life of great bliss in the presence of God. If they did not become Christians, they would go to hell to suffer cruel and everlasting torment." The "chieftains" knelt again and kissed Oñate's hand.

As is so often the case, we have only the Spanish side of the story. Yet what accounts for the apparent acquiescence on the part of the Pueblo leaders in what must have seemed to them a bizarre and incomprehensible ceremony? Why did they not fight the invaders, as the Zuni of Hawikuh had in 1539 and 1540? Were they intimidated by the sheer might of Oñate's caravan into a passive submission? Or were they biding their time?

On top of an old pueblo site called Yunge Oweenge, virtually within the village of San Juan, Oñate built his capital of New Mexico, which he called San Gabriel. Here he erected the province's first church. As far as he could judge, the Indians were perfectly happy to share their homes with the Europeans. From this base, Oñate now undertook a sweeping, five-month reconnaissance of his new dominion. With a small exploring party, he rode north to Taos, east to Pecos, south into the Galisteo Basin, and west into the Jemez country. All the while, he searched in vain for ore deposits that might turn Nuevo

México into a bonanza on the scale of Zacatecas. In September, he led a foray out onto the plains to hunt bison to feed his hungry colonists. Then, in October, he abruptly decided to explore far to the southwest, in quest of a route to the Pacific Ocean, which rumors and bad maps had placed far nearer than the 600 miles as the crow flies that actually separated San Gabriel from the closest sea, the Gulf of California.

Awash in the reverie of his new empire, Oñate overlooked certain signs that all was not right with the Puebloans. The commander's chief concern was not with rebellious Indians, but with mutineers within his ranks. When four disgruntled fortune seekers stole horses and headed for Mexico, Oñate sent soldiers under two of his trusted lieutenants in pursuit. This posse caught up with the deserters only after a ride of hundreds of miles. They slit the throats of two mutineers on the spot; the other two got away.

It is not surprising that Oñate failed to recognize the first signs of Puebloan resistance, for they were cloaked in seamless secrecy. And by the beginning of October, the conquistador had yet to visit Acoma. Of that cliff-top pueblo west of the Rio Grande, he had heard only the vaguest gossip. He would learn only later that in early September, as he had presided over a week-long celebration of the founding of San Gabriel, dazzling the Indians with a pageant re-creating the glorious triumph of Spain over the Moors, spies from Acoma had slipped into the throng, where they took careful notes in their heads.

Today's Acomans, who number 6,000, live in several villages—principally Acomita, McCarty, and Anzac—scattered across a 400,000-acre reservation that occupies some of the most beautiful country in New Mexico. Only about thirty people still live in Sky City, the ancient pueblo built atop a butte surrounded on all sides by 400-foot cliffs, where all the Acomans dwelt in 1598. Though it retains a strong conservative streak in its culture, Acoma presents a tourist-friendly face, as pueblos such as Santo Domingo and Jemez do not. Beside an off-ramp from Interstate 40, the Sky City Casino, open twenty-four hours a day 365 days a year, waylays sightseers and truck drivers. Every hour during the daytime, buses full of visitors rumble up a paved road, carved into the cliff in the 1940s to accommodate a John Wayne western, to plunk them down for guided walking tours of Sky City.

Along with the Hopi villages of Walpi and Oraibi, Acoma (in the form of Sky City) lays claim to being the oldest continuously inhabited town in the United States. Archaeologists grant a founding date some-time before A.D. 1200, while tribal elders maintain that the village is far older. In Oñate's time, Acoma was by far the best-defended pueblo in Nuevo México, with only steep hand-and-toe trails giving access to the summit. Some 500 adobe rooms, marshaled into quadrangular blocks, made up the village, whose drinking water was supplied by bedrock cis-terns that caught rainfall. What one Spaniard called "the best situated Indian stronghold in all Christendom" imparted to its residents a proud autonomy matched by only a few other pueblos in the Southwest.

On his way to the Great Salt Sea, Oñate camped at the foot of the Acoma butte at the end of October. The record of what happened next remains highly ambiguous, but a plausible scenario can be cobbled out of the Spanish documents. The spies who had visited San Gabriel had reported back to Acoma. A chieftain known as Zutacapán resolved to make war upon the invaders, but other leaders took a contrary view. Even as Oñate, with only thirty soldiers, slept at the foot of the butte, the Acomans were in the midst of a strenuous debate about how to deal with the interlopers.

The peace party, it would seem, prevailed. Acomans swarmed down from their stronghold to offer gifts to the Spaniards. Oñate was convinced that these credulous natives thought that the neighing horses were speaking to each other, a fancy he encouraged in order to inculcate further "fear and respect."

Now the Acomans made signs to invite the Spaniards up to their pueblo. With part of his force, Oñate climbed the hand-and-toe trail. Serene in their assumption of Spanish superiority, the soldiers fired their harquebuses from the summit as a salute to the men guarding camp below. An Acoman, one of Zutacapán's confederates, led Oñate away from his entourage, toward a kiva in a corner of the village. Gesticulating eagerly, the man urged the conquistador to climb down the ladder that protruded from the hatchway in the roof to see some marvel inside. That marvel, however, was twelve armed lieutenants of Zutacapán, ready to deal Oñate his death blow. At the last minute, mindful no doubt of certain traps he had eluded fighting the Chichimecas, the Spanish leader declined, foiling the plot.

This scenario, as reconstructed by biographer Marc Simmons, leaves virtually unexplained the riddle of how the Spaniards ever learned what was really going on at Acoma. The pueblo's own oral traditions about this potentially momentous event have never, so far as we know, been shared with Anglos. Suffice it to say, however, that in hesitating to enter the kiva, Oñate survived the closest call he would undergo in New Mexico. Had the Acomans succeeded in killing the conquistador, the subsequent history of the Southwest would have taken a far different course.

Whatever his true feelings as he visited the sky-top pueblo, Oñate completely underestimated the Acoman threat. Back at the foot of the butte, he called together the pueblo's leaders and inflicted upon them an oath of submission very like the one he had exacted from the "chieftains" at Santo Domingo. The Puebloans, Oñate believed once again, freely and willingly pledged obedience to the Spaniards, upon pain of death should they lapse.

From Acoma, Oñate rode blithely on toward the Pacific. A few days later, he camped at the base of a towering sandstone butte, a favorite stopping place for travelers as far back in time as they can be traced in the Southwest. That butte today is the centerpiece of tiny El Morro National Monument. It is also called Inscription Rock.

I had visited El Morro before, but never with my head so full of history. On the afternoon of the same day that I had toured Hawikuh

with Lena Tsethlikia, I stopped at the monument, just off State Highway 53 between Ramah and Grants. Once more I hiked the trail that
loops around the soaring, 200-foot-high butte on the north, climbs it
from the west, traverses its spiny summit fins, and descends on the
east. Atop El Morro stands a ruin called Atsinna, ancestral to Zuni, its
thousand rooms occupied in the thirteenth and fourteenth centuries.
Atsinna has only been partially excavated, but the block of stabilized
rooms along the tourist trail gives a vivid sense of what a blissful place
the village must have been, commanding lordly views over the basins
stretching away on all sides. Unfortunately, the path itself, as it crosses
the summit bedrock, bears all the hallmarks of the heavy-handed trail-
building technique favored by the Park Service and the Civilian Con-
servation Corps in the 1920s and 1930s: steps, staircases, and grooved
passageways dynamited and chiseled out of the gracefully weathered
sandstone.

The reason travelers always stopped at El Morro is a natural
"tank"—a virtual reservoir created by a huge funnel that spills from
the summit down to a hollow in the earth tucked into a corner of the
southeast face of the butte. With every rainstorm, the funnel floods in
a crashing waterfall. In all of New Mexico, there is no more reliable
natural tank than what the Spaniards called El Estanque del Peñol.
Long before Coronado, the Anasazi camped here, leaving enigmatic
petroglyphs carved in the gleaming white stone.

Here, too, Oñate camped on October 29, 1598. And seven years
later, on the way back from a second, successful journey to the Gulf of
California, he camped again, and decided to etch his name in the rock.
Now I slowly walked the guardrail-equipped path that meanders from
left to right beneath the southeast face of the butte. I passed the faint
vestiges of a dizzy hand-and-toe trail that was the ancients' shortcut to
the summit, passed the tank itself, brimming far deeper than head-
high with a milky green water, and soon came to Oñate's inscription.
The words are jammed together, as was the fashion of the day, and certain conventions abbreviate words too tedious to carve at full length.

Allowing for the separation of distinct words, what I saw before my eyes, only three feet away and a little above my head, the letters dappled by the shadows of the leaves of a small cottonwood that guards this nook, was:

paso por aqui el adelantado don ju°
de oñate del descubrymiento de la mar
del sur a 16 de abril de 1605

("There passed this way the Adelantado Don Juan de Oñate, from the discovering of the South Sea, on the sixteenth of April, 1605." *Adelantado* was an honorary title for the conqueror of a new land.)

Even though Oñate had carved his motto directly on top of an Anasazi petroglyph, I felt a thrill at seeing the old inscription. Here, after all, was the first graffito ever scratched in the Southwest! The inscription would be virtually illegible today, thanks to weathering, but for the practice of monument superintendents in the 1910s to 1930s, who systematically retraced the letters with pencil lead to make them stand out.

Oñate here started a grand tradition. El Morro bristles today with hundreds of inscriptions ranging from 1605 to 1898. Scores of others were effaced in the early decades of the twentieth century, by work crews under the direction of monument rangers, as too recent to be interesting. Some of these workers proved overzealous, erasing signatures carved as early as 1667. According to an early superintendent, one inscription wiped out during these years was that of Kit Carson, possibly etched in 1863 as he rounded up Navajos for the Long Walk. (Carson was illiterate, but by that date he had learned to sign his name to official army dispatches he dictated to others. As it was a Navajo worker who allegedly removed the signature, and as Carson lives on in Navajo tradition as the arch-villain of their history, the erasure may have been less careless than deliberate.)

In any event, the first Anglos to leave their mark on El Morro were a pair of explorers, who carefully etched, on the shaded north wall of the butte:

Lt. J. H. Simpson U. S. A. & R. H. Kern Artist
visited and copied these inscriptions
September 17th 18th 1849.

Charles H. Lummis, the maverick artist, photographer, editor, writer, explorer, self-taught archaeologist, and ceaseless celebrator of the Southwest—it was Lummis who coined the very term "the Southwest," as well as the slogan, "See America first"—wrote a hymn of praise to El Morro, in the form of an essay called "The Stone Autograph-Album," published in *Some Strange Corners of Our Country* in 1906. In the years just before the butte was made a national monument, with characteristic flair Lummis pronounced, "It is the most precious cliff, historically, possessed by any nation on earth, and, I am ashamed to say, the most utterly uncared-for." Two decades later, Lummis underscored his encomium: "No other cliff on earth records a tithe as much romance, adventure, heroism. . . . Oñate here carved his entry with his dagger two years before an English-speaking person had built a hut anywhere in the New World, and 15 years before Plymouth Rock."

From Oñate's graffito I strolled a few dozen yards to the right, and found the other carved record that equally thrilled me to behold. It is the only known inscription from the architect of the reconquest, twelve years after the Pueblo Revolt, Diego José de Vargas Zapata Luján Ponce de León. Like Oñate's, Vargas's is no mere signature, but a boast:

aqui estubo el Gen$^l$, D$^n$, D$^o$,
de varg$^s$, q$^n$, Conquisto
á Nra, S$^{ta}$, Fé, y á la R$^l$
Corona todo el nuebo
Mexico á su costa,
AÑO DE 1692.

("Here was the General Don Diego de Vargas, who conquered for our Holy Faith, and for the Royal Crown, all the New Mexico, at his expense, Year of 1692.")

While Oñate camped at El Morro, one of his lieutenants, on the way back from chasing the deserters into Mexico, was trying to catch up with his commander. This man was Captain Gaspar Pérez de Villagrá. In his impatience, he had chosen the dangerous gambit of traveling alone, and now he made the mistake of passing by Acoma.

Villagrá had high ambitions not only as a soldier and explorer, but as a writer. Upon his eventual return to Spain, he penned an epic poem based on Oñate's expedition, published in Alcala in 1610 under the title, *Historia de la Nueva [sic] México*. Following an honored Renaissance tradition, Villagrá imitated Virgil's *Aeneid*. The opening stanza, translated a bit awkwardly into English, begins,

> Of arms I sing, and of that heroic son.
> Of his wondrous deeds and of his victories won.
> Of his prudence and his valor shown when,
> Scorning the hate and envy of his fellow men,
> Unmindful of the dangers that beset his way,
> Performed deeds most heroic in his day.

The *Historia* has twice been translated into English, in a prose rendering by Gilberto Espinosa in 1933, and in a faithful (though unrhymed) verse translation by three Hispanic experts in 1992. Throughout most of the twentieth century, scholars have tended to look askance at the epic as a historical work. The best-known example of what Villagrá was attempting is Luís de Camões's magnificent *Os Lusíadas* (1572), an epic poem based very loosely on the explorations of Vasco da Gama and other Portuguese mariners. Camões, however, is not taken seriously as a documentarian of those landmark voyages.

Yet in proportion to how bad the *Historia* is as a poem (and it is quite bad), it may be valuable as a historical source for Oñate's *entrada*.

As Marc Simmons points out, the poem is "the first published history of any part of the future American nation, preceding by fourteen years Captain John Smith's *General History of Virginia.*"

One of the most vivid passages in the epic recounts Villagrá's narrow escape as he passed Acoma in October 1598. Indeed, much of Canto Nineteen reads as unintentional comedy, unless one pauses to imagine the genuine ordeal the author so floridly hymns.

As he approached Acoma, Villagrá noticed Indians "lying in wait on either side of the road I must take, like so many crouching tigers ready to pounce upon their prey." (As narrative, Espinosa's prose translation is preferable to the more recent verse rendering.) The only thing that saved the poet was the proud steed he rode, for the Acomans' fear of horses was so intense, he claimed, that "They will not under any circumstances approach within more than six arms' length of a horseman."

Nonetheless, Zutacapán himself greeted Villagrá, encouraging him in sign language to climb up to the pueblo to receive water and provisions. The wary traveler insisted that he had no time to spare for such a delay. As he started to ride off, Zutacapán called after him, asking how many other "Castilians" were following in the captain's wake. Villagrá bluffed, boasting that "one hundred and three well-armed men were but two days' journey away." (As always in reading the *Historia*, one wonders just how such linguistic exchanges could have taken place. Villagrá certainly spoke no Keresan, and Zutacapán cannot have commanded more than a smattering of Spanish words.)

Villagrá rode long into the night, then hid off the trail in a campfireless bivouac. Shortly after dawn, it began to snow hard. The captain pushed on toward El Morro. Back on the trail, he came to "a pile of brush across the road." Carelessly, he rode his horse through the brush, only to discover that it was an Acoman trap—a deep pit concealed by a brush roof. It is possible that pointed stakes were planted on the floor of the pit (as Puebloans were known to construct hunting traps), for the horse was killed in the fall.

Badly shaken, Villagrá continued on foot, abandoning his helmet, harquebus, shield, and coat of mail, keeping only a sword and a dagger. The snowstorm raged on. "In order that I might not be tracked," the poet insisted, "I put my shoes on backward so that the heels faced to the front. . . .

"For four whole days I wandered, suffering terribly from both hunger and thirst." Lost and in despair, Villagrá decided to kill and eat his dog—a companion he has neglected to mention until this point in the epic. It is here that the poet's ordeal reaches its bathetic nadir:

> I gave [the dog] two mortal wounds, at which the dying beast fled from me. I called to it in anger and the noble creature, forgetting my shameful treatment, crawled toward me, licking his wounds, and then, as if to please me, licked my hands, staining them with the blood which flowed from his cruel wounds. O, sir, I was ashamed that I should be guilty of such base conduct! Especially did I regret it when I realized that I had no fire with which to roast the meat. . . .
>
> Leaving the poor creature dead, I set forth in downcast mood to combat this sad fate which so afflicted me.

At this juncture, Villagrá was saved by a minor miracle. Three of Oñate's men, out in the storm looking for stray horses, stumbled instead upon the bedraggled captain.

Even Villagrá's harrowing tale somehow failed to alert Oñate to the full threat that Acoma posed. The conquistador's nephew and second-in-command, Juan de Zaldívar, was at the moment riding southwest with thirty soldiers to join Oñate's party. Yet the commander failed to send a messenger back to warn his nephew to give Acoma a wide berth. Speculates Marc Simmons, "possibly . . . he assumed that young Zaldívar, being an able soldier, could handle any difficulty that might arise."

Zaldívar did not set out from San Juan until November 18. Oblivious to the danger, he not only rode straight to Acoma, but stopped there to try to trade hatchets and tools for corn. On December 3, seven men climbed the hand-and-toe trail to the mesa-top pueblo. The Acomans gave them a little food, but not nearly enough to feed all the soldiers. The Puebloans stalled, claiming they needed to grind more corn, promising to supply the Spaniards on the morrow. Zaldívar camped that night about six miles away, in an arroyo providing both firewood and water. On December 4, he climbed back up to Acoma with eighteen of his men.

In his Cantos Twenty-one through Twenty-three, Villagrá, who was not there, gives a vivid eyewitness account not only of the battle that soon broke out, but of the weeks of internal debate among the Acomans that preceded it. He even quotes verbatim the exhortations of the pueblo's leaders. These sound more like the set speeches of Virgil's heroes than like Puebloan oratory, and in all probability the poet made them up out of whole cloth. Yet no less an authority than the great historian Hubert Howe Bancroft believed it possible that Villagrá got his details straight from the mouths of Acomans several weeks or months later.

Thus Zutacapán, the "Lucifer" among the "savages," according to Villagrá, addresses his Acoma listeners in such Roman accents as, "Tell me, how could there be a greater misfortune, a more terrible disgrace upon all of us, than to submit to the slavery and subjection offered us and be obliged even to feed these strangers? I swear by all the living gods that not a man should remain alive rather than submit to this tyranny."

For Villagrá, the events of December 4 issue from a premeditated trap laid by Zutacapán and his followers. This may well be true, for the Acomans had nearly succeeded in luring Oñate into the fatal kiva more than a month before. (Yet the primary source for Simmons's recreation of that October contretemps is Villagrá himself.)

A more likely cause for the battle that broke out at Acoma emerges in a letter written less than three months later, from the newly appointed treasurer of New Mexico to an official in New Spain. As the Spaniards milled about on the mesa top, waiting to receive their corn, "there arose a minor incident," reported the treasurer, "when a soldier named Vivero took two turkeys from the Indians, and they killed him from one of the terraces." Whether Vivero's foolish deed was an act of outright theft (domesticated turkeys were highly prized among the pueblos) or a trading transaction gone wrong, we have no way of knowing.

In Villagrá's telling, on the other hand, the Acomans disperse the nineteen soldiers by leading them one by one to separate houses to gather the promised corn. A "fearful war-cry" signals the attack, led by Zutacapán, whose battle pledge is worthy of Aeneas himself: "Death, death by blood and fire! Death to these thieves who have so arrogantly dared to set foot within our lofty fortress!" The fighting rages across the mesa top. "On [the Acomans] came, hurling their heavy war-clubs, darts, and spears at the little band of Spaniards. . . . The arquebuses spit forth the hidden missiles from their barrels, laying low a number of the foe. But it was only a temporary advantage."

As is obligatory in classical epic, the principals end up locked in hand-to-hand combat. After three hours of continuous warfare, "Zutacapán himself struck the brave Zaldívar a terrible blow on the forehead. Zaldívar fell, delivered unto that eternal sleep to which we are all doomed some day."

Whatever the true causes of this battle, which was to have profound consequences for New Mexico, and whatever the actual course of the fighting among the plazas of Acoma, there is little doubt about the outcome. Eleven Spaniards and two "servants" were killed, including Zaldívar and two other officers. The six who survived jumped off the cliffs, somehow managing not to dash themselves to pieces in the process, probably because they landed on sand dunes. One survivor later testified that, as he lay on the ground after his great leap, he stared up the precipice to see "the Indians jumping from rock to rock, carrying swords and hats and mocking us, while others hurled the bodies of the dead down the cliff." (The number of Acoman victims is unknown.)

The battered band that was all that was left of Zaldívar's regiment limped onward to find Oñate. On December 13, thirty miles west of

Acoma, the conquistador met an advance party who gave him the terrible news.

The retribution that Oñate would mete out was a foregone outcome. Yet the commander did not act in haste. He believed it vital to respond to the killing of his men within the sanctions of Spanish law. Because, in October, the Acoma leaders had taken the oath of obedience that Oñate had administered to them below the pueblo, he felt justified in prosecuting them, as Spanish subjects, for their misdeeds. Yet Oñate went further. Back in San Juan, he asked the Franciscan friars to judge whether the Acoma offenses were grounds for a "just war." Not surprisingly, the priests so judged.

The avenging squadron that set out from San Juan on January 12, 1599, was composed of seventy soldiers—more than half of Oñate's entire army in New Mexico—under Zaldívar's younger brother, Vicente. Nine days later, the troops arrived at the foot of the Acoma butte. They found the Puebloans armed to the teeth, not only with bows and arrows, war clubs, and stones, but with swords and protective coats of mail they had taken off the bodies of their victims on December 4. From below the mesa, through an interpreter, Vicente de Zaldívar announced that he came in peace, desiring only to find out why the Puebloans had slain the Spaniards. According to the official report, "The Indians all shouted loudly, raised their swords on high, and . . . boast[ed] that they had killed ten Spaniards and two Mexicans, and that we were all a pack of scoundrels and whoremongers." (One wonders what the Keresan word for "whoremonger" might be.) Then the Acomans rained arrows and stones down upon the assembled soldiers.

Zaldívar retreated to camp out of range of the missiles. The Acomans "spent all that night in huge dances and carousals, shouting, hissing, and making merry, challenging the army to fight."

At 3:00 in the afternoon of January 22, the battle began. It lasted two days, but in the end, it was a complete rout. Zaldívar employed a favorite Spanish military strategy. With the main body of his army, he feigned an all-out frontal attack on one side of the butte. All the Acoma warriors rushed to that side of the summit cliff. Meanwhile, the commander himself, with twelve chosen men, sneaked around to the opposite side of the mesa. Under cover of the furious exchange of fire on the other face of the butte, these thirteen succeeded in climbing the hand-and-toe trail to the top. The Acomans swarmed to defend their rear, but Zaldívar had his men firmly installed. Eventually, he managed to bring a pair of small cannons up to his fortified position.

The mismatch was inevitable—bows and arrows and hurled stones versus harquebuses, swords, and artillery fire. Toward the end of January 23 (if the official report can be believed), Zaldívar called a halt while his interpreter pleaded with the enemy "not to persist until all were killed. . . . They replied that they and their women and children wanted only to die, and that the Spaniards were scoundrels." A renewed volley of stones and arrows underscored the Puebloans' defiance.

The full horror of the carnage wreaked that day at Acoma is almost impossible to conceive. As the battle turned hopeless for the defenders, the soldiers took prisoners and tried to confine them in the kivas. But "the Indians ran from house to house and killed each other without sparing their children, however small, or their wives." Despairing of any other solution, Zaldívar set fire to the pueblo, burning many men, women, and children alive.

When it was all over, according to official count, between 600 and 800 Acomans lay dead. The Spaniards claimed not to have lost a single soldier. They took between seventy and eighty warriors captive, as well as 500 women and children. These prisoners were marched to Santo Domingo to await a trial, arriving on February 9.

The trial unfurled as a charade of cool, deliberative justice. Survivors of Juan de Zaldívar's ill-fated mission to Acoma in December were called to testify, as were the principals in the avenging massacre. A number of wretched Acoma men were even put on the stand. Each was asked "why the Indians of the pueblo had killed the maese de campo

[Juan de Zaldívar] and his men." One Acoman murmured, "They had killed them because they asked for maize, flour, and blankets." Another insisted "that the Spaniards first killed an Indian, and then all the Indians became very angry and killed them."

Every Acoman, of course, was found guilty. On February 12, Oñate handed down his sentence. Every man over the age of twenty-five was to have his right foot cut off, and was sentenced to twenty years of slavery. The women over the age of twelve and the younger men were likewise assessed twenty years of slavery. Girls and boys under twelve were taken from their families and assigned as "servants" in Spanish households (at least sixty girls ended up in slavery in Mexico). Two luckless Hopi men who happened to have been visiting Acoma at the time of the battle had their right hands cut off, then were sent home as a warning to that far western pueblo of the futility of resistance.

That Acoma exists today is a profound testament to Puebloan resilience. It would take thirty years after the carrying out of Oñate's sentence before the survivors and their descendants were allowed to begin rebuilding the pueblo on top of the butte. Under the direction of Fray Juan Ramírez, after 1629 the Acomans were put to work erecting, with adobe bricks, one of the most grandiose mission churches in New Mexico. Upon completion, San Estevan del Rey stood one hundred feet long and thirty-five feet tall. Acoma legend has it that the forty-foot roof beams were harvested from the slopes of Mount Taylor, twenty-five miles to the north, and that the Indians who carried them (each timber weighing several hundred pounds) were forbidden to let them touch the ground in transit. Though much remodeled over the centuries, San Estevan still stands near the south edge of the mesa, the cynosure of Sky City.

As I researched Acoma history, I was startled by a peculiar fact. In the first three books ever written by Anglos about the pueblo—John Gunn's *Schat-chen: History, Traditions and Narratives of the Queres Indians of Laguna and Acoma* (1917), Mary K. Sedgwick's *Acoma, the*

*Sky City* (1926), and Leslie A. White's *The Acoma Indians* (1932)—there is not a single word about Oñate's cruel punishment of the survivors of the 1599 battle. Surely the massacre itself, and the amputations and slavery that followed it, were the single most important event in Acoma's post-contact history, seared like a brand into the collective memory of the pueblo. How could it be that none of Gunn's, Sedgwick's, or White's informants saw fit even to mention that tribulation? Was the memory still too painful even to talk about?

In March 2003, I traveled to Acoma to meet Brian Vallo, a former lieutenant governor of the pueblo now in charge of its tourism effort. A good-looking dark-haired man in his late thirties, Vallo has been entrusted since 1990 by the Acoma tribal council to talk, as he put it, with "folks like yourself."

Early on in the interview, I asked Vallo point-blank if Acoma oral tradition about Oñate's sentence jibed with the Spanish record. He seemed to grow uncomfortable. "Anytime something like that is discussed internally," he answered me, choosing his words carefully, "there's always a sense of secrecy. There's a reluctance to share the people's different renditions of those occurrences with outsiders."

I waited for further clarification. Shifting in his chair, Vallo acknowledged, "Based on our oral history, a lot of Acoma elders from about thirty years ago would have supported the idea of Oñate's sentence being carried out."

Two years ago, a highly respected Southwest historian made news by postulating in his most recent book that Oñate's sentence had never been executed. According to him, it was a standard Spanish trick for the governors and soldiers to threaten severe punishments, only to have the Franciscan friars plead for mercy, thereby winning the hearts of the Indians. Though there is not a shred of direct evidence that the priests interceded to prevent the carrying out of Oñate's dire sentence, this is exactly what the historian maintained must have happened.

This argument gladdened the hearts of the members of a New Mexico society devoted to Hispanic history, which invited the historian to speak and sign books. To my mind, however, this revisionist hypothesis seemed not only sophistry at its feeblest, but a deep insult to the Acomans themselves. Oñate's own formal account of the trial, moreover, closes by saying, "The said sentence was carried out as decreed in the pueblo of Santo Domingo and other towns nearby, where the Indians whose hands and feet were to be cut off were punished on different days."

The inconclusive hour I spent with Brian Vallo was not, of course, the first time I had tried to peer under the veil of secrecy that cloaks the pueblos today. Still, throughout our interview, it was striking to observe how deliberately Vallo edited his utterances. Finally he confronted my nosiness. "I hope that in the process of sharing this information," he said, as though reciting a prescription, "while limited and vague, and not consistent with what people read in books—I hope that we're educating you that stories are what have allowed us to maintain our culture. In our case, it's all oral." He fixed me with a steady gaze. "There's a lot I can't tell you. And I won't."

That secrecy was a key to survival under the Spanish. Four hundred and five years after Zaldívar's massacre and Oñate's punishment, 324 years after the Pueblo Revolt, and 312 years after Vargas's reconquest, Acoma, like other pueblos, guards its integrity by wrapping it inside a syncretic belief system that somehow welds Catholic faith to the kachina religion, Anglo notions of the past to oral tradition. There was no better way to see that syncretism in full bloom, I knew, than to take the guided tour of Sky City, as I did upon leaving Vallo's office.

It was my fifth such tour during the past two decades. Our group of thirty rode the bus from the visitor center up to the mesa top, debarked, and formed an expectant circle. We hailed, it turned out, from all over the United States and a couple of European countries. Most of the older men wore baseball caps with such logos as "North Carolina National Golf Club" and "Napa Auto Parts." Our guide was a stocky, crew-cut, middle-aged man named Leo Patricio.

In the name of its burgeoning tourism, Acoma stations vendors hawking sugar-coated fry bread and homemade jewelry along the route of the guided walk. But a sly irony lies just beneath the surface. Sky City has no plumbing or electricity, and inevitably, the first question one tourist asked, as she pointed at the cliff-edge outhouses, was, "What are those?" Leo gave the same deadpan answer my last Acoma tour guide had a few years before: "Those are our ATMs. They only take deposits."

Slowly we made our way to San Estevan del Rey, inside of which, uniquely at Sky City, no photography is allowed. Leo pointed to the bell in the nearest tower and said, as if teaching a kindergarten class, "We *were* under the Spanish crown at one time." But then he added a legend I had never heard before. "Our oral history says that that bell was traded from Mexico for four boys and four girls." He paused, then added softly, "Now who would do a thing like that? We call that kidnapping."

Inside the church, I admired once more the brown-and-red wall murals that mingled Puebloan rainbow and cloud symbols with Christian crosses, the painting on buffalo hide of Saint Stephen's (Estevan's) stoning. Leo mentioned that September 2 was the feast day of Saint Stephen, then went on to say, "You come up and celebrate with us. The public is welcome." As if sensing the apparent paradox that stared us in the face inside the mission, now he editorialized (just as all my previous Acoma guides had), "There's no contradiction at all between the two religions."

During the Pueblo Revolt, the Indians burned to the ground most of the hated churches, yet the Acomans spared San Estevan del Rey. Choosing a quiet moment, I asked the question that had vexed me for fifteen years: "Why didn't Acomans burn down this church during the Pueblo Revolt?" Leo stared, nonplussed, then gave a puzzling answer, "We did. We did. The renovation was in 1802." I let it go.

We left the church and stood on its porch, gazing over the cemetery just to the east. "We don't like to say the dead are 'buried,'" Leo commented. "We say they're 'replanted.' We believe in reincarnation.

The Bible believed it, too, until the fourteenth century, when they changed it." I was still turning this revelation over in my mind, when Leo murmured, as if to himself, "Forty-two of our people died building this mission."

Next Leo explained the *shibop*, the Acoma term for what outsiders more commonly know as the *sipapu*—the hole in the earth from which all human beings emerged during the Creation. "The original *shibop* is just over there," he said, waving vaguely to the west. Many Puebloans locate the original *sipapu* near the mouth of the Little Colorado River. But then Leo added, "It's also believed that the *shibop* is across the Bering Strait in Siberia. That's where we migrated from."

Though I was tempted to regard Leo's spiel as a confused hodgepodge of oral tradition and Western science, what he had to say was no less fascinating for that. As our group moved through the narrow lanes north of the church, Leo summarized the Oñate story. Unlike Brian Vallo, he recited the carrying out of the terrible sentence without batting an eye. Several tourists gasped or winced.

Then Leo recounted the Pueblo Revolt, followed by Vargas's reconquest. Beneath the gentle, accommodating tone of his voice, I heard the immemorial pain, as he stopped in his tracks and spoke: "Vargas came to Acoma in 1692. He said, 'I'll forgive you if you accept Catholicism.'" A potent pause, as Leo's gaze flitted from one tourist's face to another. (Were we, at the moment, the children of the conquistadors?) Then, softly, "Forgive us for what?"

After the attack on Acoma, the last vestiges of overt Puebloan resistance to the Spanish collapsed. Oñate had achieved his dream of conquest. He was ruler of all Nuevo México.

Yet the eight years that remained of his tenure as governor would be stained with failure, bitter conflict, and deep personal discouragement. Having turned into the "petty despot" conjured up by biographer Marc Simmons, Oñate brooked not the slightest sign of disloyalty among his underlings. By 1600, many of the settlers and soldiers were fed up with the new colony; yet their governor interpreted even the request to return to New Spain as tantamount to treason. There is evidence that Oñate was behind the ambush and murder of two of his once most trusted lieutenants who dared initiate a return to the south.

Despite the glowing reports about the prosperity of the colony that the governor sent back to Mexico City, the fact was that no one had yet found any gold or silver in the province. And by 1601, colonists and Indians alike were on the verge of starvation. Ever restless, Oñate set off on one exploring mission after another. His successful journey to the Gulf of California in 1605 was a triumph of sorts. But during an earlier sojourn out onto the plains of Quivira—that chimerical land of bison and rumored riches—while he was gone from San Gabriel, most of the population of the capital fled south. In a fury, Oñate ordered the deserters pursued, under a sentence not only of execution but of beheading, but it was too late.

These refugees brought back to Mexico City shocking claims against the governor. A Franciscan averred that, as the colony fell on lean times, Indian chiefs had been tortured and killed to force them to confess the whereabouts of secret stores of corn. Thousands of Indians, the friar went on, had already died of starvation. "They had been reduced to such extremity," he reported, "that he had seen them eating branches of trees, earth, charcoal and ashes."

At last Oñate accepted the inevitable, resigning as governor on August 24, 1607. He lingered on in New Mexico for two more years before returning to New Spain. In the meantime, a royal viceroy prepared formal charges against him. Of the thirty counts, Oñate was eventually convicted on twelve. These included the murder of several deserters, robberies committed by his soldiers, the giving of "glowing accounts of the land when it was really poor," living "shamefully with women in the colony," and, most damningly, the brutal treatment of the Indians of Acoma. For his crimes, Oñate was sentenced to permanent banishment from the colony he had brought into being, as well as four years of exile from Mexico City. He was also fined 6,000 ducats, and ordered to pay for the costs of his case.

In the 1620s, now more than seventy years old, Oñate petitioned the king for exoneration from his crimes and reinstatement of his honorary title of *adelantado*. Nothing came of his plea. The last conquistador died in obscurity, back in Spain, in 1625.

In New Mexico today, Oñate is not forgotten. For years, the predominantly Hispanic town of Española has sponsored an annual Oñate fiesta in July. In 1992, the outgoing Hispanic senator from New Mexico pushed through legislation for an Oñate visitor center to commemorate the province's first governor. The building stands beside State Highway 68, on the outskirts of Alcalde, a small town just north of Española, only a long stone's throw from where Oñate established his capital of San Gabriel in 1598. With $108,000 of taxpayer money, the center commissioned an Albuquerque artist to make a bronze sculpture of the founder of Nuevo México.

The statue, mounted behind the visitor center, captures Oñate in all his conquistadorial glory, rearing on horseback in full armor, his staff raised to smite some enemy, a wrathful grin twisting his lips. As if to echo the man's hard nature, the statue is surrounded by black boulders, cholla, and prickly pear.

In 1998, Hispanic citizens organized several commemorations of the 400th anniversary of the conquest. A Civil War reenactor named Roberto Valdéz announced that with friends, wearing authentic sixteenth-century soldiers' clothing and gear, he would retrace the route of Oñate's *entrada* on foot, from Ciudad Juárez in Chihuahua all the way to Valdéz's hometown of Española. The local paper, the *Rio Grande Sun*, reported that Valdéz was "unsure about how to include New Mexico's Indian pueblos into the project." With a keen grasp of history, Valdéz added, "When two cultures meet . . . anywhere on this Earth, there's always been conflict."

On January 5, 1998, some unknown activists—most likely Puebloans—figured out just how to include themselves into the commemoration. In the dead of night, they sneaked into the visitor center and cut off the right foot of the Oñate statue. Calling themselves the Brothers of Acoma, they bombarded the New Mexico media with photos of their booty.

The center's director found this hard to swallow. "There's no animosity between Hispanos and Native Americans around here," he told the *Rio Grande Sun*. "Most of the people around here are mestizo, they've got Indian blood. I'm mestizo myself." In the director's opinion, the Brothers of Acoma was "a made-up name," the vandalism the act of "some 'extreme' environmental group." "I'd say this was done," the man added, "by someone from out of state who wasn't even Native American." The paper went on to editorialize that unspecified "officials" believed no such group as the Brothers of Acoma existed.

A week later, the statue had a new right foot, courtesy of the Albuquerque sculptor, who billed Río Arriba County $10,000 for his repairs. The artist sounded miffed by the desecration. "What Oñate did," he told the *Sun,* "might seem cruel and unusual, but what about what the Indians did to him?"

The very sentiments, one imagines, of the conquistador himself. For the last few years, due to lack of funding, the visitor center has been sporadically closed for months at a time. Out back, unvisited by the oblivious tourists whizzing by on their way to Taos, Oñate rears his horse against the enemy on all sides, sneering at fickle fate.

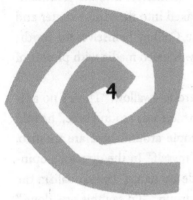

# 4

# TROUBLOUS TIMES

By the time Pedro de Peralta arrived in New Mexico, in the winter of 1609–10, to succeed Oñate as governor, the total Spanish population of New Mexico had dwindled to about 200, virtually all of them lodged at San Gabriel. Peralta's main achievement would be to move the capital to Santa Fe, which he founded in 1610. (In building San Gabriel within the precincts of an existing pueblo, Oñate had violated a Spanish law aimed at preventing colonists from disrupting existing Indian settlements.) Peralta brought with him twelve soldiers and eight more Franciscan priests. The governor is memorialized today in various Santa Fe monuments, as well as in the name of the Paseo de Peralta, the street that makes a loop around the downtown area.

Yet even before Peralta arrived, the colony of Nuevo México came very close to being abandoned. In a long history riddled with woeful ironies, here lies one of the most poignant. In 1608, weighing all the reports he had received from colonists and deserters alike—the tales of near starvation, of mistreatment of Indians, of the failure to find gold or silver—the viceroy in Mexico City made a summation to the Spanish crown of the state of affairs in the far northern province. On September 13, 1608, the Council of the Indies formally recommended that New Mexico be abandoned.

It would have taken only a single expedition with carts to arrive from New Spain, pack up the settlers, and trundle south down the Rio Grande, leaving the bloodstained land to the Puebloans, who had lived there in sovereign independence for centuries, perhaps for millennia. How different would Southwest history be, had New Mexico been abandoned in 1608? Would the Spanish have eventually changed their minds, and sent out new conquering expeditions? (Since 1573, by explicit order of the king, the leaders of such expeditions had been forbidden to use the very word "conquest.") Would Anglo-Americans instead have been the "discoverers" of this new land, arriving no earlier than the 1820s and 1830s, as mountain men trapped beaver up the Arkansas River, down to the Chama and the Rio Grande, and west to the Salt and the Gila?

One can only guess—for it took but a single Franciscan to foil the abandonment. Fray Lázaro Ximénez, who had already recommended giving up the colony, returned in December from a second trip to New Mexico with the glorious but problematic news that by now, no fewer than 7,000 Indians had been converted and baptized. In the logic of Catholic thinking, it was unconscionable to abandon Christianized natives. Once baptized, an Indian risked far greater spiritual ruin in the temptation to return to old, discredited gods than did a "heathen" who had never been converted in the first place. The crown actually pondered the option of removing all 7,000 converted Puebloans by force to New Spain, so that the Franciscans could continue to minister to them. In the end, however, King Philip III suspended the order of the Council of the Indies. New Mexico must not be abandoned, no matter what the cost or hardship.

With Peralta began an insidious pattern of conflict between church and state in the remote northern colony that would checker the eighty-two years between Oñate's arrival and the outbreak of the Pueblo Revolt.

It was to this perennial conflict that one of the most penetrating scholars of the period, France Scholes, applied the memorable epithet, in the title of a 1942 monograph, *Troublous Times in New Mexico.*

In the summer of 1612, a supply train from Mexico City arrived with one Fray Isidro Ordóñez in tow. Ordóñez, who was, in the words of historian Carroll Riley, "very much a loose cannon," almost immediately became Peralta's nemesis. The friar's first act, however, was to present the prelate of the colony's priesthood with a letter from Mexico City (very likely forged) removing that worthy from his office and installing Ordóñez himself as prelate. In this Machiavellian schemer, Nuevo México would see the first in a succession of power-crazy priests and governors.

Ordóñez seems to have formed a violent dislike of the governor from the first day he set foot in Santa Fe. In the summer of 1613, their simmering quarrel reached an absurd boiling point. Ordóñez demanded from the governor an escort of soldiers to take him to Mexico City, where, he darkly promised, he would file a report about "serious matters" afoot in the colony. He also promulgated a decree against anyone sending any kind of dispatch to the capital without Ordóñez's own approval, upon pain of excommunication and a heavy fine.

On July 7, at Mass in Santa Fe, the priest (perhaps under the orders of Fray Ordóñez, who was present) threw the governor's chair into the street outside the church. Peralta picked up the chair and plunked it down near the baptismal font, where he sat among the Indians rather than his fellow officers. After the gospel had concluded, Ordóñez stood up to give a speech that shocked the whole congregation. "Do not be deceived," the self-appointed prelate warned. "Let no one persuade with vain words that I do not have the same power and authority that the Pope in Rome has, or that if his Holiness were [here] in New Mexico he could do more than I. Believe that I can arrest, cast into irons, and punish as seems fitting to me any person without exception who is not obedient to the commandments of the Church and mine."

One is left to imagine the bewilderment of the "Christian Indians" who witnessed this display of dueling tempers. Who was in charge, after all, in this strange new Spanish world?

On the very next day, when Peralta declined to assign three particular soldiers to the prelate's convoy, Ordóñez, in France Scholes's words, "flew into a rage, denounced his opponent as a Lutheran, a heretic, and a Jew, and threatened to arrest him." On learning of these aspersions, Peralta marched with soldiers to the convent to confront his antagonist. Somehow, the governor's pistol was discharged, wounding a Franciscan. (The record is ambiguous as to whether Peralta himself deliberately fired the gun.)

In due time, Ordóñez sent four soldiers and a friar off on a journey to Mexico City to request formal permission to arrest the governor. Unable to find messengers of his own to head to the capital to present his side of the story, because of Ordóñez's threat of excommunication and a heavy fine for such missions, Peralta set off southward himself. In the meantime, with oily blandishments, Ordóñez had won a number of soldiers over to his side. A small party with the prelate at their head set out in pursuit of the governor. On the night of August 12–13, Peralta was apprehended in a camp near the pueblo of Isleta, arrested "in the name of the Inquisition," and jailed in the convent of the Sandía mission. He would spend the next nine months as Ordóñez's prisoner.

In a single year, the newly arrived Franciscan had converted himself from an ambitious priest into the supreme ruler of Nuevo México. Back in Santa Fe, Ordóñez ransacked the governor's papers for incriminating material, of which he found enough to send batches to Mexico City as justification for the arrest he had already carried out. And he delegated a friar to go from door to door in Santa Fe, reading out loud a document in Peralta's hand that referred to the citizens as "half-breeds."

Some sort of monomania must have fueled Ordóñez's tyranny. Like many a despot, he saw traitors on all sides. During the months of his reign over the miserable colony, wrote one witness, "Excommunications were rained down.... Existence in the villa was a hell."

Peralta was freed only upon the arrival of the governor appointed to succeed him. (Unlike the prelacy of New Mexico, the governorship was rotated at fairly short intervals, usually from two to four years.) In November 1614, stripped of nearly all his worldly possessions, the ex-governor hobbled south on horseback. Once he reached Mexico City, though facing grave charges himself, he must have filed his own affidavits about the prelate's misdeeds. Unfortunately, no record of them survives.

Ordóñez remained in power for another two and a half years. At first he professed to be on excellent terms with the new governor, but his habitual distrust of rivals soon reduced that relationship to an impasse almost as nasty as the battle of wills that had led to Peralta's arrest. Ordóñez was finally removed from New Mexico in the winter of 1616–17, but only through the Church's sly maneuver of creating a new post, the *custodia,* to supersede the prelacy.

Much of this prolonged struggle between prelate and governor reads today as bad comedy. Yet if Ordóñez's tyranny turned the colony into a veritable hell for the settlers, it had an even more lugubrious impact on the Puebloans. On hearing that a Cochiti man had been murdered by Indians from Jemez, Ordóñez sent soldiers to seize the alleged perpetrators and bring them to Santo Domingo. There he had one Jemez man hanged on the spot, and ordered the execution of the others. The latter sentences may not have been carried out, but they set the mold for a fierce resentment of the Spanish on the part of Jemez, which would only grow more bitter over the next sixty-five years. Not surprisingly, Jemez would play a leading role in the Pueblo Revolt, and an even more pivotal one in the resistance after Vargas's reconquest of 1692.

Further twisting the screw of Puebloan discontent were the practices, introduced by Oñate, of the *encomienda* and the *repartimiento.* The former granted landed settlers the right to collect regular tribute from a specified number of Puebloans, usually in the form of corn or animal hides. The latter demanded a similar tribute in the form of forced labor. Both practices had been made explicitly illegal by the Spanish crown, but they flourished in New Mexico. For Puebloans barely able to feed and clothe their own families, these tributes worked a severe hardship.

Another illegal practice was the slaving expeditions carried out by governors against the nomadic tribes on the periphery of the Pueblo world. These had as an excuse the effort to protect the Puebloans from attacks by raiders, mostly Apache. But the taking of Apaches as slaves led to the predictable retribution of Apaches attacking and burning yet more pueblos, usually those farthest from the military presence in and around Santa Fe.

Meanwhile, churches were being built at a breakneck pace, and Indians converted and baptized. Scholes, the pioneering scholar of this period, relied heavily on mission documents as sources for his historical works about seventeenth-century New Mexico. As a result, he has often been criticized for importing (whether or not consciously) a pro-Church bias to those works.

If so, a corrective pendulum swing in the other direction can be found in the pages of Ramón A. Gutiérrez's *When Jesus Came, the Corn Mothers Went Away*. This brilliantly readable, provocative, and much criticized book, published in 1991, paints the Franciscans in New Mexico in lurid and extreme colors. Gutiérrez is the main spokesman for the idea that these friars sought out martyrdom at the hands of natives as the most perfect of deaths. And he argues that "a hypnotic spell beckoned the Franciscans to New Mexico. There, in a new missionary field . . . the most radical members of the order flocked to usher in Christ's second coming."

Gutiérrez raises the crucial question of why so many Puebloans were willing to be baptized and to convert. At his gala festival inaugurating the first church in New Mexico in 1598, Oñate had re-created a pageant that Cortés had used to great effect among the Aztecs in 1524. Before the assembled Indians, Oñate had knelt, kissed the hands and the hems of the skirts of the Franciscan friars, then demanded that the natives do likewise. At the end of the pageant, Oñate had again gotten down on his knees, praying in a loud voice for the conversion of the infidels. His men fired their harquebuses into the air, and Oñate erected a large cross on the spot.

In Gutiérrez's gloss, "Kneeling before the Spaniards was a radical and humiliating gesture for the Puebloans. Never had they approached their leaders or their gods on bended knee. Now, not only were they expected to kneel before the Franciscans, but every time they greeted a priest they were to kneel and kiss his hands and feet."

Other factors made the conversions logical. If Spanish sources are to be believed, priests sometimes produced miracles to demonstrate the puissance and benevolence of their God. At the Hopi pueblo of Awatovi in 1632, skeptical shamans presented Fray Francisco de Porras with a thirteen-year-old boy who had been blind since birth, challenging the friar to give the child sight. The father knelt, prayed for a miracle "for the confusion of these infidels," grabbed a handful of dirt, spat into it, then rubbed the mud on the boy's eyes. Suddenly, the blind youth could see. Other Hopis rejoiced, but the shamans felt tricked. A year later, they poisoned Fray Francisco.

In other carefully staged dramas, Puebloans sentenced to death by the governor and turned over to soldiers to be executed would be saved at the last minute by friars pleading leniency. Oñate had explained the usefulness of such theatrics: "[The Puebloans] will recognize the friars as their benefactors and protectors and come to love and esteem them, and to fear us."

The cross itself was the pervasive emblem of the new religion. Gutiérrez argues that the similarity of the cross to the prayer-stick Puebloans had employed since long before the advent of the Spanish smoothed the way for acceptance of the symbol of Christ's crucifixion. Carroll Riley likewise postulates that the cross bore an uncanny resemblance to the anthropomorphized four-pointed star so prevalent among petroglyphs conjuring up the kachina phenomenon, although rock art expert Polly Schaafsma casts doubt on this linkage.

The overarching explanation as to why so many Puebloans converted to Christianity, however, lies in their gift for adaptability and secrecy. As a conquered people, the Puebloans quickly understood that even more than gold and silver, the Spanish desired to save the souls of the thousands of unbelievers they had come among. To undergo conversion and baptism, nonetheless, was more than a simple matter of feigned acquiescence: the Puebloans also felt free to take what was useful from the new religion and meld it to the kachina faith. It is this process that has resulted in the seamless syncretism of today's Pueblo belief system, in the assertion, so alien to the Western rational mind, that Leo Patricio had offered our tour group at Acoma, "There's no contradiction at all between the two religions."

Yet underneath the apparent acceptance of the cross and the Church, a profound malaise and resentment simmered for eight decades, a bitterness that Popé would tap in 1680. No symbol of the Christian faith was more potently laden with meaning for the Puebloans than the church bell, whose ringing every morning summoned children and adults alike to service. In the Pueblo Revolt, not every mission church would be destroyed, but virtually every bell would be. At San Lázaro, the Galisteo Basin pueblo partly excavated by private owners since the early 1990s, diggers found the church bell smashed into a hundred pieces.

All across the colony of Nuevo México, the Franciscans built churches directly on top of existing pueblos. Usually, the new mission obliterated the villagers' most important kivas, thus stamping the superiority of the Catholic over the kachina religion into the very architecture. In several state and national monuments, and in one national historic park, the ruins of such missionized pueblos have been stabilized and restored to make the sites accessible to tourists, who stroll through them on designated pathways numbered with posts keyed to edifying passages in the trail guides.

Over several months in the spring of 2003, I visited five such ruins. No more vivid diorama of life in seventeenth-century New Mexico exists today. The churches themselves, built of adobe and stone in the same style as the pueblo rooms, have weathered so handsomely that it is hard to see them as grandiose monuments to oppression. They tower as high as forty feet above the ground. Twentieth-century excavators devoted their efforts, for the most part, to the missions, leaving the surrounding roomblocks unexcavated: today, the buildings in which the Puebloans lived sleep beneath vague earthen ridges covered with grass and cactus.

Three of these ruins—Abó, Gran Quivira, and Quarai—are incorporated into a single unit, as the Salinas Pueblo Missions National Monument. Lying some fifty miles as the crow flies southeast of Albuquerque, more than eighty south of Santa Fe, they are in the middle of nowhere in terms of modern settlement patterns. In consequence, they are relatively little visited. Yet each has a lonely beauty of its own, and each brims with the history of the difficult decades that preceded the Pueblo Revolt.

The "Salinas" of these pueblos' common name refers to the extensive salt beds nearby. Salt was so valuable a trading commodity in the pre-Columbian Southwest that those beds, as much as anything, were the villages' original *raison d'être*. Yet, as the southeasterly-most pueblos in all of New Mexico, they became acutely vulnerable to Apaches and Comanches roaming the plains to the east, who raided more and more boldly as the seventeenth century wore on.

On a cold March day with a fierce wind lashing out of the east, I strolled, the only visitor, through the mission at Abó—a graceful oblong structure made of well-shaped brownish orange stones. Then I meandered out past the humble roomblocks hidden in the ground, and finally, off the tourist track, down a dry wash for half a mile until I found several low cliffs covered with beguiling petroglyphs, probably carved in the fifteenth century. Abó was first occupied around A.D. 1300. The mission was built, we think, in the 1620s. Between 1672 and 1675, having fallen on desperate times, the pueblo was abandoned for good.

A rather heavy-handed excavation and restoration of the Abó mission in the 1930s has left important research questions unanswerable. Yet the single most intriguing puzzle about the place stared back at me as I lingered by a numbered post. At Abó, the Franciscans did not obliterate the kiva of their heathen charges. Instead, it seems, they built (or allowed the building of) a kiva right in the middle of the mission's west court patio. Was this a sign of an atypical tolerance on the friars' part? Had they permitted Indian dances and secular meetings right here, in the shadow of the walls of the house of God? The 1930s excavators found that the kiva had never had a roof, and it was full not only of ashes but of kitchen rubbish. This gave rise to the speculation that the Spaniards had allowed the building of the kiva only to treat it as a garbage bin—one more way of heaping humiliation on the benighted pagans whom the friars had come to save.

Like their neighbors to the south, at Gran Quivira, the denizens of Abó were Tompiro. Upon abandoning their villages in the 1670s, they joined the Piro pueblos—most likely, their linguistic cousins—to the west on the Rio Grande. Despite having fiercely resisted the Spanish during Oñate's time, the warriors of Abó and Gran Quivira would play no part in the Pueblo Revolt. Eventually they drifted south to settle near the El Paso area. Like Piro, Tompiro is a lost language and culture.

On a much warmer day in April, I drove thirty miles from the sleepy town of Mountainair, down an empty road that made four beelines straight south punctuated with three jogs straight east, to arrive at Gran Quivira. The site struck me as the most improbable of any pueblo I had yet visited in New Mexico or Arizona. So flat was the basin stretching away on all sides, I might, I thought, have escaped the mountains and mesas of the Pueblo homeland to creep to the very edge of the Great Plains. Yet a single bulging outcrop of bedrock had allowed the construction of a village here. Gran Quivira, every bit as appealing to the eye as Abó, is made of gray limestone, rather than the warm-toned sandstone otherwise so prevalent all over the Southwest. Though it is a harder stone to work, the builders here had shaped their blocks to fit with cunning precision one against another.

Gran Quivira is also far older than Abó, its roots reaching back to pithouses gouged in the earth around A.D. 800. At peak population, this isolated pueblo was home to between 1,500 and 2,000 natives. A first church was built at Gran Quivira in 1636; a second, never completed, in 1659. Here, uncharacteristically, the friars put up their mission not smack on top of the central roomblocks, but off to the side, on lower ground. The statement of Catholic supremacy is correspondingly muted.

An excellent job of excavation and stabilization was carried out here in the 1970s. Not content simply to rehabilitate the mission, the archaeologists excavated many Puebloan roomblocks as well. As a result, Gran Quivira gives the best picture in all the Southwest of what a missionized pueblo must have looked like. And in the course of their work, the diggers made a fascinating discovery: several ordinary rooms fitted out with all the paraphernalia of a kiva. In the 1660s, apparently, after dutifully attending Catholic Mass in the mission, the Indians would slip into these hidden chambers to commune in earnest with the gods that had never failed them.

Gran Quivira succumbed, around 1670, to the same misfortunes—drought, famine, and disease, as well as Apache raids—that depopulated Abó. After a continuous occupation of almost 900 years, the isolated pueblo on the salt plains was abandoned to the coyotes and the winds.

Later the same day, I drove north to the third Salinas pueblo, Quarai. Sheltered beside a spring-fed stream on the east slope of the Manzano Mountains, Quarai seemed to me more cozy than lonely. The mission, built of a deep red sandstone, looks virtually European in its ruined grandeur. Like the mission at Abó, Quarai's church encloses a puzzle—a rectangular kiva in the middle of the convent. We know the kiva was built at the same time as the church, in 1630, but everything else about it remains a mystery.

The Puebloans who lived here were Tiwa rather than Tompiro, related thus to such Rio Grande pueblos as Isleta and Sandía. Yet Quarai suffered the same fate as its neighbors to the south. Abandonment came in 1677, only three years before the Pueblo Revolt. A despairing dispatch from the last priest at Quarai, shortly before the dispersal of its last inhabitants, reads like a message in a bottle:

> The drought and famine continue. Many are sick, some are dying. . . . The terror and outrages continue. Some are leaving every day. . . . We must leave, all two hundred families, and go north to Tajique where there is a mission and a settlement. If that, too, is unprotected, we will go on to Isleta to be with other Tiwa-speakers.

In contrast to the Salinas pueblos, Pecos, which lies just off Interstate 25 between Santa Fe and Las Vegas, is a regular tourist destination. One of the largest and most important of all the pueblos, Pecos was skillfully excavated by Alfred V. Kidder over twelve field seasons after 1915. When Kidder brought nearly all the leading Southwestern archaeologists together for a meeting of minds here in 1927, the Pecos Conference, which still convenes every August, was born. Out of that first conference emerged the classification system for Anasazi-Pueblo prehistory and history that is still in wide use today: Basketmaker II, Basketmaker III, Pueblo I, Pueblo II, Pueblo III, Pueblo IV, Pueblo V. (There was no Basketmaker I, because the Basketmaker II culture, now dated roughly from 1200 B.C. to A.D. 500, seemed so sophisticated to the assembled savants that they felt the need to postulate a prior, as yet undiscovered, Basketmaker I phase. BM I remains undiscovered: instead, Archaic flows seamlessly into BM II.) Kidder so loved the Pecos ruin that he was buried there upon his death in 1963, though out of respect for the wishes of his family, the rangers will not reveal the location of his grave.

Kidder is revered today as one of the giants of Southwestern archaeology. More than any other scholar, he brought rigor to the discipline, insisting on finding proof of prehistoric events in the dirt of excavations themselves, rather than (as was often true before his time) in the uncritical acceptance of Puebloan oral traditions.

At Pecos National Historic Park, another loop trail with numbered posts takes the visitor on a useful tour of the sprawling ruin. Several Puebloan roomblocks have been restored and stabilized, and a reconstructed kiva, complete with modern ladder, serves as a favorite lecture hall for tour guides. What impressed me most on this, my third visit, was none of these prettified showrooms of ancient life, but the sheer volume of the unexcavated buildings stretching from south to north, buried beneath brush and cholla. Kidder had been so moved by the prodigal abundance of Pecos that he chose it for that reason for his life's work. The pueblo's midden, shelving off to the east from the principal roomblocks, was, in his words, "the greatest rubbish heap and cemetery that had ever been found in the pueblo region."

As usual, I found a bevy of serious photographers parked with their tripods on all sides of the towering mission, a marvel of brownish red adobe. This church, however, post-dates the reconquest of 1692, built to replace the larger mission that the Puebloans gleefully razed to the ground during the Revolt. Unlike the Salinas pueblos, Pecos was occupied after the reconquest, until its final abandonment in 1838.

Four successive seventeenth-century missions were erected on the site of the present church, beginning around 1621. The first of them was the grandest in all New Mexico, a veritable cathedral 150 feet long from entrance to altar. Its very existence, however, seemed all but apocryphal, until the original foundations were almost accidentally rediscovered by archaeologist Jean Pinkley in 1967. According to Pecos historian John L. Kessell, this first mission required 300,000 sun-dried adobe blocks to build, each weighing forty pounds. The walls were as thick as twenty-two feet at the maximum. Roof beams were as long as forty-one feet. Six towers and a crenellated parapet made the mission look, in Kessell's words, "as much like a fortress as a church." All the labor, of course, was carried out by Puebloans, reduced by the megalomaniac dream of Father Andrés Juárez to virtual slavery.

The fifth of the missionized pueblos I visited in the spring of 2003, called Giusewa, has by far the loveliest setting, tucked in a bend of the

Jemez River beside State Highway 4, between forested 1,500-foot-tall slopes that soar toward mesa rims crowned with Ponderosa pines. Compared to Pecos or even Gran Quivira, Giusewa is a diminutive pueblo; there is no room in the small basin formed by a tributary creek joining the Jemez River for a village to grow to more than modest size. The ruined mission of San José de los Jemez is modest, too, and as beautiful as any in New Mexico. Yet no less than the vanished cathedral of Fray Andrés at Pecos, this church represents a monument to oppression.

An original mission was founded here around 1600 by Fray Alonzo de Lugo. Assigned to minister to the Jemez people, the friar faced an impossible task, for these tough, independent mountain dwellers were scattered among at least eleven different villages, some of them on distant mesa tops at altitudes above 7,500 feet. Fray Alonzo dutifully visited eight of these remote pueblos, but chose the most convenient, down in the river valley, as the site for his mission. Then he set about attempting a standard Spanish ecclesiastical practice of the day, called the "reduction" of the natives. Fray Alonzo pleaded with the mesa-top dwellers to give up their villages and congregate at Giusewa. Met with stony refusal, the friar gave up and left in 1601. A succession of later priests likewise failed to reduce the Jemez.

San José Mission, built around 1621, and the partially excavated pueblo surrounding it are incorporated today in Jemez State Monument. A single ranger tends the site from a shack beside the highway. Most visitors, I had noticed on previous stops at Giusewa, spend about five minutes in the ruin, clicking a few snapshots of the church before heading on to more sybaritic venues, such as the hot springs just up valley or the motels and bars of Jemez Springs, just below. Last spring, I stopped by on a Jemez Pueblo holiday. Four young girls and boys, dressed in semitraditional garb, were dancing dispiritedly before the mission, to the beat of a young drummer. The girls, wearing painted cardboard butterfly wings, shook feathers in either hand. The dancers' parents sat at picnic tables on the periphery, eating snacks and cheering the children on. "You doin' good, Laura," I heard a mother call out.

The Anglo tourists, however, were lingering longer than the usual five minutes. They had something other than the church to point their cameras at: real Indians, wearing Indian clothes, dancing Indian dances. Behind the young performers, the crumbling walls of San José nicely framed their portraits.

Exacerbating the already strained relations between church and state in New Mexico, its fourth governor, Juan de Eulate, who came into office in 1618, called a halt to the building of a number of churches —including Fray Andrés's monumental mission at Pecos—on the grounds that the demands on Puebloan labor required to do the building were inhumane. Eulate also encouraged the Puebloans to venerate the "idols" and perform the dances that the friars had done all they could to extinguish.

The governor, however, was no benevolent champion of the Indians. It was a personal antipathy against the Franciscans that motivated his seemingly tolerant reforms. Later Eulate would face charges in Mexico City for having waged slave-taking forays even against peaceful nomadic bands. He was also taxed with having seized Puebloan orphans and selling them on the market in Mexico. As vain and pompous a man in his own way as had been Ordóñez, Eulate no sooner arrived in the colony than he announced that "the King was his ruler and he did not have to acknowledge the authority of the Pope or the Church."

At El Morro, I had puzzled out a long inscription that, although its author is not named, is attributed to Eulate on the basis of its date. In this windy boast, the governor congratulates himself for having pacified the Zuni pueblos and sworn their inhabitants to vassalage—"all of which he did," claims Eulate, referring to himself in the third person, "with clemency and zeal and prudence, as a most Christian and great gentleman, a most extraordinary and gallant soldier of imperishable and praised memory." Some skeptical passerby later saw fit to scratch out the epithet "great gentleman" ("*gran caballero*"), whose characters can just be discerned in the grazing light of a summer sunset.

In 1626, the Holy Office of the Inquisition was formally introduced to New Mexico. The idea of the Inquisition had been born in A.D. 1231, when Pope Gregory IX had established the office to bring to trial and execution such heretics as the ascetic Cathars, who roamed across Languedoc in southwest France. In its Spanish guise, beginning in the second half of the fifteenth century, the Inquisition became synonymous with persecution, mostly of Jews and Muslims, in the name of Catholic orthodoxy. The very name of the first Spanish grand inquisitor, Tomás de Torquemada, still evokes the terror that issued from his systematic torture and burning at the stake of some 2,000 suspected heretics.

In New Mexico, at first, the Inquisition was used not so much against Puebloans as against settlers. Among the scores of accusations brought against Spaniards in the colony were grave matters of witchcraft and pacts with the devil, but also such seemingly ludicrous charges as the employment by frantic wives of Indian love potions to try to win back the affections of their unfaithful husbands. A number of cases of bigamy were likewise prosecuted. The overall impact of the Inquisition, however, was to give ambitious Franciscans yet another weapon in their struggle to seize power from the colony's governors.

No Franciscan was more ambitious than Fray Alonso de Benavides, who arrived in New Mexico as the new custodian in 1625, and who became the commissary of the Inquisition the following year. Benavides's great dream was to elevate the province to the dignity of a diocese, with himself as the first bishop.

To that end, Benavides wrote two versions, in 1630 and 1634, of a work usually called simply the *Memorial*, though the actual title of the first volume tellingly translates as *A Harvest of Reluctant Souls*. Scholars have been grateful to Benavides ever since, for if Gaspar Pérez de Villagrá's fanciful epic poem, *Historia de la Nueva Mexico*, is the colony's first history, Benavides's *Memorial* represents the first ethnography, however crude and limited by Catholic preconceptions. There are short chapters on a number of the most important pueblos, as well as an attempt to identify and characterize some of the more shadowy nomadic tribes on the outskirts.

Some of Benavides's descriptions of the customs of the Puebloans are quite bizarre. For instance:

The women who wanted men to crave them would go out into the countryside fat and fine, and raise up a rock or a long stick on the top of a hill. There they would offer up cornmeal, and for eight days, or as long as they could, they would not eat. This sort of thing certainly upset their stomachs, and provoked them into vomiting. They whipped themselves cruelly. When they couldn't stand this any more, and had gone from fat to thin, with figures like the devil, they would saunter up confidently to the first man they saw and get him excited. The man would give them blankets, which was their principal aim.

Like many another friar, Benavides misjudged the Puebloans' apparent willingness to be converted. In a chapter called "How Well They Take to Christian Practices," he claimed,

When we ring the bell for mass, they all come as well scrubbed and neat as can be. They enter the church to pray as though they had been Christians forever.... All these people make their confessions in their own tongues. They ready themselves for confession by studying their own sins, bringing them along recorded on a series of knotted strings.... If we travel down the roads, and they see us from their pueblos, or their croplands, they all come out to greet us with very great delight. "Praised be Our Lord Jesus Christ," they say. "Praised be His Holy Sacrament."

The potent foreshadowing of 1680 embodied in those knotted strings, Benavides would not live to appreciate. It did not take long, however, for the custodian to receive vivid evidence of the hatred for the brown-robed men of God that lurked under the surface of the charade of Puebloan piety. At Zuni, in 1630 or 1632, the resident priest was murdered, as was another friar who had left Zuni to travel to the Mexican state of Sonora.

The quasi-omniscient Very Rev. James H. Defouri, that indefatigable chronicler of the martyrs of New Mexico, writing in 1893, gives us an eyewitness account of the treacherous killing of Fray Francisco Letrado at Zuni:

> Father Francisco was on the point of celebrating mass, but the Indians did not come. After repeated signals, he went out to see the cause of the delay. Meeting some of them he invited them to come, but as they refused, he reproached them for their want of religion. They became angry. Perceiving that they were prepared to do him harm, he fell on his knees, holding with both hands a crucifix, and in that attitude he was pierced with innumerable arrows.

A few years later, priests at Taos and Jemez were also murdered by the Puebloans, and the miracle-working Fray Francisco de Porras at Hopi was poisoned. According to Defouri, the latter friar died with the psalm "*In te, Domini, speravi*" on his lips.

After killing the priests at Zuni, the Puebloans, knowing retribution must come, fled en masse to their mesa-top refuge of Dowa Yalanne. An expedition of soldiers failed to dent the precipitous defenses of this natural fortress. Only in 1635 did the Zuni dare to descend and take up residence again in their low-lying villages.

Under the governorship of Luis de Rosas, from 1637 to 1641, relations between church and state were strained almost to the breaking point. Rosas's innovation was to install the Indians in workshops of his creation, the goods they turned out to be sold for the governor's personal profit. The friars were outraged, ostensibly because Rosas was exploiting Indian labor, but also because the workshops denied these men of God the kinds of help from Indian "servants" they had grown to take for granted. Rosas also conducted the most ambitious slave-raiding expeditions against the Apaches yet attempted in New Mexico.

In 1636, Rosas and one of the friars, Fray Antonio de Arteaga, engaged in a melodramatic exchange in the middle of a church service that must have baffled Puebloan witnesses every bit as thoroughly as the contretemps between Ordóñez and Peralta in 1613. Aiming his remarks at the governor, Arteaga sermonized that "all Catholic princes were subject to the laws of the Church." Even the king of Spain was so constrained. Furthermore, "any man who refused such obedience would be a heretic." Unable to bear such pronouncements, Rosas exclaimed, "Shut up, Father, what you say is a lie." According to Scholes, the Indians present were "scandalized" by the governor's outburst.

Only months after his term as governor had ended, Rosas was killed in Santa Fe by a soldier who, returning from an extended leave in New Spain, found his wife hiding underneath the ex-governor's bed.

In the middle of Rosas's reign, a terrible smallpox epidemic swept through the pueblos. At least 3,000 Indians died. This epidemic, which coincided with a lasting drought, proved to the Puebloans that the friars' magic was worthless. According to Ramón Gutiérrez, it also "indicated that the native gods were angry." With the 1640 epidemic, a movement to revive the kachina religion—often enacted in dances and rites defiantly carried out under the noses of the priests—swept the Pueblo world.

This provoked a predictable counterreaction. The priests, whom Oñate had scripted to play the role of saviors and protectors of the Indians, could also prove themselves apt disciples of Torquemada. At their most extreme, some of the punishments carried out by friars against Puebloans bespeak a cruelty, guided by religious bigotry, whose horror still reverberates more than three centuries later. At Hopi, Fray Salvador de Guerra brutally flogged a Puebloan for "worshiping idols" until "he was bathed in blood," then poured hot turpentine on his wounds. (The man died from the treatment.) At Taos, according to Gutiérrez, Fray Nicolás Hidalgo "punished his insolent children by castration and acts of sodomy." The friar also fathered a number of illegitimate children by Indian women. A priest at Awatovi, alarmed that his affair with an Indian woman had aroused the jealous wrath of a leading Puebloan, ordered two soldiers to kill the man. Then, to cover up his own role in the plot, the friar contrived to have the soldiers arrested, brought to a swift trial, and hanged.

In the mid-1640s, as part of the backlash against the revival of the kachinas, Governor Fernando de Argüello Carvajál had forty Indians whipped and imprisoned for "sedition." No pueblo suffered more than Jemez. On the flimsiest of evidence, Argüello accused Jemez leaders of aiding the Apache and Navajo enemy, and summarily hanged twenty-nine of them.

By the 1640s, then, after four decades under the quixotic and often mutually contradictory despotisms of Spanish church and state, the Puebloans had seen their way of life profoundly disrupted. Complicating the situation was the fact that not a few of the conversions were genuine. Thus within each pueblo, a tense struggle was acted out between Christianized Indians (mostly young) who were loyal to the friars and the more conservative and usually older Puebloans (particularly the shamans) who clung to the kachina faith. According to Gutiérrez, there were instances in which the "traditionalists" seized half-breed children fathered by concupiscent friars and beat them to death.

At the same time, overwhelmed by the suffering caused by the *encomienda* and the *repartimiento*, many Puebloans simply fled their home villages. Improbable though it seems, some of these refugees allied themselves with their enemies, the Apaches, and took their revenge by raiding Spanish settlements and supply trains. (The suspicion of such defections at Jemez was part of what had prompted Argüello to carry out his mass hangings.)

It was during this decade that the seed of the Pueblo Revolt was sown.

During my rambles across New Mexico in search of rock art, I found
the occasional petroglyph or pictograph that vividly recorded these
years of oppression. Rock art is extremely difficult to date, but many
images that I stumbled upon—some of them on the margins of panels
that exuberantly celebrated the pre-contact glory of a way of life
presided over by the kachinas—were unmistakably intended to pro-
claim the gloomy truths of a world changed forever by the coming of
the Spanish.

In 1598, Oñate had found a roundabout way to climb the *bajada*
separating the Río Abajo from the Río Arriba. But Santa Fe Canyon,
which carves a gorge through the basalt cliffs of the "jump," soon
became the Camino Real that every train of immigrants and soldiers
rode from the capital of New Spain to the capital of New Mexico.

Today, Santa Fe Canyon is a parcel of Bureau of Land Management
quadrangles crowded from the south by small homesteads and ranch-
erías, mostly Hispanic-owned. The perpetual stream that winds through
the valley floor carries the sanitized but still foul-smelling effluent
from Santa Fe's waste treatment facility down to the tributary's junction with the Rio Grande (located, perhaps symbolically, smack in the
middle of the Cochiti reservation).

On the south-facing rim of Santa Fe Canyon, several hundred feet
above the stream, I found petroglyphs of three Spanish soldiers, complete with cornered hats, on horseback. All three were riding northeast, up-canyon. It was not hard to imagine an artist hiding on the rim,
watching the invasion as it passed below. Near one soldier, an upright
sword, complete with hilt, had been carved; the weapon seemed all the
more ominous for its detachment from any human actor.

The Pajarito Plateau is a vast tableland sloping south and east from
the Jemez Mountains to the Rio Grande, dissected by many sharp
canyons and arroyos. In the thirteenth and fourteenth centuries, this
may have been the most densely populated region in all of what is now
New Mexico. Unlike the Galisteo Basin, which a century later would be
the center of the Pueblo world, with its huge aggregated villages, the

settlement pattern on the Pajarito was defined by scores of small pueblos, many located less than half a mile from one another. Literally hundreds of such ruins lie secluded in the piñon and juniper forest that swathes the plateau, although one valley full of them, Frijoles Canyon, forms the restored centerpiece of Bandelier National Monument.

The rock here is neither basalt nor sandstone, but volcanic tuff, the congealed debris of several colossal eruptions that occurred long before humans entered the region, but not so far back in geologic terms. Tuff forms a gravelly, soft stone ranging in hue from gray to orange. Here the Puebloans learned a new way to make a house, simply by carving out arching hollows in the tuff, probably with tools no more sophisticated than fire-hardened pointed sticks. These "cavates," as archaeologists call them, look superficially like cliff dwellings, but really have nothing in common with the Anasazi villages of the Four Corners area—mud-and-stone buildings erected within the shelter of arching natural alcoves. Cavates tend to be diminutive and close to the base of the cliff, but what makes them beguiling to the eye is that each architect has scraped and carved his home (no two alike), complete with little storage niches, benches, and granaries, straight out of the bedrock.

Hiking the Pajarito Plateau over the years, I had always thought that here the Puebloans had crafted an ideal marriage of landscape to living space. Yet the paradox that hangs over this sweeping shelf of arable, well-watered terrain is that it was almost completely deserted by the time Coronado entered the Southwest. At a loss to explain this mini-abandonment, archaeologists vaguely invoke climate changes that have yet to be firmly documented.

I had thus assumed that I would learn little or nothing about the conflict between Spaniards and Puebloans on the Pajarito Plateau, but Rory Gauthier proved me wrong. Park archaeologist for Bandelier National Monument, Gauthier, who grew up in nearby Los Alamos, dropped his usual chores on a balmy late October day to hike with me to several little-known but deeply evocative corners of the plateau.

On a blithe ridge near the Bandelier outlier called Tsankawi, I followed Gauthier past a number of cavate dwellings, then some faint petroglyphs of kachinas grooved in the soft stone. In all its crumbly splendor, tuff makes a poor canvas for rock art, but this had discouraged the local engravers not one whit. Suddenly we came to a startling design, hard to make out in the slanting mid-morning light, but unambiguous in its purport. At about half life-size, some Puebloan artist had carved a conquistador on horseback galloping from left to right across a flat vertical wall of tuff, sword raised menacingly in his right hand.

The implications of this petroglyph are buttressed by a small number of field studies dating fugitive reoccupations of the Pajarito Plateau. Sometime after Oñate's *entrada*, a limited number of Puebloans— most likely Tewa, from such nearby villages as Santa Clara, San Ildefonso, and San Juan, or Keres from Cochiti, whose forebears had claimed much of this tableland—had returned to these ancestral haunts, perhaps to hide from soldiers who were hunting them down. The petroglyph of the rampaging conquistador was a lasting emblem of the fear that had driven these refugees here.

Gauthier also led me to a site that, while off-limits to tourists today, lies not far from the monument headquarters. In many of the cavates, the dwellers had smoothed the walls with a surface of brown clay. Years of campfires inside these cramped precincts had coated the upper walls and ceiling with a layer of black soot. Upon this *tabula rasa*, in a small number of cavates, artists had used some kind of sharp tool to etch half-mystic designs with a filigree delicacy rare anywhere in the Southwest.

To protect the wall beneath this particular cavate as we entered the dwelling, Gauthier and I climbed a stepladder that he had lugged up the hillside. Sitting cross-legged inside, I let my headlamp play across a congeries of overlapping drawings, ranging from abstract grids to half-formed humanoids to what Gauthier interpreted as a *koshare*—a kachina clown—shinnying its way like a koala bear up a tree.

The cynosure of this cavate art gallery, the finest yet found at Bandelier, is a design that pulses with a strange mixture of native and Spanish connotations. This eerie figure, lightly but expertly traced in the flaking soot, shows a human head haloed by a band from which radiate twenty-one triangles, forming what looks like an ethereal crown. In a brilliant study of this single image, a graduate student at the University of Pennsylvania, Matthew J. Liebmann, argues convincingly that the head, carved no doubt by a Puebloan refugee, idiosyncratically blends the horned or feathered headdress of a kachina with the haloed crown of a European saint, or, more particularly, of the Virgin of Guadalupe (paintings of which circulated widely in New Spain). Even the stylized facial features blend European and native conventions: the curving eyes and nose, according to Liebmann, "are undoubtedly in the European style," while the rectangular mouth is pure kachina. Hunkering in this little-visited cavate, I beheld as perfect an emblem of the syncretic welding of Catholic onto kachina religion as it would be possible for a Puebloan artist to conceive.

Thirty miles northeast of Bandelier, I found another teeming body of rock art that reflects the intrusion of the conquerors on the conquered. On Black Mesa, where the Rio Grande spills abruptly out of a tight canyon, an estimated 20,000 petroglyphs abound, making up one of the richest museums of outdoor iconography in the Southwest. I befriended Katherine Wells, an artist who owns 165 acres of prime land here (which will revert to the Archaeological Conservancy upon her death). Wells guided me to some of the most startling panels on her property, etched on basalt boulders that have tumbled from the mesa top down toward the river.

One remarkable image, almost surely from before 1540, depicts a mountain lion in profile, feet curled like pinwheels, with a human head face-on, bristling with spikes as if to allude to the sun; a snake bisects its throat. Only a few hundred yards away, Wells showed me an isolated image of another kind of lion—a heraldic, curvilinear beast straight off a Spanish coat-of-arms, copied no doubt by some impressionable Pueblo artist after 1598.

Near the heraldic lion, etched on the south face of an otherwise unremarkable boulder, I found a circular design quartered with four triangular marks, crossed diagonally with a double-headed arrow. The petroglyph looked remarkably like an old-fashioned compass. I took out my own pocket compass, then held it level before the boulder. The needle pointing toward magnetic north settled into an alignment exactly parallel to the "needle" on the rock carving.

Higher on the slope, I found an absolute masterpiece: an upright carving of Awanyu, the plumed serpent ultimately of Toltec origin, fully eight feet tall. Above its head, presumably added later, was a neatly incised Christian cross. I assumed the cross was the work of a converted Puebloan after the conquest, but when I mentioned it to Polly Schaafsma, she referred me to an obscure passage from the dispatch of an officer at Abiquiu in 1763. Under the orders of the governor of New Mexico, this functionary "went to the said district with the intention of destroying and annihilating, in as much as possible, the adoration sites [adoratorios], and places where they might have been [worshiping]; or places where detestable idolatry, superstitions, or vain observations might be committed presently."

On the west side of a high peak called El Cerro de los Pedernales, the official found three caves that his Indian guide indicated were sites "where witches in various animal forms went to request from the devil what they wanted." The interiors of the caves were covered with rock art, which the pious Spaniard did his best to obliterate. The key passage: "With the figures erased and crosses drawn on the same large rock . . . I returned to this said pueblo." After carving the crosses on top of the effaced petroglyph panels, the official had bade a priest among his company formally to exorcise the site.

On Black Mesa, however, the superb Awanyu had been left undefaced. My ultimate guess is that crosses carved on rock art panels—of which I would eventually see scores—had been added both by Spanish officers and priests and by Christianized Indians. (In Britain and France, I had seen menhirs, or standing stones, the work of artists who had lived some 3,000 years before the birth of Christ, that had been recarved into crosses in the Middle Ages.)

Later, at El Morro, I would see another example of a Christianized petroglyph, a design that seems to have gone undocumented by scholars and rangers preoccupied with puzzling out the myriad Spanish and Anglo inscriptions that surround it. Someone had added a small cross to the top of a stepped pyramid, thereby converting the standard Puebloan icon for a rain cloud into a stylized church.

Farther up the slope at Black Mesa, I found yet another masterpiece: a life-sized humanoid carved upside down, as if plunging headfirst toward some invisible doom, with fingers spread in helpless anguish, an arc and spiny rays sprouting from his blank, round head. Perhaps a shaman in mid-trance—and many rock art experts believe that upside-down figures symbolize death, worldwide. On a nearby boulder was carved what had to be a Franciscan priest in buttoned robe and hat, his right hand tucked piously behind his back. The patina of this pair of images (the coloration of the stone where it has been grooved, which darkens slowly with age) suggested that the two might be contemporary. In any event, it seemed unlikely that the juxtaposition of the pair was accidental. Here, I believed, I was witnessing a powerful tableau of the demise of the old religion, the faith of divinatory trance and health-giving kachina, under the onslaught of men of God in brown robes, wielding crucifixes, promising a fiery hell to the unconverted.

So, after the 1640s, the dismal pageant of Spanish rule in New Mexico trudged toward an apocalypse that, however unforeseen by governor and custodian alike, must have seemed almost inevitable to the Pueblo leaders who conceived it. The nineteenth governor of the colony, Bernardo López de Mendizábal, who held office from 1659 to 1661, enacted what seems today an extraordinarily enlightened reform. He not only sharply curtailed the amount of forced labor the missionaries could demand from their Puebloan "servants," but he explicitly encouraged the resumption of kachina dances and rituals. For his troubles, López was eventually arrested, imprisoned, and charged before the Inquisition. In the judgment of historian Carroll Riley, "In trying too much, too fast, López succeeded in intensifying the very trends he sought to reverse." With his departure from New Mexico, the friars launched what Riley calls a "Franciscan war on native religion."

As so often proves the case in the years preceding a historic cataclysm, natural disasters took a toll that added to the misery of the colony. With a woefully inadequate harvest in the fall of 1667 began five years of famine. A second smallpox epidemic struck in 1671. The Tompiro pueblos, including Abó and Gran Quivira, were forced to the brink of starvation before they were abandoned in the 1670s. In the course of the 130 years since Coronado's *entrada*, the total Puebloan population had been reduced by more than 75 percent, from an estimated 80,000 to less than 20,000.

Meanwhile, such nomadic enemies as the Apaches, Navajos, and Comanches, with whom in better times the Puebloans had carried on a wary trade of goods, perceived the weakness of their sedentary neighbors and intensified their raids on the pueblos. To fight them, the Spanish enlisted Puebloan war captains in their counterattacking and slave-raiding forays. In general, the Puebloans, even as they fought side by side with Spanish soldiers, were denied the use of horses and harquebuses. Yet even so, through close observation, the canny war captains learned much about European styles of warfare. Unwittingly, the Spanish were training the fighting force that would soon turn against them.

Though the colony still could number its Christianized Indians in the thousands, by the 1670s a profound disillusion with the Catholic religion had set in among the pueblos. For all their praying, the Franciscans had failed to bring the rain that would make the corn grow, had failed to thwart the Kliwa—the "refuse wind," as the Taos named the evil deity who inflicted smallpox upon the people. The shamans moved beyond their skeptical contempt for the brown-robed friars.

This map of New Mexico, drawn in 1657 by the French cartographer Nicolas Sanson, illustrates the geographical confusion of the day. Florida adjoins present-day Kansas (Quivira); California is an island, and the Rio Grande (Rio del Norte) drains into the Gulf of California rather than the Gulf of Mexico. Yet recognizable Puebloan groups are indicated (Taosij, Queres, Tompires, Piri, Zuni, and Moqui, as well as the poorly identified Tigues attacked by Coronado), and Apaches of all kinds surround the Puebloans on three sides. (Courtesy of the Harvard Map Collection)

Deciding that these men were the true witches among them, the shamans put hexes and curses of death upon their heads.

If there was a single precipitating event for the Pueblo Revolt, it was the paranoid roundup of miscreants enacted by Governor Juan Francisco Treviño shortly after taking office in 1675. Judging that the Tewa were at the heart of the growing malcontent in the colony, Treviño ordered the arrest of forty-seven "sorcerers," mostly from Tewa pueblos. One was hanged at Nambé, one at San Felipe, another at Jemez, as an instructive lesson to the others. Another committed suicide by hanging. The other forty-three were brutally flogged and held as prisoners.

In response, the Tewa took an action that Puebloans had never before dared to attempt. They marched en masse to Santa Fe, accosted the governor, and demanded the release of the shamans. Caught off guard by this show of force, Treviño relented and released his prisoners. This uncharacteristic backing down on the part of their Spanish rulers only served to fuel the hopes of the rebellious Tewa.

His very name, as far as we can judge, unknown to any Spaniard, Popé—a shaman from San Juan Pueblo, some forty-five years old— returned to his home and began to brood on the vision that had been forming in his mind even before the flogging he had publicly endured. Distrusting some of the San Juan leaders, he moved to Taos. In the kiva, he beseeched the kachinas and the gods. Meanwhile, in secret meetings with shamans and war captains from other pueblos, he hatched the plan that would change New Mexico forever.

On August 9, 1680, the slim young runners Catua and Omtua were handed the knotted cords and given their instructions. They set out jogging from Tesuque Pueblo, headed south into destiny.

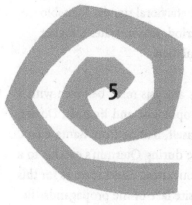

# 5

# POPÉ'S APOTHEOSIS

Now, the great mystery. What happened in New Mexico between 1680 and 1692?

Having burst free from the fatal trap of their fortress in the center of Santa Fe, Otermín's caravan of a thousand men, women, and children (including a certain number of loyal Indians, many originally from Mexico) began their crawl down the Rio Grande toward El Paso. The first question is an obvious one. That caravan must have been intensely vulnerable to attack. Why did the Puebloans not ambush it at every bend of the great river, raining arrows upon the bedraggled survivors, completing Popé's dark vision of wiping the Spaniards from the face of the New Mexican earth?

One answer is offered by Edward P. Dozier, in his 1970 book, *The Pueblo Indians of North America*:

Certainly, the Pueblos must have realized how vulnerable the refugees were, but they let them go, watching their movements closely but not attempting to harm them. In comparison to the

atrocities of the Spanish, the Pueblo behavior was humane. . . .
The Pueblos rarely matched the cruelty meted out to them by
Spanish officials. From any kind of behavioral standard, Pueblo
conduct throughout the Spanish period demonstrates a higher
ethic than that of the intruding population.

This may well be true, but Dozier's analysis must be taken with a
grain of salt. A highly respected anthropologist and linguist, Dozier,
who died in 1971, was a Puebloan himself, hailing from Santa Clara.
To attribute the Puebloans' forbearance during Otermín's exodus to a
higher standard of humaneness—without citing direct sources for this
explanation—may simply be the opposite face of the propaganda that
so often colors the Spanish record.

It may be, alternatively, that the Puebloans could not countenance
any further loss of life, which would have been inevitable in any attack
on the southward-marching caravan. If Otermín's body count of 300
Indians slain in the escape from the fortress on August 20 is not wildly
inflated, the momentous deed of driving the Spaniards out of New
Mexico had already cost the Puebloans dearly.

There are two sources for an understanding not only of what happened among the Pueblos after the Spanish were driven out, but of
how the Revolt was conceived and carried out. One is the archive of
Spanish documents, particularly the testimony of Indians captured
and questioned (probably under torture) on Otermín's way south in
1680 and in his failed attempt to reconquer the colony the following
year. The other is Puebloan oral tradition.

Let us begin with the Spanish record, which, while it furnishes the
skeletal framework within which scholars have always sought to
understand the Revolt, at the same time throws an obstacle course of
puzzles and perplexities across our path.

As has been mentioned, in an official dispatch Otermín sent to the
Franciscan *procurador general*, who was hurrying north with soldiers and
provisions to resupply the colony, written while still in the middle of his

demoralized trudge down the Rio Grande, the governor blamed himself for the Revolt, "His divine Majesty having thus permitted it because of my grievous sins." In this dispatch, Otermín confessed to "a certain negligence" in not at first believing the Indians were in full revolt.

As early as August 23, near San Marcos, Otermín captured a Tewa "rebel" named Antonio who was hiding in a cornfield near Los Cerrillos. This poor wretch, who spoke Spanish, declared under solemn oath (no doubt hoping to save his own skin) that he had come to Santa Fe only after learning that the Spaniards had broken free of their stockade and were moving south. Portraying himself as a dazed nonparticipant in the Revolt, he "recognized among the pillagers Indians of all nations" who were busy sacking the *casas reales*, "taking out a large amount of property belonging to the señor governor." One of these vandals paused long enough to tell Otermín's captive, "We are quits with the Spaniards and the persons whom we have killed; those of us whom they have killed do not matter, for they [the Spanish] are going, and now we shall live as we like and settle in this villa and wherever we see fit."

Two days later, an even more vivid testimony came from another captive, identified as one Pedro García (by 1680, most Puebloans had been given arbitrary Spanish names). A few miles from Galisteo Pueblo, García was dutifully weeding the cornfield of his Spanish master, when a Puebloan named Bartolomé, apparently a loyalist, came up to him, weeping, and said, "What are you doing here? The Indians want to kill the custodian, the fathers, and the Spaniards, and have said that the Indian who shall kill a Spaniard will get an Indian woman for a wife, and he who kills four will get four women, and he who kills ten or more will have a like number of women." So much for the monogamy that the friars had forced down the throats of the Puebloans, for whom the taking of multiple wives had been an immemorial custom.

"They have said," Bartolomé went on, "that they are going to kill all the servants of the Spaniards and those who know how to speak Castilian." García himself would thus be a victim. "Hurry! Go!" Bartolomé implored the man in the cornfield. "Perhaps you will be lucky enough to reach the place where the Spaniards are and will escape with your wife and an orphan girl that you have." Under oath, García recited the names of Spaniards he knew had been killed on August 10 in and around Galisteo, beginning with the four Franciscans who had hoped to find refuge there. García had fled his post to join Otermín's caravan, only to have rebels from Santo Domingo seize his wife and girl when he was almost in sight of the Spanish troops.

As the survivors straggled south, they came upon one burned and looted *estancia* after another. Often the dead, including women and children, lay sprawled on the floors, their bodies stripped. At times, Otermín's soldiers saw large numbers of Puebloan warriors massed on the mesa tops overlooking the Rio Grande. Rather than attack, however, these sentinels merely watched the Spaniards plod onward.

Day after day, as he beat his ignominious retreat, Otermín was at a loss to comprehend what had happened. And each day, he expected reinforcement from Lieutenant Governor Alonso García, whom the governor had put in charge of all the Río Abajo country. When García failed to show up or even send messengers, Otermín began to wonder whether all the Spanish inhabitants in the southern part of Nuevo México had been massacred. Only when he encountered the old Indian in the cornfield, near La Alameda, did the governor learn that García had passed by some fourteen or fifteen days earlier, leading some 1,500 refugees toward El Paso.

Meanwhile, the lieutenant governor labored under the reciprocal delusion that Otermín and all the citizens of Río Arriba had been wiped out. For on August 26, near the pueblo of Socorro, García heard the testimony of one Luis Granillo, a Spaniard who had been appointed *alcalde mayor* of the Jemez and Keres pueblos. Granillo reported that shortly before he himself had fled from Jemez, an Indian had returned from the Tewa country "highly elated," bragging that "Now we have killed the Spanish governor and a great many other Spaniards. . . . We have killed them all from Los Taos to the pueblo of Santo Domingo. . . . Not one will be left alive." The messenger then exhorted his fellow

Jemez to kill all the Spaniards resident in the pueblo. Granillo escaped, but the friar assigned to the pueblo was beaten, taunted, paraded naked around the plaza, and killed.

Sometime around September 3, Otermín reached Isleta Pueblo. It was here that, during the preceding two weeks, he had counted on joining García's men, reorganizing his forces, and marching back north to reconquer the colony he had so shamefully lost. Instead, he found Isleta deserted of Spaniards and Indians alike. (For fear of the pueblo's loyalty to the Spaniards, Popé and the other leaders of the Revolt had decided not to include that village in the plot. As Otermín would later learn, most of the Puebloan inhabitants of Isleta had fled south with García.)

Desperately short on food, the caravan trudged on, while the governor's annoyance about García's supposed betrayal mounted into a fury. Only on September 6 were the two leaders reunited. Otermín at once arrested García, but, after being persuaded to hear the lieutenant governor out, pardoned him and continued the march toward El Paso.

That same day, Otermín cross-examined yet another Puebloan, who had been captured at La Alameda. This was a frail old man of more than eighty years, who, when asked his name, gave it as Don Pedro Nanboa. The titular "Don" must have struck even the irascible governor as a bit ludicrous, but from this elder he gained a little more insight into the cataclysm that had fallen around his shoulders. The invariable formula of these interrogations betrays an incredulity born of blind faith in their Catholic and Castilian superiority: "Asked for what reason the Indians of this kingdom have rebelled, forsaking their obedience to his Majesty and failing in their obligation as Christians. . . ."

Yet Nanboa gave Otermín the most straightforward answer he had yet received: "He said that for a long time, because the Spaniards punished sorcerers and idolaters, the nations of the Teguas, Taos, Pecuríes, Pecos, and Jemez had been plotting to rebel and kill the Spaniards and the religious, and that they had been planning constantly to carry it out, down to the present occasion." The old man went on to declare "that the resentment which all the Indians have in their hearts has been so strong, from the time this kingdom was discovered, because the religious and the Spaniards took away their idols and forbade their sorceries ... and that he has heard this resentment spoken of since he was of an age to understand."

With twenty-first-century hindsight, one is tempted to wonder how the Spaniards in New Mexico could have remained utterly oblivious to this searing bitterness under the Pueblo surface. How could any colonial power round up forty-seven shamans, hang three and flog the rest, and not sow the seeds of a ravenous hunger for vengeance? From the seventeenth-century point of view, however, Benavides's honeyed portrait of well-scrubbed Indians eagerly running to church as the bell pealed, of men and women waving from their fields and uttering such homilies as "Praised be our Lord Jesus Christ," makes perfect sense.

On September 13, near a southern pueblo called Fray Cristóbal, with all 2,500 survivors gathered in a single camp, Otermín called a grand council to discuss what might be done. The eight Franciscans who had escaped martyrdom declared themselves willing to follow any course of action the governor might order. It was the joint opinion, however, of Otermín's five *maestres de campo* that sealed the decision. As Charles Wilson Hackett, the pioneering compiler of English translations of the Spanish documents about the Revolt, paraphrases the lament of the governor's most trusted officers, "They agreed that because of the miserable condition of all, and especially of so many women and children, and since there was little prospect of any alleviation of their hunger, or any way to avenge or restrain the taunts of the enemy in that desert place, the retreat should be continued."

Despite the defeatist tone of that resolution, the official dispatch announcing it still bristles with outrage at what the Puebloans had wrought—"the destruction, treason, rebellion, and uprising committed by the Christian Indians, who with diabolical plotting and conspiracy have destroyed the temples, profaned the holy vessels and things pertaining to divine worship, of which they have made trophies, and have gone so far as to set fire to the temples and images."

The formerly meek and tractable Puebloans had now become, in the language of this dispatch, a formidable foe, "what with the cunning and audacity of so many enemies, treacherous and skilful alike on horseback and with firearms, lances, and other weapons which they have used in this uprising."

On September 29, the throng of refugees reached La Salineta, a camp a few miles north of El Paso, where they mustered and recuperated. Nuevo México was lost, and Otermín, mired in disgrace, struggled to comprehend what had come about, and why.

Meanwhile, what was going on in and around Santa Fe? Not a single eyewitness account of the immediate aftermath of the expulsion of the Europeans exists in the Spanish record. This has not kept romantic historians from trying to re-create the orgiastic scenes of liberation that must have ensued.

In *The Pueblo Revolt* (1970), for instance, Robert Silverberg paints a lurid picture of Popé becoming, as it were, more Spanish than the Spanish:

> He took up residence in Santa Fe, moving into the adobe palace so lately occupied by Governor Otermín. Donning a fantastic outfit of gaudy-hued robes, and wearing a bull's horn on his forehead as a symbol of his power, Popé strutted and capered through the white man's capital, demanding that his subjects bow to him precisely as though he had succeeded to Otermín's rank and grandeur. Sometimes he even climbed into Otermín's old carriage of state and had himself drawn through the streets of the city.

No source is cited for this vignette, which most likely sprang full-blown from the author's overheated imagination, as, consistently throughout the book, he "dramatizes" history in quasi-novelistic fashion. (Alas, for a quarter-century, Silverberg's was the only popular account of the Revolt in print.)

Quite an opposite you-are-there dramatization can be found in the pages of Joe Sando's *Pueblo Profiles* (1998). Sando is a well-educated scholar from Jemez who, among other contributions, wrote the first and to date only history of his home pueblo, a fascinating book called *Nee Hemish* (1982). In the more recent work, Sando has the Pueblo warriors watch the departure of Otermín's refugees from the surrounding hills. Then they gather in the Santa Fe plaza to make victory speeches. "Each speaker thanked the Great Spirit and the twin war gods, Maseway and Oyoyeway, the deities that had rescued the people just as the old men had said they would."

Popé is the final speaker:

> According to tradition, he said: "Within and around the world, within and around the hills and mountains, within and around the valleys, your authority returns to you. Therefore, return to your people and travel the corn pollen trail again. A trail with no pebbles, no boulders, and no obstructions. Go home and enjoy your families, the birds, the clouds, the mist, the rain, the lightning, the wind, the rivers, the mountains, the trees, and the sky. . . . Lastly, don't forget, each morning before our father, the sun, makes his appearance, to take feathers in one hand and corn pollen in the other hand and offer them to the deities in the mountains, in the clouds, in the valleys, to the north, to the west, to the south, to the east, to Sipofinae and to Waynema. *Sengi di ho!*"

With its rhetorical symmetries and parallelisms, this speech certainly sounds like Puebloan oratory. In the simple phrase, "according to tradition," Sando appeals to the unassailable authority of oral tales handed down from one generation to the next. He does not need footnotes or bibliographical citations.

Native American oral traditions are often extraordinarily precise over long periods of time. But from the moment I first read Sando's rendering of Popé's speech, I had my doubts as to whether so long an utterance could have been passed down verbatim across 318 years. And later, when I interviewed Sando and learned just how vague and ambiguous the traditions from 1680 seemed to be, my doubts were intensified. Perhaps Sando's version of Popé's speech should be taken with the same grain of salt as Villagrá's epic poem about the conquest.

It took Otermín more than a year to gather his forces and his nerve before attempting to retake the colony from the Puebloans. He did not set out from El Paso until November 5, 1681. Even so, the governor was dismayed by his army, which was mostly made up, in Hackett's assessment, of "mere boys and raw recruits." Of the settlers and soldiers who had fled south with the governor the previous year, fewer than six signed up for the expedition of reconquest.

In the end, Otermín's force consisted of 146 soldiers, 112 Indian allies, 36 "servants," possibly as few as 3 Franciscans, and 948 animals. Slowly the procession wound its way up the Rio Grande. In ruined churches, the soldiers found melancholy talismans of the Puebloan fury: smashed bells and burned statues of saints and crucifixes. In the nearby cornfields, they discovered skulls and disarticulated bones. Not a single pueblo along the way was inhabited.

By early December, the reoccupying army had drawn close to Isleta. Scouts who had sneaked within fifteen miles of that village reported seeing columns of smoke rising from the adobe houses. Otermín took seventy of his best soldiers and marched north to attack.

The dwellers at Isleta were taken completely by surprise. They made a halfhearted attempt to fend off the invaders with volleys of arrows, but upon Otermín's ordering them to surrender, they laid down their arms. The governor was led to believe that the Isletans had thought the enemy coming from the south was made up of Apaches, not Spaniards.

After such an auspicious beginning, Otermín had reason to hope for full success. But at Isleta, which the governor made his base camp for the reconquest, the expedition stalled. Small reconnaissance parties ventured out from that pueblo to gauge the state of things farther north, in the Tewa and Keres country. A larger troop under Juan Domingo de Mendoza marched up the Rio Grande, with orders to tell the leaders of each pueblo, "Wait for the Spaniards and surrender to them peacefully." But Mendoza found, successively, La Alameda, Puaray, Sandía, San Felipe, Santo Domingo, and Cochiti deserted. The inhabitants had fled to the hills and mountains.

Only at Cochiti did Mendoza at last make contact with the rebels. There, he saw nearly a thousand warriors ranging the mesa rims above the pueblo, calling down taunts to the Spaniards to fight. Instead of launching a battle, however, the Cochiti leader, Alonso Catití, came down to parley with Mendoza. The Puebloan made a show of contrition and promised to bring in his people to surrender.

It took two days for Mendoza to suspect that Catití's performance was a ruse. While he waited for the surrender, the Cochiti men had sent runners north to recruit warriors from other pueblos for an all-out attack on the small Spanish force. Sensing a trap, Mendoza prudently withdrew and headed back toward Isleta.

Though furious with Mendoza for his timid response to the Cochiti threat, Otermín soon had problems enough at his base camp. On December 23, fifty northern Puebloans on horseback surrounded Isleta, calling out to the natives to join them, threatening death if they refused. This odd "siege" lasted a week, during which more than a hundred Isletans defected to the rebels. Otermín himself seemed paralyzed, and his soldiers had lost the heart to fight. At last the governor decided to abandon the reconquest and head back to El Paso, taking with him the 385 Isletans who had remained loyal (and whom the warriors from the north might well have slaughtered as soon as the Spanish left).

Although in two months, Otermín had burned eight pueblos to the ground, his long-fancied *reconquista* had turned into an utter failure. The most tangible result of the expedition lay in the testimony of nine more Indian captives, who were cross-examined at Isleta. In two weeks, Otermín learned ten times as much about the Revolt as he had in the sixteen months since it had exploded around him in Santa Fe.

The testimonies of those captives, which are preserved in the Spanish record, comprise the bulk of the written primary sources for the origins and execution of the Pueblo Revolt. What we know of Popé lies largely in those coerced confessions, over which at first Spanish officials, then Anglo scholars, then at last Puebloans themselves, have ruminated ever since.

On December 18, Otermín heard the translated testimony of a man from Tesuque named Juan, about twenty-eight years old. Tesuque was the pueblo from which the runners with the knotted cords had set out the previous August: its leaders were clearly among the principal actors behind the Revolt. Harangued with the florid interrogatory formula as to why the Indians had rebelled, "forsaking the law of God and obedience to his Majesty, burning images and temples, and committing the other crimes which they did," Juan gave a prompt answer: "He said that . . . the chief mover of it is an Indian who is a native of the pueblo of San Juan, named El Popé, and that from fear of this Indian all of them joined in the plot that he made."

Sixteen months after he had been driven out of New Mexico, Otermín thus heard for the first time the name of the ringleader of the Revolt. During the next two weeks, five of the other captives would also identify Popé as the chief mover, and a sixth who did not know Popé's name would characterize him as "an Indian from San Juan . . . who came down through all the pueblos in company with the captains and many other people, ordering them to burn the churches, convents, holy crosses, and every object pertaining to Christianity."

Juan's examiner asked him why the Puebloans were so willing to obey Popé. He answered that

> the common report that circulated and still is current among all the natives is that the said Indian Popé talks with the devil, and for this reason all held him in terror, obeying his commands. . . . It

was a matter of common knowledge that the Indian Popé, talking with the devil, killed in his own house a son-in-law of his named Nicolás Bua, the governor of the pueblo of San Juan. On being asked why he killed him, [Juan] said that it was so that he might not warn the Spaniards of the rebellion, as he intended to do.

The phrasing of this confession must be screened through a Spanish filter. It is not likely that Juan, who was apparently not a "Christian Indian," actually said that Popé talked with the devil. Whatever the Tewa name of the spirit or deity with whom Popé spoke, Franciscan orthodoxy would translate it into "the devil," for all the rites of kachina worship were, in the minds of the friars, the works of Satan. As Carroll Riley points out, among the Franciscans in New Mexico there was "a strong tinge of Manicheism." Absolute good warred with absolute evil among the pueblos. To the friars, the devil was no abstract theological concept: he was a personifiable force who worked his deadly spell every time a Puebloan put on a mask and danced in the plaza.

Otermín must have listened to Juan in rapt astonishment, for now the Tesuque man went on to describe how the plot of the Revolt had been hatched on August 9, 1680.

He said that [Popé] took a cord made of maguey fiber and tied some knots in it which indicated the number of days until the perpetration of the treason. He sent it through all the pueblos as far as that of La Isleta . . . and the order which the said Popé gave when he sent the said cord was under strict charge of secrecy, commanding that the war captains take it from pueblo to pueblo.

Strictly speaking, maguey, a species of agave, does not grow in New Mexico. The phrasing in the original Spanish document, which was first published only in the year 2000, is *mecate de palmilla*, literally "cord of yucca."

Once the Spaniards had been driven out, Juan explained, Popé ordered a rigorous purification of Puebloan life. The people were to rid themselves of everything Spanish and Catholic. This meant not only burning the churches and their statues of Christ, the Virgin, and the saints, but discarding the Spanish names that had been imposed on them and divorcing the wives whom they had married under Christian law. The Puebloans were forbidden to utter a single Castilian word. Popé further dictated an even more extreme reform: the people were told to burn all the seeds of the foods the Spaniards had introduced (which included wheat, fruit trees, melons, and chile peppers), and "to plant only maize and beans, which were the crops of their ancestors."

The twenty-eight-year-old from Tesuque was a gold mine of information. Juan went on to say that in all, there were twenty-two Puebloan leaders of the Revolt. Besides Popé, he named Luis Tupatú from Picuris and Alonso Catití, with whom Mendoza had parleyed over a feigned surrender at Cochiti within the previous week. Juan called Catití "a coyote of the Queres nation," i.e., a "half-breed," the son of Indian and mestizo parents. Now both Otermín and Mendoza learned of another facet of the trap Catití had plotted against the Spanish soldiers, but which he had not been able to carry out: "He declared also that the plan of the coyote Alonso Catití was to order all the Indian girls to wash themselves and put on their mantas and induce the Spaniards to sleep with them; that then the Pecuríes and Teguas would come to take off the horses while the Queres and other nations would kill the Spaniards." Four other captives would soon corroborate the coyote's plan to have "the prettiest girls . . . provoke the Spaniards to lewdness."

In the following days, Otermín learned more about Popé from other captives. The visionary shaman's program to rid the Puebloan world of everything Spanish went beyond abjuring wheat and cherry trees: the Indians were also to turn loose all their livestock—horses, cattle, mules, and pigs being likewise tainted by their introduction to

New Mexico by the Castilians. To undo the curse of baptism, Popé bade each Puebloan who had received that sacrament to wade into the Rio Grande and scrub himself clean with yucca root. Two young brothers from San Felipe claimed "that he who should utter the name of Jesus would be killed immediately."

Popé supervised the resumption of the old kachina rites. Once more, the Spanish filter transforms the very words in which the interpreter rendered the informant's report: "[Popé] saw to it that they at once erected and rebuilt their houses of idolatry which they call estufas, and made very ugly masks in imitation of the devil in order to dance the dance of the cacina." (Soon after first contact, the Spaniards—not the Puebloans—had called the kivas they found in every village "*estufas*," under the initial misconception that they were designed to serve as steam baths.)

One very old man, a native of La Alameda, also named Juan, told Otermín that he remembered Oñate's coming to New Mexico eighty-three years before! He professed to be at a loss as to why the Indians had rebelled, "being so old," as he sardonically reported, "they never communicated anything [to him]." This graybeard maintained that he felt deceived by the shaman from San Juan, whose name he did not know but whose promise that everyone should "live in great ease" if they followed his commands, Juan had initially believed. Instead, during the past year and a half, "they have had very small harvests, there had been no rain, and everyone is perishing."

Otermín's most valuable informant was an eighty-year-old man from San Felipe, a shaman named Pedro Naranjo, who spoke good Spanish. Naranjo insisted that the Puebloan leaders had been planning the Revolt since the time of the governorship of Hernando Ugarte y la Concha, who had held office from 1649 to 1653. Sometime before the idea of the knotted cords had come to Popé, a pair of deerskins painted with pictures had circulated secretly in the Pueblo world, being carried as far as Hopi. These tableaux, Naranjo hinted, amounted to a call to rebellion, but they were rejected at Hopi. The San Felipe man bore vivid witness to Popé's loathing of all things Christian. He had caused the instant execution of a number of Puebloans who, as sincere converts, opposed the Revolt. "The God of the Spaniards," Naranjo paraphrased Popé, "was worth nothing and theirs was very strong, the Spaniards' God being rotten wood." (The allusion is to the wooden statues in the missions.) Popé also insisted that "he who might still keep in his heart a regard for the priests, the governor, and the Spaniards would be known from his unclean face and clothes, and would be punished." Under Popé's powerful influence, Alonso Catití had come to San Felipe to exhort everyone to go to Santa Fe and kill the governor and all the Spaniards. Naranjo had heard Catití threaten to behead anyone who did not enlist in this vendetta.

The deepest insight into the origins of Popé's apocalyptic vision that has come down to us lies in four sentences of Naranjo's testimony. The details, however, are so tantalizing and opaque that this passage in the Spanish record has become a kind of Yorick's skull, upon which, for decades, scholars have woven intricate soliloquies of conjecture. As Naranjo told Otermín,

It happened that in an estufa of the pueblo of Los Taos there appeared to the said Popé three figures of Indians who never came out of the estufa. They gave the said Popé to understand that they were going underground to the lake of Copala. He saw these figures emit fire from all the extremities of their bodies, and that one of them was called Caudi, another Tilini, and the other Tleume; and these three beings spoke to the said Popé, who was hiding from the secretary, Francisco Xavier, who wished to punish him as a sorcerer. They told him to make a cord of maguey fiber and tie some knots in it which would signify the number of days that they must wait before the rebellion.

One further remark of Naranjo's adds a shade of meaning to this vision. The people had rebelled, the San Felipe man averred, "because they had always desired to live as they had when they had come out of the lake of Copala." (Of the possible meanings of Copala, Caudi, Tilini, and Tleume, more below.)

By the time Otermín had listened to the testimony of the last of his nine informants, on January 1, 1682, one thing had become abundantly clear. The northern Puebloans would never surrender. Instead, they would fight to the death before once more accepting Spanish rule.

So much for the Spanish record. What, then, of Puebloan oral tradition?

Long before I had gone to New Mexico to begin my search for an understanding of the Pueblo Revolt, I had known that by far the hardest part of my task would be penetrating that tradition. You did not simply walk into the visitor center or tribal headquarters of a pueblo and start asking questions about a matter as serious as the Revolt. There was a time-honored protocol to be observed, a process of building trust that might lead to a platform from which I could be allowed to ask such questions.

Nonetheless, I made preliminary inquiries at a number of pueblos. At each, I was told, "Oh, you'd have to talk to the governor about that." Not so easily done—for the governor was always busy.

The awkwardness of simply visiting one of the more conservative pueblos strikes even a casual passerby. San Felipe, for instance, has recently built a casino right beside Interstate 25, twenty-six miles north of Albuquerque. Above the neon-bordered doorway is a sign announcing "Katishoya"—San Felipe's Keresan name for itself. The accompanying billboard purrs,

WELCOME TO

CASINO HOLLYWOOD

LET US ENTERTAIN YOU

Inside, slot machines jangle their nonstop trickles of coins, as bored Puebloan blackjack dealers await their victims.

Casino Hollywood, however, is a mere facade. From the Interstate, a back road leads two and a half miles northwest to San Felipe itself— "the least-visited of all the pueblos," according to one guidebook. An old sign proclaims "Welcome to the Pueblo of San Felipe," then immediately lays out the ground rules:

NO PICTURE TAKING & SKETCHING

ALLOWED—ABSOLUTELY NO LIQUOR

PERMITTED. SOLICITORS, BILL

COLLECTORS MUST HAVE

GOVERNOR'S PERMISSION

Driving the dirt streets of the poor but handsome village, as kids and old women stare, the outsider feels as though he has stumbled into some Third World backwater. A sign in front of the Saint Philip church threatens a $3,500 fine to be levied against any tourist who dares to take a picture of the adobe building.

Similarly in Santo Domingo, often called the most xenophobic of all the pueblos, nine miles north of San Felipe on the Rio Grande. A sign in front of the harmoniously shaped Santo Domingo mission, its stepped-cloud doorway flanked with painted horses and deer heads, pleads:

PLEASE!

DO NOT TAKE PICTURES

DO NOT OPEN GATES

DO NOT PICK UP THINGS

FROM THE YARD

DO NOT CLIMB OR JUMP

ON THE WALLS.

THANK YOU.

Elsewhere around the pueblo, other signs enjoin the visitor against driving into the main plaza, taking pictures of anything, sketching, entering any of the "show" kivas, or using a cell phone—each transgression punishable by a $500 fine.

On a recent visit, I walked into the Santo Domingo visitor center. I mentioned to the receptionist that I was interested in the Pueblo Revolt. "You'd have to talk to the governor about that," she said. Overhearing our exchange, another woman, who turned out to be the governor's sister, joked, "He's old enough to know about the Revolt."

I engaged the woman, whose name was Rita Pacheco. "The kids don't seem to know about the Revolt," I offered.

"Kids just aren't interested in learning history in any culture," she countered, slipping away from my intrusion.

"Don't they teach about the Revolt in the schools, though?" I persisted.

"I wonder," said Pacheco, turning back to her work.

Both before and after numerous impasses such as this, I sought out individual Puebloans who might be more willing to talk. These were men and women who, though fiercely loyal to their home pueblos, had gone on to get university educations, sometimes in anthropology. They tended thus to straddle two worlds—the xenophobic intellectual and spiritual milieu in which they had grown up, and the rational, supposedly open forum of academe.

In the end, most of what I learned about Puebloan oral traditions of the Revolt came from the mouths of five such remarkable individuals. They were Joe Sando, from Jemez; Brian Vallo, from Acoma; Tessie Naranjo, from Santa Clara; Peter Pino, from Zia; and Herman Agoyo, from San Juan—Popé's pueblo.

I headed into these interviews, however, with a preconception based on my own thoroughly Anglo-American education. The Pueblo Revolt was, in the words of one scholar, "the point of highest drama in New Mexico's long history." Whatever its final outcome, the expulsion of every last Spaniard in 1680 had been a brilliant revolutionary stroke, unparalleled among Native American peoples who resisted colonial powers in what is now the United States. Surely, I naively thought, the Revolt lingered on in Puebloan memory as a glorious triumph—the proudest chapter in their post-contact history in the Southwest.

Yet one of the first things Brian Vallo told me flatly contradicted that assumption. The former lieutenant governor of Acoma, now in charge of the pueblo's burgeoning tourism enterprise, Vallo said, "The kids here don't know the story of the Pueblo Revolt." He paused, while I gave him a puzzled look. "The elders don't want them to know," Vallo continued. "When I was a kid, I asked my great-grandfather about it. He said, 'I'm not going to tell you. You don't need to know.'"

"Why?" I wondered.

Vallo carefully framed his answer. "What the elders do tell the kids is our migration story. But not about the atrocities, the fights. That doesn't give you life, it doesn't give you anything good." Here, I thought, might be a clue as to why none of the first three historians of Acoma had written a word about Oñate's terrible sentences after the massacre in 1599. "Atrocities and fights," even when the Puebloans had won, were painful to remember, not readily recounted to outsiders.

"If you ask some people even of my generation"—Vallo is in his late thirties—"they wouldn't have a clue about the Pueblo Revolt. They know it happened—'Oh, yes, there was a fight, we fought with [the Spaniards]'—but not anything more than that."

Vallo had already warned me that, in deference to Acoman notions of secret lore, "There's a lot I can't tell you. And I won't." Was the pueblo's knowledge of the Revolt off-limits to nosy intruders such as myself? Or was the memory really so dim?

That would be my first question for Joe Sando, whom I met at the Indian Pueblo Cultural Center in Albuquerque. A slight, silver-haired fellow in his eightieth year, Sando proved to be a man of few words and an acerbic humor.

"Why don't the Pueblo people know the story of the Revolt very well?" I bluntly began.

"Because they didn't write the books," Sando snapped. "Most of the books were written back East." Gradually, however, the man softened. "When I was growing up," he mused, "I didn't know anything about the Revolt. It was only when I went to college that I learned about it."

I knew that Sando had borne the brunt of intense criticism from his own people when he had published the history of Jemez in 1982, in *Nee Hemish*. I also knew that he was now laboring over a new book about Popé. To write these works, I thought, was to concede that the university-trained intellectual in the man won out over the Puebloan traditionalist. Still, the books were meant to reach not only a broad audience of Anglos, but his own kith and kin. As he told me, "I want our people to learn the story again. A twelve-year-old boy at Jemez doesn't know who Popé was."

One of the central mysteries of the twelve-year interregnum in New Mexico is what became of Popé. Shadowy rumors in the Spanish record hint at his dying or being killed sometime before 1689. I asked Sando, "What happened to Popé?"

"No one knows," he replied, and added cryptically, "All we know is that he was replaced."

Historians have also suggested that, in the severity of his threats against nonparticipants in the Revolt, and in the radical purism of his purgation of all things Spanish, Popé was too extreme for his own people. When I ventured this theory, Sando frowned. "He did kill his son-in-law," he granted. "But as for getting rid of all the Spanish things—that wasn't Popé. He wasn't that fanatic. The writers made that up."

I came away from my meeting with Sando perplexed. Nothing that he had told me exceeded the bounds of the books he might have first read in college, the documentary record of Otermín's lost colony and failed reconquest published in 1942 by Charles Wilson Hackett and Charmion Clair Shelby. If that was all he knew, from what source had he gleaned his verbatim transcript of Popé's victory speech in the Santa Fe plaza, as published in *Pueblo Profiles*? (To have asked Sando that question would have seemed rude and confrontative.) Or were Sando's terse, summary comments during my interview all that he thought another writer from the East had a right to hear?

Back in 1994, on my first visit to Jemez Pueblo, archaeologist Bill Whatley had told me that the tribe's elders in charge of their people's migration story (of which, after years of work at Jemez, Whatley had been privileged to learn only bits and pieces) could recite the whole story in intricate, vibrant detail, taking twelve hours to complete the task. (As many scholars have pointed out, the authors of the *Iliad* and the *Odyssey* were illiterate.) If the Jemez elders still knew exactly what had happened in, say, A.D. 1270, as their people made their way from the north and west to their present heartland, why might they not retain a comparably rich story of what had happened in 1680?

It was a problem I would never solve. Indeed, in general, the reliability of oral tradition remains one of the most vexed and controversial issues in anthropology.

Both Tessie Naranjo and Herman Agoyo corroborated Vallo's and Sando's testimony about learning little or nothing about the Revolt as they grew up. "As a child, I didn't know about the Pueblo Revolt," Naranjo told me over lunch in a Santa Fe restaurant. "It probably wasn't until I went to the university that I began examining it. Then I put together a real strong consciousness about it using the [Spanish] documents."

Yet Naranjo, who is a writer, artist, and historian, took umbrage at my suggestion that the tribulations of 1680 were dimly remembered today among the pueblos. "I get stunned when I hear a statement like that," she objected. "The memories are vague, but the emotions are strong. You behave according to your emotions. Nothing has to be said. You carry the pain for all those [ancestors] who went through that pain.

"Even the younger people—it's through osmosis, from generation to generation, carrying the emotions of the ancestors who lived through that."

Said Agoyo, an ex-governor of San Juan, whom I met in his office within the pueblo: "Much of what I know about the Revolt comes from Hackett and Shelby. I didn't learn about it in school. And here at San Juan, there's not a great pride about Popé. I think it was such a horrible event. People were always living in fear. Everything about the Spanish presence was negative. So Popé became a forgotten man."

Agoyo was willing to entertain the idea that Popé's rejection of everything Spanish was too extreme a reform. When the conquerors returned in 1692, they found abundant evidence of the Puebloans continuing to ride horses and herd cattle and pigs, to plant fruit trees and melons. As Agoyo put it, smiling ruefully, "It's hard to give up your TV set after you've watched television."

Alfonso Ortiz, who died in 1997, was a San Juan man who earned a Ph.D. and became a leading Pueblo anthropologist. His probing 1969 book, *The Tewa World,* is a landmark example of a Native American turning the tools of academic inquiry upon his own culture. Like Joe Sando, Ortiz also earned the bitter enmity of many people at San Juan for his efforts. Shortly before he died, Ortiz wrote an article for *National Geographic* about the Pueblo world. I was told by a Santa Fe archaeologist that not a few of Ortiz's former friends at San Juan attributed his death to this betrayal of Puebloan secrecy.

In a Santa Fe library, I bumped into the Anglo historian David Grant Noble. He told me that, some years ago, Ortiz had told him, "The Pueblo Indians have an amnesia about the Revolt. It was a very negative, traumatic event, and they put it out of their collective memory. So there aren't stories passed down in the oral tradition about it." Here was the strongest statement that I had yet heard about what I was coming to think was not so much a body of lore carefully guarded from outsiders, but a lacuna in the Puebloan memory—an "amnesia," in Ortiz's well-chosen word.

Grateful though I was to my five university-educated, outward-looking native informants, it seemed important, for balance, to try to penetrate the bureaucracy of at least one pueblo to trace what I could of the collective legacy of a people's experience of the years from 1680 to 1692. I decided to focus on Jemez, where I had first felt the itch of curiosity about the Revolt in 1994, and which, I had concluded, was perhaps the most central of all the pueblos to the story. I was not prepared, however, for the scarifying encounter that would ensue from my dogged effort to gain a hearing at Jemez.

I was aware that Jemez remained one of the most conservative of the pueblos: no casino, little tourism, and an absolute ban on non-Jemez living in the village—even those few outsiders who work for the tribe. Before I had headed out to New Mexico in the spring of 2003, I had tried many times to call the Jemez governor, Raymond Loretto. "He's in a meeting," a female clerk invariably told me. "You might try again tomorrow about this time."

At last I managed to snag two minutes of the governor's attention. I explained that I was seeking the Jemez point of view on the Revolt; I would hate to have the Spanish record be my only source. I could feel the man's resistance pulsing over the telephone line. "I'd have to bring that up with the tribal council," he said before hurrying off to his next meeting.

Once in New Mexico, it would take me two months to win an audience at Jemez, not with the tribal council, but with a group called the Cultural Committee. The meeting was scheduled for 6:30 on a Tuesday evening in May. I drove eighty miles from Santa Fe, arriving half an hour early, and entered the conference room of the governor's office—a fluorescent, sterile modern chamber, not unlike a high school teachers lounge.

I sat in a chair against the wall, while one Jemez man after another slowly filed in and took a seat around a long rectangular table. Two Anglo archaeologists from the Santa Fe National Forest (on whose land lie many ancestral Jemez sites) shared my bleacher seats, while Mehrdad Khatibi, the Iranian-born Department of Resource Protection officer for the tribe (and the man who had arranged my audience) sat with his confrères at the table. The Jemez men had each shaken my hand and offered their first names, but now they sat ignoring me as they drank Diet Cokes and ate Hostess Cupcakes, while cracking jokes with each other in Towa, the language spoken only at Jemez.

Six forty-five P.M. passed, then 7:00. There was no sense of urgency in the room. Impatient and exhausted, I toyed with a fantasy of acting like a stereotypical Easterner and thereby ruining any chance of getting a foot in the Jemez door: I might have waved my hand and blurted out, "Can we get started here, 'cause I've got a long drive back to Santa Fe tonight?" Instead, I kept my silence and tried to hide my impatience, as I had in many another encounter on Indian reservations.

At last, around 7:15, the lieutenant governor whispered, "Well, I guess we can begin." There were now eleven of us in the room— myself, the two archaeologists, Khatibi, and seven Jemez men. These were not elders from the tribal council, but men in their twenties and thirties. Now the lieutenant governor said, "Will the war captain please lead us in prayer." We all stood; I stared at the floor as a young man to my left delivered an extended incantation in Towa. His prayer was punctuated by the group's murmuring a single syllable in unison at apparently predetermined intervals, like the Amen's in a Catholic Mass (or perhaps, given the man's role in the tribe, the Olé!'s in a bullfight).

I was invited to sit at the rectangular table. Though nervous, I was eager to explain my mission. But suddenly, there was another rapid exchange in Towa. Then Tom Lucero, also of the Department of Resource Protection, turned to the two archaeologists and apologetically asked them to leave the room. Apparently what I was about to discuss was too sensitive for them to hear. Veterans of the protocol, the two got up and left without a word.

I thanked the assemblage and spoke for ten minutes. I explained the research I had already attempted for my book, the difficulty I had had gaining insight into the Pueblo version of things, the rampant biases of the Spanish records. I said that the Pueblo Revolt deserved to be better known by all Americans.

While I spoke, eight faces stared at me, seven of them completely blank. When I finished, there was a long, painful silence. Then a fellow opposite me, slouched back in his chair, said evenly, "What's in it for Jemez?"

I was taken off guard. "Nothing, financially," I began, then lamely mentioned a scholarship donation I had made to Zia Pueblo after interviewing Peter Pino.

"We're not interested in 'donations,'" my antagonist said witheringly.

It got worse. The young man on my immediate left explained, "If you get to write this book—the first book authorized by Jemez—you'll be way up here." He held a level palm above his head. "You'll be some-body."

I knew what he meant, and it wasn't good. In Pueblo culture, it is a grievous error to attempt to stand out as better than one's peers. Anthropologist Florence Hawley Ellis, who had worked at Jemez in the 1940s and 1950s, claimed that in Pueblo society a man with a new pickup truck might find it vandalized, a beautiful woman might be "accidentally" killed.

Perhaps to be provocative, I said, "I'd hate for Joe Sando to be the only person speaking for Jemez in my book."

The reaction was electric. The lieutenant governor demanded, "Did you tell the governor you talked to Joe Sando?" I shook my head. I hadn't had the chance to tell the governor anything. My first inquisi-tor added bitterly, "Joe Sando wrote his book. He got rich and famous. And he didn't give anything back to the pueblo."

Sando's *Nee Hemish* had been published by the University of New Mexico Press, and by now it was long out of print. I doubted very much that the book had made its author either rich or famous—but that was my Eastern, Anglo take on what those words meant. When I had interviewed Sando in Albuquerque, he had complained acidly about the accusations *Nee Hemish* had elicited from his home pueblo. "The tribal council condemned my book," he had said, "but they never even read it. I didn't tell any of our people's secrets." Sando sighed: "Sometimes pueblos are like Third World countries. They're very jealous of anybody who's educated. Most of the young people at Jemez are aware that the old people are holding them back."

In the governor's conference room, the mention of Sando had unleashed a hubbub of comments in Towa. The man opposite, still slouching back in his chair, fixed me with his stare and said, "The thing that really bothers me is that you keep talking about 'my book.' This is all about you. Where are we in all this?"

The fellow on my left gave me a hard but earnest look, saying, "We just don't want to get screwed . . . again."

The meeting ended with my promise to put all my hopes in writing in a letter to the lieutenant governor, yet even as I uttered that pledge, I doubted that I would have the heart to follow through on it. The Cultural Committee promised in turn to get back to me. I staggered out of the conference room, to find the archaeologists still waiting patiently in the hallway. I gave them a rueful smirk and headed for the door. Mehrdad Khatibi came hurrying after me. "Thanks for coming," he said. I turned my rueful look on him. "No, I think you broke the ice," he pleaded. If so, I thought, it would take decades for the glacier of Jemez secrecy to surge toward the valley of my understanding.

▼
▼

Secrecy. Of all the traits that stamp Puebloan culture, secrecy is the hallmark. And no wonder: in the seventeenth century, when Spaniards hanged and whipped shamans for practicing "sorcery," burned their kivas and kachina masks, preached to them daily about the eternal flames of hell they must endure unless they embraced Catholicism, the Puebloans learned to hide the religion that had sustained their ancestors—as in the secret, ordinary rooms at Gran Quivira where twentieth-century excavators found all the paraphernalia normally stored in the kivas. In the view of many accomplished scholars, including France Scholes and Elsie Clews Parsons, the Puebloans developed secrecy as a defense against Spanish oppression.

With the 1870s, as Anglo ethnographers began to study the pueblos, often moving in and staying for extended periods of time, a new assault on the integrity of Puebloan culture was launched—all the more insidious because it was couched not in the punitive strictures of Franciscan friars and Spanish governors, but in the sincere curiosity and admiration of anthropologists. For several decades, Puebloans freely volunteered all kinds of information about their lifeway to these gentle inquisitors, never dreaming (for the most part) that they were compiling treatises that would be published in Washington, D.C., Cambridge, Massachusetts, or New Haven, Connecticut.

In *Nee Hemish*, Joe Sando wrote, "There is still some fear that someone like Elsie Clews Parsons may come to stay in the village again." Parsons, who would go on to compile a monumental two-volume work called *Pueblo Indian Religion* (1939), showed up at Jemez in the early 1920s, moved into an adobe house more or less uninvited, and lingered on for months, asking incessant questions. According to Sando, Parsons "enjoyed the usual Pueblo Indian hospitality; always friendly and eager to please, the people were unaware that the anthropologist was collecting secret religious data."

In 1925, Yale University Press brought out Parsons's monograph, *The Pueblo of Jemez*. When several Jemez subsequently read the book, they were shocked and horrified, for Parsons had published detailed accounts of secret ceremonies as well as colored drawings of sacred altars and kachina masks.

Exactly how Parsons gained access to the most sensitive cultural material remains a matter of controversy. In her monograph, she makes no bones about the sacredness of certain Jemez rites and artifacts. Forbidden to attend a kachina dance and exiled to a house with its windows covered with opaque sacking, she sneaked out and tried to watch the ceremony from an alleyway, until a messenger sent by the governor ordered her back to her quarters. One wonders what really went on in the exchange Parsons coyly renders thus:

When the man who drew the masks figured in the colored plates [in the monograph] handed over to me his pictures he remarked, "They would put me in jail for this. . . . It is our life. They say if we tell about it, we are going to die." Another artist, even more fearful, said, "They would kill me for this."

Parsons's gleeful tone is less a matter of personal insensitivity than a reflection of the science of the day. She had been a student of the great ethnographer Franz Boas, who essentially believed that the culture of "primitive" peoples, since they were doomed to extinction, should be recorded whether or not they wanted it to be.

At Zia, the pueblo only ten miles downstream from Jemez, Peter Pino told me an even more doleful tale of ethnographic betrayal. To that village came Colonel James Stevenson and his wife, Matilda Coxe Stevenson, in 1879. The couple stayed among the Zia intermittently until 1888, compiling copious notes. After the colonel's death, in 1894 his wife published an extensive monograph, titled simply *Sia*, as a U.S. Bureau of Ethnology report. The mind-set of the day is all too plainly revealed in the laudatory comments in the preface by John Wesley Powell—pioneer of the first descent of the Colorado River, and by the 1890s director of the bureau. "The work," Powell wrote, "was carried forward with indefatigable energy and zeal, and resulted in the accompanying report, which is a unique and exhaustive account of a decadent and rapidly changing people."

According to Pino, "The Stevensons gained the trust of the Zia people. Matilda Coxe Stevenson used flashlights and matches to convince the people she had magical powers. She convinced them that they should give her all their information, which at first they did.

"She wanted to take a vessel from the Snake Society. The tribal council said no. So she stole it under cover of night, took it away in a wagon the next morning. For that, she was forcibly expelled from Zia.

"It's all written up in her report. She thought the Zia would all be extinct in ten or twenty years, so no Zia would ever [become literate and] read her report."

Indeed, Stevenson's own version of this incident makes the modern reader's flesh crawl. She and her husband had become aware of secret snake dance ceremonies carried on in a secluded building six miles from the pueblo. The man Stevenson called the "vicar of the snake society" reluctantly guided the Anglo pair to this house. "Some diplomacy," she wrote, "was required to persuade the vicar to guide Mr. Stevenson to the cave in which the vases are kept when not in use." On seeing these pots, James Stevenson's greed became insatiable. "These vases belong to the superior type of ancient pottery, and they are decorated in snakes and cougars upon a ground of creamy tint. Mr. Stevenson was not quite satisfied with simply seeing the vases, and determined if possible to possess one or both." The "vicar" told him no, in no uncertain terms: "[The pots] were made by our people of long ago; and the snakes would be very angry if the Sia parted with these vases."

James Stevenson pushed his appeal all the way to the tribal council. The answer was still no. The *ho'naaite*, a chief official of the Snake Society, tried again to explain: "It would excite the anger of the snakes, and perhaps all of our women and our little ones would be bitten and die."

What happened next, according to Matilda Coxe Stevenson, strains the reader's credulity. She writes that the vicar approached her and her husband furtively at midnight, smuggling one of the sacred pots inside a sack. "He would not allow a close examination to be made of the vase, but urged the packing of it at once; he deposited a plume offering in the vase, and sprinkled meal upon it and prayed while tears moistened his cheeks."

Had the Stevensons bribed a corrupt Zia man? Or had they returned to the cave, stolen the pot, and later made up the story of the midnight exchange? We cannot know.

"The vase was brought," Matilda smugly concluded, "to Washington and deposited in the National Museum." Ninety-four years later, in 1982, the sacred vessel was finally repatriated from the Smithsonian Institution and returned to the Zia people.

According to Pino, one reason the Stevensons were able to take advantage of the Zia was that the people had reached the lowest ebb in their long history. "The elders tell us," said Pino, "that there were 15,000 Zia in five villages when the Spanish came." (Most anthropologists would set that number lower, though still in the thousands.) "By 1891, our population was reduced to ninety-seven. We lost a lot of people to the Navajos, the Apaches, and disease." Today, the Zia number 800 people, living on a reservation of 122,000 acres.

Beginning in the 1920s, the Puebloans faced yet another serious threat to the integrity of their culture. Under new policies of the Bureau of Indian Affairs, Native American children all over the West were shipped off to boarding schools. Their hair was cut short, they were dressed in "American" clothes, and they were forbidden to speak their native tongues, under punishments ranging from beatings to the proverbial washing out of their mouths with lye. Under such benighted laws as the Religious Crimes Code, the Puebloan religion was once more suppressed.

The effect of all these intrusions on traditional life—on the part of Franciscan friars, prying ethnographers, and educational zealots ("Kill the Indian, save the man" was a slogan of the turn of the twentieth century)—has been to drive Puebloans deeper into the refuge of secrecy. It has only been in the last three decades that Puebloans have claimed a new dignity and begun to reassert their independence from mainstream America. The causes are many: the liberalism of the late 1960s and early 1970s, giving rise to native movements such as the American Indian Movement, AIM; the passage of NAGPRA (the Native American Graves Protection and Repatriation Act) in 1990, which has allowed tribes to reclaim from museums not only sacred objects once dug up by archaeologists, but the very skeletons of their ancestors; and even the financial success of Indian casinos.

Yet, ironically, this new empowerment has only turned the pueblos, at the spiritual and religious level, more xenophobic. Since Anglo-Americans first started flooding into the Southwest in the 1820s and 1830s, it has never been more difficult than it is today, in 2004, to attend a Puebloan dance, to visit an ancestral ruin, or to ask questions (as I had hoped to do at Jemez) about the past. Fieldwork by anthropologists among the Pueblos has become all but impossible. As one archaeologist told me, speaking of the tongue spoken only at Jemez, "It's sort of sad. No linguist will ever again be allowed to study Towa."

In the late 1980s, Jane Anne Ball, a graduate student at the University of Minnesota, spent fifteen months at Jemez trying to study a ticklish but significant phenomenon—intra-pueblo factionalism, the kind of conflict that had memorably torn the Hopi village of Oraibi asunder in 1906. Her unpublished dissertation reads, in one sense, as a book-length sigh of frustration. Ball was never allowed to spend a single night at Jemez: had a family let her stay with them, she wrote, the offenders would have been "summoned to the Tribal Office and fined or threatened with possible expulsion." Only at the very end of her dogged research effort did any Jemez people begin to teach her a few words of Towa.

Yet Ball keenly understood the roots of Jemez distrust. Quite aside from the legacy of Spanish persecution, Puebloan secrecy has its own internal mandates. Even within the village of Jemez, ritual knowledge is meant to be "owned" only by certain members, the "made" people who (to quote Ball) "have been initiated into a number of ritual or ceremonial organizations." A woman healed in a curing ceremony must guard the secrets that ensure her health. Ball reported that numerous times, when she asked a Jemez man or woman a question, the answer was, "I don't even want to know about that."

Jemez distrust applies within the pueblo. So innocuous a query, Ball learned, as "Just how many cattle do *you* have?" or "So when did you plant your chile?" might veil a serious accusation. Every Puebloan believes that witchcraft is a rampant threat. "All facets of Jemez life," wrote Ball, "seem to be concerned not so much with maintaining harmony but in discovering who is responsible for *disrupting harmony*."

Work such as Ball's has led recent theorists to dispute the idea that Puebloan secrecy arose as a response to Spanish persecution. Rather, it is increasingly seen as intrinsic to the culture, at least since it was radically reorganized by the kachina phenomenon around A.D. 1325. In a provocative 1980 paper called "On Secrecy and Control of Knowledge: Taos Pueblo," Elizabeth A. Brandt rejects the old view, as memorably encapsulated by Edward Dozier (himself a Puebloan) twenty years before. "The unsuccessful attempts of recent ethnologists to break the Pueblo iron curtain," Dozier wrote in 1961, "appear to demonstrate that these Indians still believe that the release of ceremonial knowledge will be used against them. They, therefore, guard tenaciously their native ceremonial system from all outsiders."

The "iron curtain," Brandt persuasively argues, is the wrong metaphor. Secrecy is not a simple us-them barrier, Puebloans versus outsiders. Rather, the very fabric of Puebloan society, with its cross-cutting moieties, clans, societies, and kiva groups, requires an intricate network of internal secrecy to keep it from collapsing. At Taos, Brandt found that a Puebloan would often seek to disguise from his best friends the identity of his kiva group. Another theorist postulates that 90 percent of a pueblo's secret knowledge belongs to less than 10 percent of its members. Knowledge shared too widely loses its power. As Brandt puts it, "Religious leaders are the only ones who possess the secrets; and in order to retain their internal control over the community, the secrets must not be exposed."

In almost every dealing I had with Puebloans, even with my five university-trained informants, at some point I had run smack into what Brandt calls "the polished evasion of questions"—one more strat-egy developed over the ages to ensure secrecy. Likewise, the reluctance on the part of the pueblos to put any part of their history or belief sys-tem into the written record—even if that record be penned by one of their own, an Alfonso Ortiz or a Joe Sando—sprang from the fear that the power of knowledge evaporates when it is too widely shared.

Ruminating on all this, I thought, *No wonder it's so hard to find out what happened between 1680 and 1692.*

Faced with this blank gap in history, scholars, both Anglo and Puebloan, have returned again and again to the twelve "declarations" of Otermín's captives—three seized on his flight south in 1680, nine in his failed reconquest the following winter—to eke some meaning out of their reluctant utterances. In particular, they have puzzled over Popé's vision in the Taos kiva, as reported by Pedro Naranjo on December 19, 1681.

One of the most penetrating analyses was published by Alfonso Ortiz in 1980, on the occasion of the tricentennial of the Revolt. In "Popay's Leadership: A Pueblo Perspective," the scholar, himself a Tewa from San Juan, begins by musing on the shaman's name. Ortiz observes that among the leaders of the Revolt mentioned in the various documents—Luis Tupatú, Alonso Catití, El Taqu, Saca, and Francisco, and the like—only Popé has a non-Hispanic name. This could mean that even before the Revolt, he had "rejected his baptismal name, the Church, and Spanish culture generally by the time his name first began to appear in the documents."

What does Popé (or Popay, as Ortiz spells it) mean in Tewa? Previous translators had rendered it as "squash mountain" or "red moon," but Ortiz thinks it means "ripe cultigens." (The intricate linguistic reasoning behind the scholar's assertion need not be gone into here.) The significance of "ripe cultigens," according to Ortiz, is that "because the name is generic, and, therefore, potent, it could not be conferred on an infant. . . . So potent a name had to be earned."

From all this subtle parsing, Ortiz concludes that Popé was a member, and perhaps the chief, of the summer moiety at San Juan, thus one of the most important figures in the Tewa world. Moieties divide all the members of a society into two groups or affiliations—summer or winter people at San Juan, wren or turquoise people at Zia, and the like. This in turn may explain why the Tewa warriors took the unprecedented step in 1675 of marching on Santa Fe to demand Governor Treviño's release of the forty-three "sorcerers" he had flogged and imprisoned. Popé was too important a man to be allowed to languish as a captive. The Spaniards ought to have taken notice, and perhaps singled out the San Juan shaman from the others; but in their arrogance, Ortiz argues, they thought one sorcerer was little different from the next. In any event, Popé's credibility throughout the Pueblo world at the onset of the Revolt—"across two dozen communities speaking six different languages, and sprawled out over a distance of nearly 400 miles"—may have stemmed from his exalted status not only as chief of the San Juan summer moiety, but as a dissident who had defiantly rejected everything Spanish even before 1680.

All this chain of logic remains highly tentative, of course. Ortiz turns next to the vision in the Taos kiva, in which Popé was instructed by the fire-emitting "demons" named Tilini, Tleume, and Caudi. "I cannot find a remembered or modern version of the last two," writes Ortiz, "but Tilini is clearly the Tewa culture hero Tinini Povi, or 'Olivella Flower Shell Youth,' one of the most revered figures in Tewa tradition." Thus "Popay was actually doing a very wise and very traditional Pueblo thing: invoking sacred culture heroes as his ultimate rationale and guides for the rebellion he was planning." Ortiz further speculates that the other two names are not Tewa at all, but Tiwa and Keresan. The upshot is to dignify Popé as a major religious leader, with influence beyond his own Tewa pueblos, for only such a shaman could have earned the right even to address such deities.

The trouble with arguments such as Ortiz's is that, as a Puebloan, he feels free to pick and choose among the Spanish documents, usually in such a way as to cast a more favorable light on his forebears' doings. The Tesuque captive, Juan, it will be remembered, told Otermín that "it was a matter of common knowledge" that Popé had killed his own son-in-law, Nicolás Bua, for fear he would betray the plot. Ortiz summarily rejects this statement: "If Popay was a chief religious leader, as I contend, he could not have taken life—any kind of life—or knowingly participated in its taking." This is dangerously close to circular reasoning.

What of the underground "lake of Copala," to which the three spirits told Popé they were headed, and which was also, according to

Pedro Naranjo, the place from which all Puebloans had emerged into an elysian world long ago? The latter hint suggests the underground Third World, widespread in Puebloan creation myths, from which all humans emerged into the present Fourth World through the hole called the *sipapu*. Yet no Puebloan who has pondered Naranjo's cryptic utterance has yet firmly linked Copala with that Third World.

Barbara De Marco, a University of California at Berkeley linguist involved in the Cíbola Project, an ambitious ongoing effort to publish and retranslate all the documents pertaining to the Revolt from their original handwritten texts (rather than the copies Hackett and Shelby used in 1942), has made an exhaustive search for the name Copala in Spanish archives. She finds allusions to lakes in the Mexican states of Jalisco and Sinaloa, as well as to a fabulously wealthy "kingdom" of Copala, and concludes that the name may be a variant of Cíbola itself, whose mythical Seven Cities launched the conquistadors north from New Spain. All of which only further muddies the waters of Naranjo's testimony.

There is yet another Yorick's skull in the Spanish record, found not in the testimony of the twelve captives, but in Otermín's own account, written in the middle of the siege of Santa Fe, of the rebellion that had broken out during the previous few days. Otermín, one recalls, had seized the messengers Omtua and Catua and tortured them to reveal what they knew of the plot. In the governor's paraphrase, "They said that . . . it is a matter of common report among all the Indians that there had come to them from very far away toward the north a letter from an Indian lieutenant of Po he yemu to the effect that all of them in general should rebel, and that any pueblo that would not agree to it they would destroy, killing all the people. It was reported that this Indian lieutenant of Po he yemu was very tall, black, and had very large yellow eyes, and that everyone feared him greatly."

Upon this gnostic formulation, commentators have improvised further fantasias. In 1967, Fray Angélico Chávez, both a Franciscan priest and an esteemed historian (the historical library of the Palace of the Governors in Santa Fe is named after him), published an article called "Pohé-yemo's Representative and the Pueblo Revolt of 1680." Chávez identifies the "Po he yemu" of Otermín's dispatch with the Tewa god Pose-yemo, literally "he who strews the morning dew"—i.e., a rain-giver. But he is not willing to accept Popé as the god's lieutenant (in Spanish, *teniente*, or representative). Instead, by a very circuitous path, he invokes a controversy at Santa Clara recorded in 1766, involving a family named Naranjo, "whose antecedents were Negroid and who, most significantly, were accused of having fomented Indian insurrections in the past." Thus an otherwise undocumented "big Negro or black-complexioned mulatto named Naranjo" becomes the architect of the Revolt, rather than Popé. Alluding to the Moor Esteban's mischief at Hawikuh in 1539, Chávez slyly remarks, "It is not the first time that an African spoiled the best-laid plans of the Spaniard in American colonial times, but it [Naranjo's alleged fomenting of the Revolt] was the most dramatic."

Thinly veiled, but at the heart of Chávez's contorted argument, is a racial bias. A black man such as the hypothesized Naranjo was, according to Chávez, "more active and restless by nature than the more passive and stolid Indian." Subscribing to the old myth of the peaceful Puebloans, Chávez (perhaps swayed by his own Franciscan bias) goes so far as to maintain that for eight decades before the Revolt, "the ordinary run of Pueblo Indians had been happy with the many material benefits brought them by the padres. . . . The pueblo people in general, besides being satisfied with things as they were, were slow to respond to a war cry." No Indian could have spearheaded such a rebellion: it took someone "descended from Negroid-Amerindian servants, brought from New Spain by the first colonists." These descendants, intermarrying with Puebloans, had "native and acquired capabilities . . . superior to those of the inbred pueblos who knew little outside their individual restricted cosmos."

From other Puebloans cross-examined in the first days of the Revolt, Otermín gleaned variant spellings of the nebulous deity Po he yemu. A Keresan man gave the name Payastiamo, while a Jemez informant rendered it as Payastiabo. Both said this god or spirit lived in the northern mountains. In *Pueblo Nations* (1992), Joe Sando pulls rank as a Puebloan himself to claim that these testimonies have come down in the oral tradition in the form of a "legendary joke" perpetrated upon the Spanish. "The joke," Sando writes, "consists of the fact that these three names, Payastiamo, Poheyemo, and Payastiabo, are the names of deities whom the Pueblos address in their prayers to intercede for them with the One beyond the clouds. He generally lives to the north, in the highest mountain, or in the clouds. But the Spaniards concluded that he was indeed the leader of the revolt."

One comes away bleary-eyed from these intense textual exegeses. (When I asked Tessie Naranjo, the Santa Clara artist and writer, if she was descended from the big black Naranjo with the yellow eyes who had masterminded the Revolt, she snorted in derision.) However clever they are at sketching out plausible narratives, these analyses seem to me to overlook a fundamental fact. In all their tantalizing suggestiveness, the "declarations" of Otermín's captives, as they have come down to us, are fundamentally unreliable. The drift of meaning inevitable in translating from Puebloan languages into Spanish must have introduced fatal corruptions into those texts. (It had occurred to me to wonder whether "Po he yemu" was merely a variant of "Popé," with some qualifying suffix. As for whether the San Juan shaman could have been tall, dark-skinned, with yellow eyes—why not? No other description of the man has come down to us.)

Another source of corrupted meaning lies in the fact that these statements were most likely extracted under torture. Desperate to save their lives, Otermín's informants must have racked their brains to tell the governor what they guessed he wanted to hear. Otermín does not bother to report the fate of the informants after they had spoken. Given that he had summarily executed all forty-seven captives he took as he burst out of the Santa Fe stockade, it would not be surprising if, as soon as Pedro Naranjo and Juan from Tesuque and Juan and Francisco Lorenzo from San Felipe and the very old Juan from La Alameda, who remembered the coming of Oñate, and the other five captives—if, as soon as they were done confessing, Otermín had had them taken out back and shot.

Having failed to reconquer the colony he had lost, Otermín was relieved of his governorship in 1683. After that date, he fades into obscurity.

Once more, as in 1608, the Spaniards came close to giving up for good on Nuevo México. Ironically, the goad that kept alive a Spanish interest in the northern colony came from a threat a thousand miles to the east. In 1682, Robert Cavelier, Sieur de La Salle, completed the epic first (European) descent of the Mississippi River, claiming all the land in that vast drainage for France. Two years later, he set off on an even more ambitious expedition. With 180 sailors, he planned to reach the mouth of the Mississippi by sea, sail up the river some 200 miles, build a fortress, recruit 15,000 Indian allies, and set out to the west to conquer the "indolent and effeminate" Spaniards who occupied all of northern Mexico.

That expedition ended up as one of the most colossal failures in New World exploration. La Salle sailed past the mouth of the great river without recognizing it, finally anchored in what is now Matagorda Bay in Texas, and built a makeshift fortress. Essentially lost (the key to the party's disorientation was that no way of accurately measuring longitude had yet been invented), La Salle and his men spent a year and a half setting out on reconnaissance missions. Eventually they hoped only to find the Mississippi and ascend it to the French forts from which the explorer had set out in 1680. Illness and Indian attacks took a terrible toll. La Salle was ambushed and murdered by his own men. In the end, only a handful of survivors reached Montreal and were returned to France in 1687.

Unaware of the fate of La Salle's second expedition, but fully cognizant of the French threat, the Spanish crown determined to rebuild a stronghold in New Mexico to fight off an invasion from the east. There was also, of course, as in 1608, a passionate Franciscan concern with saving the souls of the Indians they had baptized before 1680, lest they slide back into pagan perdition.

It was not until 1689, however, that the next serious attempt to reconquer New Mexico was launched. Under Governor Domingo Jironza Petríz de Cruzate, an army of eighty soldiers set off up the Rio Grande. This expedition remains poorly documented, but it seems that Jironza's main achievement was to fight a fifteen-hour pitched battle against the pueblo of Zia, in which fifty of his own eighty soldiers were wounded, but 600 Zia men, women, and children were killed. After this carnage, Jironza turned around and limped back toward El Paso.

If nothing else, Jironza's barbarous thrust into New Mexico should have demonstrated how determined the Puebloans were, nine years after they had perpetrated the Revolt, to keep the Spanish out of their homeland. Yet from that 1689 foray, and from the occasional report of an Indian defector arriving in El Paso to ally himself with the former enemy, the Spanish gleaned that the Puebloan world was in grievous disarray. That patchwork of gossip and innuendo is all that remains in the Spanish record of what happened in New Mexico between 1682 and 1692.

That even this patchwork exists depends on the diligence of a remarkable explorer and friar named Silvestre Vélez de Escalante. In 1776, with a fellow friar, Francisco Atanasio Domínguez, Escalante made a pioneering voyage through many parts of the Southwest that no Spaniard had yet seen, crossing the southern Rocky Mountains, the Colorado Plateau, and the Great Basin in search of a route linking New Mexico with the Catholic missions in California. (Grand Staircase–Escalante National Monument in southern Utah is named after the friar.) During the next two years, in Santa Fe, Escalante copied down original documents that have since vanished from the archives.

His *Extracto de Noticias* remains unpublished in either Spanish or English, but serves as an invaluable source for scholars.

Escalante's documents reveal that one Puebloan, who had escaped from several years' captivity among the Apaches, reported in 1682 that Popé had been deposed. Luis Tupatú, of Picuris Pueblo, was now the chief leader, with Alonso Catití as his principal deputy. The confederation of pueblos was apparently crumbling, for Catití had led an attack on Hopi, killing ten men. Other informants during the next few years reported that Ute Indians raiding from the north had made major inroads among the pueblos. Apaches and Navajos also benefited from the absence of the Spaniards. Adept at stealing horses and firearms, these nomads quickly learned to use them. With no mounted soldiers to oppose them, they raided the Pueblos with devastating frequency.

Alonso Catití had died, probably in 1684. Popé was apparently reinstalled as leader in 1688, but may have died shortly thereafter. By 1690, Luis Tupatú seems to have been the only principal leader of the Revolt still alive.

As the 1680s wore on, according to the witnesses Escalante saved from oblivion, Zuni and Hopi waged war against one another. Acoma was undergoing a dramatic internal schism, which would eventually result in the expulsion of a substantial minority who would found the nearby pueblo of Laguna in 1699. The Keresan pueblos, joined by Jemez, Taos, and Pecos, had taken up arms against the Tewa pueblos and Picuris. Meanwhile, drought and famine continued to threaten the Puebloans' very existence. An old legend has it that the Rio Grande completely dried up at one point during this period. Popé's vision of a life of "great ease" once the people had rid themselves of everything Spanish had proved a hollow illusion.

In Escalante's *Extracto*, there lurks a vignette of Popé in action that casts a new light on the scope of his plot against the Spanish. The source is a Christian Indian from Isleta named Alonso Shimitihua. According to Shimitihua's testimony, as he retreated south with Otermín's caravan in September 1680, he had a sudden change of heart.

Fired with messianic zeal, he turned back north, determined to convince the whole rebel horde to atone for their sins and return to Christianity. Two other Tiwa men accompanied him. At La Alameda they were captured by a war captain, who tied them up and carried them north to an audience at Santo Domingo with Alonso Catití.

Shimitihua was shocked and dismayed to see that Catití's house was lavishly decorated with booty from the churches the rebels had looted and burned. Several lieutenants were wearing the gowns of murdered Franciscans, one with an altar cloth tied around his head. Catití listened to Shimitihua's mad entreaty, then took the three Tiwa men to meet Popé.

The San Juan shaman was so outraged at the Christian turncoat's proposition that he stabbed Shimitihua with a knife, shouting out that no such God as the Christians worshiped had ever existed. Meanwhile the other two Tiwa men hastily confessed that they had only pretended to go along with Shimitihua's program, hoping in truth to persuade the rebels to march on El Paso and kill all the Spaniards. Popé was much taken with this idea. He sent these two Tiwa back south to recruit allies among such border tribes as the Mansos and Sumas. An advance guard, made up mostly of Piros and Tiwas, was intercepted by Apaches before they could reach El Paso; five Puebloans were killed, and the rest fled back north. At last discerning the hopelessness of his mission, Shimitihua escaped and made his way back to El Paso, where he told his outlandish tale—most of which in all likelihood was true.

In 1691, Diego José de Vargas Zapata Luján Ponce de León y Contreras was made the new governor of New Mexico. Forty-seven years old, born in Madrid, Vargas had come to the New World in 1673 and worked his way up the ladder of colonial bureaucracy. He arrived in El Paso to take over as governor in February 1691. During the next seventeen months, he gathered information and prepared an army to march north. On August 10, 1692, he made a formal announcement of his expedition of reconquest, promising to reclaim "the provinces of New Mexico from the apostate, uprisen Indians, traitors to his majesty." It was no coincidence that the proclamation came on the twelfth anniversary of the outbreak of the Pueblo Revolt.

Vargas's army was actually smaller than Jironza's—fifty soldiers, ten armed civilians, and 100 Indian allies, many of them Piro and southern Tiwa who had come south with Otermín. But in the field, Vargas would prove himself the brilliant general that Otermín and Jironza had manifestly failed to impersonate.

The great surprise, as Vargas pushed north in the late summer of 1692, was how little resistance his army met. Out of the apparent ease with which that army reclaimed New Mexico has grown the myth, current today, of the "Bloodless Reconquest." Yet it would take four years for Vargas fully to establish control over the shattered Pueblo world, and those years would prove far from bloodless. And in the end, the new colony that Vargas brought into being bore only superficial resemblances to the abject fiefdom Oñate had launched in 1598. Although in the light of history and anthropology, those four years remain a snarled tangle of ambiguities and mysteries, the integrity of the Pueblo world today owes everything to what happened between 1692 and 1696.

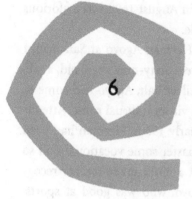

# 6

# THE BLOODLESS RECONQUEST

At the Indian Pueblo Cultural Center in Albuquerque, I asked Joe Sando, "Why was it so easy for Vargas to reconquer New Mexico?"

The Jemez elder frowned. "We weren't reconquered," he said. "We became friends."

Sando must have seen the look of surprise on my face, for he added, "Our oral history says that we went down the Rio Grande to El Paso to invite the Spanish back."

"Why would you do that?"

Sando seemed uncomfortable with my grilling. Anglo historians had made it clear that after 1680, without Spanish soldiers as a buffer, the Puebloans were more vulnerable than ever to attacks by Utes, Apaches, and Navajos. But Sando was putting a new twist on this tribulation. "The Pueblos were suffering alone," he said. "We didn't have enough guns or horses to fight off the raiders. When the Spanish came back after twelve years, they became our partners in fighting the raiders."

Needless to say, there is no echo in the Spanish record of an invitation from the Puebloans to reoccupy their homeland. In Vargas's mind, the mission on which he set out in August 1692 was a glorious campaign of reconquest, pure and simple.

A few weeks later, as I talked with Herman Agoyo at San Juan, I heard Sando's assertion flatly contradicted. Sixty-nine years old, a tall, slender, dignified man with black-and-silver hair, Agoyo had come to his own curiosity about the Pueblo past via an unusual route. Attending the Santa Fe Indian School in the early 1950s, Herman had been encouraged, like all his classmates, to master some vocational skill so he could get a job after graduating. But a ninth-grade teacher recognized the youth's intelligence, and Agoyo, who was good at sports, cherished the dream of becoming a professional baseball player. The upshot was that he applied to Manhattan College and was accepted, the only member of his graduating class to attend a four-year college. Agoyo never got a tryout with the Yankees, but in New York City, 2,500 miles away from home, he learned far more about the history of his people than he had from his parents and grandparents at San Juan. Back in New Mexico, he became a champion of Native American rights, serving (among other offices) as the executive director of the Eight Northern Indian Pueblos Council.

I mentioned Joe Sando's story of Puebloan messengers going down the Rio Grande to El Paso to invite the Spanish back. Agoyo gathered his thoughts. I sensed the man's discomfort with Sando's theory, and also his reluctance, in front of a non-Puebloan inquisitor, to criticize a friend he otherwise greatly admired. Agoyo's rejoinder thus took on an impersonal guise. "We have to refute the idea," he said, "that the Spanish were invited back. It's just twelve years later. You don't forget something so tragic in twelve years. Probably Vargas was better organized than Otermín."

Months later, over lunch in a Santa Fe restaurant, Tessie Naranjo told me, "I would go along with Herman on that." Naranjo's own path to her role as a spokesperson for the pueblos had been every bit as remarkable as Agoyo's. Having grown up at Santa Clara in a family of accomplished potters and artists, she too went to college far from home, at Northeastern Oklahoma University. She returned to her native state to earn an M.A. and a Ph.D. in sociology from the University of New Mexico. She has been influential in the movement to preserve Native American languages, crafts, and oral traditions, and has served as national chairperson for the NAGPRA commission.

Now Naranjo amplified her point. "I refuse to believe the Spanish were invited back," she said. "Yes, during that twelve-year period, the Apaches and Navajos were raising cain. My gut feeling is that when the people saw the Spanish coming, they knew the power of their machinery, their aggression. . . ." Naranjo took a deep breath. "My poor Pueblo people! Maybe they just didn't have enough fight left in them."

In New Mexico today, another vein of oral tradition flourishes, one that could not be more contrary to the beliefs of Herman Agoyo and Tessie Naranjo. It holds sway among the more chauvinistic of the Hispanic descendants of the original colonists. In this view, the coming of the Spanish to New Mexico was first and foremost a mission of civilization. Oñate and Vargas are not bloody conquerors—they are the John Smith and Miles Standish of the Southwest. This school of thought finds expression not only in such monuments as the Oñate statue and visitor center on Highway 68 near Alcalde, but in the Fiesta de Santa Fe, an annual summer pageant dating from 1712.

Among other ceremonies acted out during the fiesta is a re-creation of Vargas's "Bloodless Reconquest." A few weeks after my lunch with Tessie Naranjo, I met with Rudy Fernández, the genial president of the Fiesta Council. "The story goes," Fernández told me, "that Vargas made a promise to Our Lady of the Rosary, Nuestra Señora la Conquistadora—that doesn't mean 'conquistador,' it means 'who conquered our hearts'—that Vargas promised that if he came into Santa Fe without bloodshed, he would celebrate a feast in her honor forever. The Puebloans accepted Vargas peacefully in 1692. In 1693, he went back [to El Paso] to get the rest of the settlers. But I'll admit, it wasn't so peaceful after that.

"Our fiesta originates in the peaceful reconquest of 1692. I hate that word—it should be, the 'peaceful resettlement.' Because we had already been here.

"Every year," Fernández went on, "we have a reenactment of Vargas's entering Santa Fe in 1692. Vargas enters the city and talks to the Indians. This year, we had an Indian playing the part of Vargas, a seventeen-year-old from Tesuque Pueblo."

Tessie Naranjo had told me as much, in tones rich with chagrin. "It's disappointing that some of us don't know our history. His mother is Chicano," she said, referring to the Tesuque youth. "So he's half and half. Our mothers raise us and give us our consciousness. That Chicano part of her never gave him the consciousness that it's wrong to celebrate the reconquest.

"He told me, 'Yeah, I had a real good time. I enjoyed it.' All I could say was, 'I'm so sad that you feel that way.' I'm afraid that young fellow will never cry for his people."

Despite Rudy Fernández's tableau of Indians sanguinely welcoming the Spaniards back (buttressed in its own odd way by Joe Sando's claim of an "invitation"), the fact is that between Puebloans and Hispanics in New Mexico today, ineradicable ethnic tensions are the legacy of the reconquest. Only half joking, Tessie Naranjo told me, "When my mother, who's eighty-seven, and I drive into Española, and we're in the car after dark, she says to me in Tewa, 'Close the windows, the Spanish are all around!'"

There exists a single portrait of Diego de Vargas; painted in New Mexico in 1704, it hangs today in a chapel in Madrid. In it, the conquistador stands stiffly facing the painter, leaning with all his weight on his left foot. He is dressed in his finery, the sleeves of his coat ballooning into huge, billowy cuffs, a gaudy hat trimmed with fur held low in his left hand. In his right hand, Vargas grasps a lance, its butt planted on the ground, spear point towering above his head. His face has a blank but resolute look. A trim mustache, mirrored by a V of facial hair beneath his lower lip, might give a less adamantine man an effeminate air. Behind him on the wall of the dark chamber hang Vargas's coat of arms and a painting of a battle scene, only the edge of which we can see—perhaps a memorial to the man's own "bloodless" reconquest.

Vargas's campaign in the late summer and fall of 1692 is documented in great detail in a journal the governor kept, admirably translated and annotated by editors John Kessell and Rick Hendricks in four fat volumes published between 1992 and 1998. Thanks to these works, we can trace the reconquest—from the Spanish point of view, at least—in exquisite detail. In his journal, Vargas for the most part eschews the florid, bombastic style favored by most of the governors of New Mexico, setting down in straightforward prose what he accomplished from day to day.

Vargas left El Paso on August 21. Moving quickly up the Rio Grande, he passed one deserted outpost and ruined *estancia* after another. The first pueblos he came to, beginning with Senecú (south of present-day Socorro) were abandoned, as Vargas expected. Oddly enough, there is no mention in the journal of passing Isleta, the southernmost pueblo that Otermín had found occupied in 1681, which, after easily subduing the inhabitants, he had made the base camp for his own abortive mission of reconquest.

On September 9, having camped at a desolate hacienda near present-day Albuquerque, Vargas decided to forge ahead even more rapidly with only forty soldiers, leaving the rest of his army to catch up later. This advance guard found Puaray and Sandía pueblos abandoned. Vargas concluded that he would meet the enemy at Cochiti, where eleven years earlier Otermín had waited out his two-day stalemate with the defiant Puebloans led by the "coyote" Alonso Catití. Even before reaching Cochiti, Vargas set down in his journal the precise program of the dawn raid he would make on that stronghold. Two Franciscan friars would ride at the head of the troops with Vargas. The soldiers would surround Cochiti to prevent any Puebloans from escaping. Then the friars would demand, through interpreters, that the Indians "praise the blessed sacrament and the name of His Most Holy Mother five times," as token of their submission. No soldier would open fire until Vargas gave the signal, "upon pain of death." Vargas's confidence in the efficacy of this formulaic surrender steeps his journal entry: "Although the rebels may answer me stubbornly and rebelliously in their apostasy and not accept the goal I wish for them . . . the two very reverend fathers will persuade and exhort them through interpreters, in accord with their fervent spirit."

Vargas was in for a surprise. When he rode up to Cochiti on September 11, he found this pivotal pueblo as thoroughly abandoned as the villages farther south. Nor was there any evidence of warriors on the mesa tops keeping watch on the Spanish vanguard, as Otermín had found in 1681. Perplexed, Vargas backtracked to Santo Domingo. This pueblo, too, was abandoned. Vargas moved on southward to San Felipe, where at last he spotted Indians. Seeing the Spanish coming, the Puebloans fled their village for the mesas to the north and west. Two of Vargas's officers managed to lure a single San Felipe man on horseback down for a brief parley. "They told him," Vargas recorded, "that he and all the people of his pueblo should come down, that we were coming neither to make war on them nor to harm them. The Indian answered them in Castilian that they did not want war but peace with the Spaniards." Indeed, the San Felipe warriors would be only too glad to have Spanish help in making war on the Tewa to the north, who had become their enemies. But Vargas waited in vain for the return of the scattered San Felipeans, concluding in disgust "that their proposition about peace between us is fraudulent."

If nowhere else, Vargas reasoned, he must find Puebloans in residence at Santa Fe. He turned his small force north once more. On September 13, he rode in sight of the capital of New Mexico, which no Spaniard had seen since Otermín's caravan had burst free from their stockade twelve years before. And Santa Fe was indeed teeming with Indians.

The delicate back-and-forth of the next few days reveals Vargas's genius as a general in the best possible light. This, despite the fact that he had the usual Spanish faith in the pompous rituals of acknowledgment and submission that must have been all but incomprehensible to the Puebloans.

In the bland reenactment of this encounter carried out every summer in the Fiesta de Santa Fe, Vargas marches unmolested into the heart of the city to be greeted by Indians who readily accept the return of Spanish rule. This is hardly what happened on September 13, 1692.

It was still dark when Vargas's force approached the walls of Santa Fe. Only as the soldiers traversed the cornfields just outside the village did Indian sentinels notice their arrival. According to Vargas, men, women, and children quickly lined "the ramparts of the fortress . . . from end to end." Dawn was just starting to break. In unison, the Spaniards chanted, "Praise be the blessed sacrament of the altar" five times. Then Vargas's interpreters called out to the sentinels in Tewa.

Bizarrely enough (if Vargas is to be credited), the sentinels refused to believe at first that the massed force outside the walls was made up of Spaniards; they thought instead the intruders were "Pecos and Apache liars." An almost comic interchange followed this taunt. If they were indeed Spaniards, the sentinels challenged, why had they not fired their harquebuses? "I replied to this that I was a Catholic and they should calm themselves," Vargas later wrote in his journal. "As the sun came up, it would grow lighter, and they would see the image of the Blessed Virgin carried on the standard."

The sentinels demanded that the intruders blow a bugle, to prove they were Spaniards. Vargas not only had the bugle sounded, but the war drum as well, yet at the same time cautioned his men to hold their fire.

At last the Puebloans believed that genuine Spaniards had come to do them harm. Their response, however, was quite the opposite of the meek submission reenacted in the Fiesta de Santa Fe. In Vargas's deadpan résumé, "They replied that they were ready to fight for five days,

they had to kill us all, we must not flee as we had the first time, and
they had to take everyone's life. At the same time, they began a furious
shouting that must have lasted more than an hour."

At this point, a more impetuous general—an Oñate, say—might
well have launched a battle. As Vargas watched, more and more men
crowded the ramparts, many of them armed with stones. "In the
interim," Vargas reported, "while they were shouting and screaming,
some of their leaders stood up, shouting many shameful things in their
language."

Vargas boldly advanced another twenty paces. Through an interpreter, he again urged the Indians to "calm themselves and be assured
that I was not coming to do them any harm whatsoever." Serene in his
Catholic benevolence, Vargas told the infidels "that I had come, sent
from Spain by his majesty, the king, our lord, to pardon them so that
they might again be Christians, as they had been, and the devil would
not lead them astray." As token of his sincerity, he brandished his standard with the image of the Virgin on it, "saying to them that they had
but to look at her and recognize her to be our Lady the Queen and the
Blessed Virgin. . . . I pitied them because they believed in the devil, who
deceived them, and not in God our Lord."

The quasi-medieval pageantry of Vargas's demonstration outside
the ramparts had a strange effect on the Puebloans. Instead of launching the battle themselves, they asked the governor to remove his helmet
so they could see his face. Then, through a spokesman whose name,
the Spaniards would later learn, was Antonio Bolsas—a Puebloan who
spoke good Spanish—they poured out a litany of grievances.

They remembered the treachery of the Spaniards before 1680, who
had feigned peace with the Apaches, only to go out and kill them. How
did the Puebloans know these new Spanish might not perform the
same sort of treachery on them? "I replied," wrote Vargas later, "that
the Apaches were not Christians but traitors." Bolsas went on to com-
plain that under the Spanish, his people "had had to work very hard,
having been ordered to build the churches and homes of the Span-

iards, and they were whipped if they did not do what they were told."
Bolsas named three particularly severe taskmasters of the old regime,
men who had personally flogged the forty-three "sorcerers," including
Popé, in 1675. Vargas replied that none of those three men was among
his party.

The governor realized that his show of standard, bugle, and war
drum was working. Instead of a battle, he had begun a dialogue. Now
Bolsas weakened, hinting at clemency rather than war: "He stated the
guilty [for the Revolt] had already died and the living were not at all
guilty and most of them had been young men then." Vargas reassured
the man that he came to pardon the Puebloans, not to punish them.

Yet Santa Fe would not be so easily won. The Indians, too, were
capable of a pageantry of their own. A single Puebloan marched out,
armed with leather shield, lance, bow, and arrows, and walked up to
Vargas, who offered to shake his hand. Instead, the man demanded
that two of the Franciscan friars come inside the ramparts. At this,
Fray Cristóbal Barroso and Fray Francisco Corvera—two more friars
hungry for martyrdom?—promptly dismounted and started toward
the gate to the villa. Vargas called out, "Your reverences, stop!"—saving
them, he was sure, from certain death.

Meanwhile, Vargas's men had seen warriors from other pueblos
advancing in the distance. The army of only forty soldiers plus Indian
auxiliaries was in a ticklish position, hugely outnumbered. Vargas
brazened it out. "I replied to them that I did not fear them though they
were all together, but pitied them because they did not believe in my
good intentions. I had already told them that the devil was deceiving
them." The Indians responded with more shouted taunts, "securing
themselves in their fortifications, bringing many round stones, painting themselves red, and making gestures and demonstrations so as to
bring on war." But they did not attack.

The exchange settled into impasse. It was now eleven o'clock in
the morning. At this point, Vargas pulled off a masterly tactic. Just as
the Puebloans had cut off the water supply to Otermín's besieged

Spaniards in 1680, now Vargas sent four soldiers to circle the ramparts to higher ground and block the ditch through which flowed Santa Fe's only water supply. At the same time, he gave the Puebloans one hour to surrender. "If they did not," he threatened, "I would consume and destroy them by fire and sword, holding nothing back."

Two hours came and went. Vargas prepared his soldiers for war, making ostentatious display of ammunition and two cannons he had brought with him. The resolution of the "rebels," Vargas could plainly see, was crumbling. They sent several emissaries out to talk to the governor, the most important of whom was a Tewa "chief" named Domingo. Vargas repeated his terms. "I saw," he later wrote, "that he had a heart that could be reduced." Meanwhile, Vargas ordered the cannons and "large harquebuses" mounted in wagons trained on the ramparts.

Domingo returned to his people, apparently pleading for surrender, for warriors mocked him from the ramparts. But as they beheld the artillery trained upon them, one by one they disappeared from their posts. Domingo reemerged. "He told me very sadly," Vargas reported, "that he had already told his people how good peace would be for them, reminding them of what had happened at Zia Pueblo." Domingo was alluding to Jironza's massacre in 1689. "They should not be fools, but believe me. . . . He saw that they were not obeying him, so he came out, taking his leave of them and told me he could not do anything with them."

The day wore on. Vargas kept up his delicate balancing act, promising to pardon the Puebloans, showing his standard with the emblem of the Virgin again and again, but making it plain that if the Indians failed to surrender, he would be merciless: "I replied that I was neither afraid of them nor humbled as they were, confined, besieged, without water, and subject to my burning them out and killing them all, which I could have done in the time that had passed since I arrived."

Slowly the resistance collapsed. At some point in the afternoon, two unarmed Indians came out and pledged the peace of all the Puebloans in Santa Fe. Vargas dismounted, shook hands with these emissaries, and embraced them. Then, bravely, he marched through the gate and entered the villa. "The Indians, although frightened, began to come out to give me the peace, which I gave them all, with all my love. I . . . spoke words of tenderness and love, so that they might be reassured about my good intentions."

Late that afternoon, Vargas had a large cross erected in the middle of the Santa Fe plaza. Without firing a shot, the governor had taken Santa Fe. And so far, he could well believe that he had accomplished a bloodless reconquest.

It was not, of course, brilliant generalship alone that had won Santa Fe without a fight. In less than a month in New Mexico, Vargas had seen abundant evidence of the disarray that had swept across the all-too-briefly-united Pueblo world—the San Felipe Keres delighted at the thought of Spanish allies joining them to fight the Tewa, the Tewa themselves assuming the army that had crept up to the ramparts in the night was made up of "Pecos and Apache liars." By 1692, nearly all the original leaders of the Revolt were dead. And for more than a decade, famine and drought had worked cruel hardships on every family in the land.

Vargas, however, was too shrewd a leader to assume that, with the taking of Santa Fe, he had won New Mexico in a single stroke. During the several days after September 13, he kept up his soldiers' vigilance against any trap or change of heart that might rupture the fragile peace. One by one, leaders of outlying pueblos, having learned of the occupation of the former capital, came to Santa Fe to pledge their own people's submission to the Spaniards.

In late September, the congenitally restless Vargas set off to visit all the pueblos he knew about, to ensure that the peace he had won at Santa Fe was universal. He rode east to Pecos, north to San Juan and Picuris and Taos, then back south through the Tano pueblos of the Galisteo Basin. In October he pushed west to the Keres pueblos and to

Jemez. More often than not, he found a pueblo abandoned as he rode up to it, so great was the natives' fear of retribution. But not once did he meet with armed combat.

Increasingly confident of his reconquest, Vargas rode far to the west, to visit Zuni and Hopi. A second motivation for this long foray was the quest for a rumored cinnabar (mercury) mine somewhere in the Hopi country. Nuevo México had yet to produce any gold and silver, but cinnabar, used to process the silver in mines in northern Mexico, would amount to a valuable find.

Zuni, full of terrified men and women whom a band of Apaches had told that the Spanish would massacre them all, capitulated easily. The governor rode on toward Hopi. And here, in the words of historian Carroll Riley, "Vargas flirted with annihilation." Things went well enough at the nearest Hopi pueblo, Awatovi, whose inhabitants warily accepted the Spaniards, allowing 122 men, women, and children to be baptized. Yet no part of the Pueblo world would prove—not only now but in the decades and centuries to come—more hostile and resistant to the Spanish than Hopi. Awatovi itself would pay dearly for its submission to the Europeans only eight years later.

At Awatovi, a Puebloan named Miguel, who had befriended Vargas, warned the governor that the leaders of the other Hopi pueblos had met at Walpi and resolved to kill all the Spaniards. Undaunted, Vargas rode west to Walpi, one of the best-defended villages in the Pueblo world, perched atop a knife-edged fin of a butte that thrusts west from what is called today First Mesa. Perhaps recklessly, Vargas climbed to the top of the mesa, entered Walpi, confronted the "rebel" leader, Antonio, and ordered him to tell his men to lay down their weapons. By now, the governor must have felt that some kind of divine grace shielded him from all possible injury. Some of the warriors put down their arms; Antonio protested that the Indians who did not were from other pueblos, and that he thus had no control over them.

"I pretended not to notice," as Vargas later put it. Bluffing his way with half his men to the center of the airy village, he "told them about my coming and proclaimed possession on his majesty's behalf, both of the pueblo and them, his vassals." Vargas erected a cross in the plaza, bade a priest to absolve the infidels, and managed to baptize eighty-one more natives. One wonders what kept the Hopi warriors from attacking. Perhaps Vargas's sheer brazen self-confidence paralyzed them: it might have seemed a kind of sorcery itself, against which bows and arrows could prove impotent.

The next day, Vargas repeated his ceremony of possession in the Hopi villages of Mishongnovi and Jongopavi, on Second Mesa, performing yet more baptisms. Then he prepared a small force to march on Oraibi, on Third Mesa, the most fiercely independent of all the Hopi villages. But Miguel, his Awatovi friend, counseled him against pushing his luck too far. After a wary reconnaissance, Vargas heeded the advice and turned back. The only pueblo in all of Nuevo México to resist the 1692 reconquest, Oraibi would fester in Vargas's soul. He promised himself a future mission to subdue the stubborn village, contenting himself meanwhile with bringing back a generous sample of cinnabar for assay. (The ore turned out not to be mercury at all, but worthless hematite.)

By mid-December, Vargas was back in El Paso. In less than four months, he had claimed possession of all of the lost colony save the single village of Oraibi. And so far, the reconquest had indeed been bloodless. The task to which Vargas would devote all of 1693 was bringing colonists north to settle New Mexico once more. In due time, the Indians themselves would learn to become good Christians.

On his way to El Paso, the governor paused at El Morro to carve the boast of his great deed into the white sandstone of the soaring butte, not far from Oñate's kindred inscription from eighty-seven years before. "Here was the General Don Diego de Vargas," he etched in Spanish, or had one of his men etch, in graceful calligraphy, "who conquered for our Holy Faith, and for the Royal Crown, all the New Mexico, at his expense, Year of 1692."

The job of pacifying the colony and making it safe for settlers and

Indians alike, however, was far from finished. It would erupt, in fact, in conflagrations every bit as bloody and tragic as the ones Oñate had touched off in 1598–99. The legacy of Vargas's reconquest is alive and bitter in the Pueblo world today, 308 years after the governor thought he had at last brought it to a happy conclusion.

The year 1692 had been an *annus mirabilis* for Vargas. By his own count, he had gained the ritual submission of twenty-three pueblos, and had baptized 2,214 Indians. Nuevo México, he assumed, was his. But in 1693, almost from the start, everything went wrong for the governor.

Determined to bring back to Santa Fe a colony large and secure enough to keep the province Spanish in perpetuity, he spent months trying to recruit prospective settlers. The task was a difficult one. Life in El Paso itself was grim and dangerous, the walled outpost constantly threatened by attacks from nomadic Indians on all sides. The Revolt of 1680 had faded from no one's memory, and few were the families on the northern frontier willing to uproot and risk everything for a new life in a place rumored to be as wretched as New Mexico. Unable to outfit a party from the El Paso region alone, Vargas traveled through the northern provinces of Mexico trying to woo soldiers and settlers. In theory, the crown was all in favor of Vargas's mission, and he was authorized to promise both titulary honors and real financial aid to anyone willing to reoccupy Santa Fe. But by midsummer, when he had spent 40,000 pesos simply to recruit his settlers and buy goods and livestock to supply their journey, the treasury cut off his funds.

A less determined governor might have given up in sheer frustration. In the end, it was not until October 4, 1693, that the expedition left El Paso, crossed the Rio Grande, and headed north. At last, Vargas had assembled a force worthy of the name of a colony: 100 soldiers, seventy families of settlers, an untold number of Indian allies, and no fewer than eighteen Franciscan friars—a total of some 800 men, women, and children. With its caravan, this multitude drove 2,000 horses, 1,000 mules, and 900 head of cattle. Eighteen wagons carried tons of useful goods.

Because of the size of this reoccupying party, progress was tediously slow. The year before, prancing at the head of his advance guard, Vargas had covered the 300 miles from El Paso to Santa Fe in only twenty-four days, even allowing for his detour as he backtracked to visit the abandoned pueblos of Santo Domingo and San Felipe. In 1693, the same journey would require two and a half months. The huge herd of animals driven along with the colonists was necessary for sustenance, but it also proved a constant temptation for the nomadic raiders through whose territories the expedition plodded north.

One can only imagine the bafflement and distrust that must have coursed through the Pueblo world during Vargas's absence. This stern, brave conquistador had come to every village, enacted his rituals of cross and Virgin, lectured the inhabitants about the devil in their midst, then had the men in brown robes sprinkle water on the heads of the natives. There had been much rhetoric about a king in Spain, about vassalage and obedience, about becoming good Christians once more. And then the messianic stranger had disappeared from Nuevo México for eight months. What must it all mean?

By November 10, as he camped just south of Isleta, Vargas knew that something had gone terribly wrong in the colony he thought he had lastingly pacified. A messenger from Zia whom Vargas had sent north returned with the gloomy information that only three pueblos—San Felipe, Santa Ana, and Zia—remained loyal to the Spanish. In consequence, the inhabitants of these pueblos lived in daily fear of attacks by the Puebloans to the north and east.

Alarmed by this news, Vargas left his caravan behind and headed north with fifty soldiers. At San Felipe, loyal Puebloans gave him a much fuller picture of the unrest in the north. These informants told Vargas that the core of the resistance was made up of Tewas, Tanos, and northern Tiwas, though, much to the governor's consternation, these Puebloans had somehow added bands of their traditional enemies, the Navajo and Apache, to their considerable ranks. Visiting San Felipe, the still loyal governor of Pecos Pueblo, itself divided into pro- and anti-Spanish factions, delivered further intelligence from the eastern frontier. And he revealed to Vargas an event that had taken place the previous winter, which seemed at once the key to the chaos that had seized his supposedly tranquil colony.

The culprit was a man named Pedro de Tapia, a mestizo who had served as Vargas's interpreter the previous year. Tapia had since died at Cochiti, but his mischief lived on. According to the Pecos governor, sometime early in 1693 Tapia had met with a large gathering of Puebloan leaders at San Juan. In an official letter to his lieutenant governor, Vargas recounts what the Pecos man told him Tapia had wrought:

> He had told them that although I had pardoned them last year, I
> had said that when I returned this year, I would kill them and run
> every one of them through with a knife. I was only going to save
> and leave alive those from twelve to fourteen years of age and
> older [younger?]. With that diabolical speech, he planted this
> information among those nations.

Beside himself with dismay, Vargas added the imprecation, "may God Our Lord forgive him if this is true."

In the words of historian Elizabeth A. H. John, "[Tapia's] story was as tragically plausible as it was false, consistent with Spanish actions Pueblos had seen before and with their own ideas of vengeance." Throughout that winter and spring, the northern pueblos armed themselves, knapping arrowheads by the hundreds, against the attack Tapia had convinced them must come.

Vargas established a headquarters at Santo Domingo, from which he rode out on reconnaissance missions to the nearby pueblos. A small stream of emissaries trickled in from as far away as Tesuque. Vargas waxed eloquent as he sought to convince these men to go back to their home pueblos and to pledge the governor's undying determination to treat them kindly. No single pueblo, it seemed to him, was unanimous in its opposition to the Spaniards. Perhaps he could yet save the day by taking advantage of the ambivalence and factionalism among the Tewa, Tano, and northern Tiwa.

Meanwhile, the rest of the caravan of settlers, soldiers, and Indian auxiliaries had trundled north, joining Vargas at Santo Domingo. These pilgrims had already undergone severe privations. Despite their herd of cattle, they had grown so short of provisions that they had traded goods, including some of their weapons, for sacks of corn offered by "friendly" Indians met along the way.

On November 27, a heavy snow fell, the harbinger of what would prove one of the most bitter winters in New Mexico in recent memory. On December 3, sixteen men and women deserted the expedition, including seven soldiers, stealing clothing and horses as they fled. In a rage, Vargas condemned them as "criminals, delinquents, and traitors against his majesty," promising to mete out "whatever penalties I . . . find they have incurred according to the customs of war."

By early December, it was clear to Vargas that any showdown with the rebels would take place at Santa Fe. Rather than march on the former capital with a vanguard of trusted soldiers, as he had the previous year, he determined to push his whole entourage to Santa Fe, thereby making it clear to the recalcitrant Puebloans that he had come to plant a permanent settlement in their midst, not merely to reenact rituals of submission.

The caravan departed from Santo Domingo on December 10. Trudging through heavy snow, the settlers, soldiers, Indians, and wagons required nearly a week to cover the mere twenty-five miles to Santa Fe, on whose outskirts they arrived on December 16.

At this point, Vargas was still hopeful that the goodwill ambassadors he had sent ahead might have worked their charm, counteracting the evil prophecy of Pedro de Tapia. And when the Tewa and Tano greeted him at the ramparts not with screams and taunts, but with a "composed" dignity, his hope surged. For several hours, Vargas used every trick at his disposal. The priests sang psalms, knelt, and prayed aloud. The standard-bearer brandished the emblem of the Virgin Queen. A cross was erected. The father president of the friars formally handed Vargas a document solemnizing the repossession of Santa Fe.

Finally, through an interpreter, Vargas addressed the Puebloan leaders who had come to hear him out. Because he had pardoned these apostates the year before, he explained, the king in Spain was no longer angry with them. For Vargas's own part, "I had begun to call them my children again." The king "was also sending many priests so that the Indians might be Christians again." And the king had dispatched Vargas and his soldiers to protect them from the Apaches.

The Puebloan leaders must have listened in stoic silence, for Vargas does not record their response. It was, however, chilly enough that the governor, rather than force his way into the villa he had just formally repossessed, moved his whole caravan to the foot of a mountain to the north to pitch camp in the snow—"two harquebus shots away" from the walled town.

So began another impasse, one that would last for thirteen days—nearly two weeks of incessant misery for the freezing colonists. Already, however, by the second day—thanks once more to the governor of Pecos, who was playing a perilous role as a double agent for the Spaniards—Vargas learned of "the treachery of the Tewa and Tano nations," who had entered into a pact with Picuris and Apache men to attack and wipe out the Spanish camp. The ringleaders of this plot included the same "chief," Domingo, from Tesuque, who had tried to talk his fellow Puebloans into submitting the year before, and Antonio Bolsas, the fluent Spanish speaker who had translated from the ramparts in 1692. "He is the worst," Vargas inveighed, referring to Bolsas, "and the one who incited these people."

During those two weeks, there was a curious succession of visits and exchanges between the Spaniards and the Puebloans, chess moves in an endgame that was not likely to end in a draw. Vargas negotiated with Bolsas to trade five beeves for eight sacks of corn and a modicum of beans. The Indians handed over their foodstuffs, the governor noted, "with scorn and disrespect." The corn turned out to be the crop from 1692, not from the previous autumn's harvest. (Whether Vargas realized just how short the Puebloans were themselves on the all-precious maize, he does not indicate.)

The Spaniards were daunted by the "coolness" of the Tewa and Tano, who had the audacity to walk among the tents, observing their enemy at close hand. "They amuse themselves," wrote Vargas, "by going about in groups during the day, searching the men's camps."

The tent-bound colonists needed a church in which to pray and to observe Mass. With Castilian arrogance, Vargas demanded labor and materials from the Puebloans to refurbish the original San Miguel chapel, burned during the Revolt, which actually lay within the ramparts of Santa Fe. (Today's handsome small adobe mission of the same name, billed as the oldest church in the United States, stands on or near the site of the original San Miguel.) The blind certainty of his faith breathes in Vargas's haughty injunction to his Puebloan laborers: "I also advised them to go to work with pleasure, because it was not work to make the house of God and His Mother, the most holy Virgin, Our Lady, who was closed up in a wagon. If a lady came, they had a duty to give her a house."

There was too much snow and cold, however, for the Indians to venture into the mountains to cut the beams needed to restore the church. The "governor" of Santa Fe, known only as José, and Antonio Bolsas, offered the Spaniards a kiva instead. Vargas accepted, ordering a door to be cut in the kiva, its walls whitewashed, and an altar constructed of adobe inside. The Puebloans complied, only to have the Franciscan father president order "that the divine offices of the holy sacrifice of the mass not be celebrated in the kiva, because it had been a place the Indians had used for their prohibited juntas." All this must have sorely tested Puebloan patience.

Among the colonists was a substantial number of families who had been dispossessed of their houses and belongings in 1680. Known

as the Cabildo of Santa Fe, this group grew irritated with what it per-
ceived as Vargas's dithering. On December 17, the Cabildo presented a
petition to the governor, demanding that he kick the Indians out of
Santa Fe and send them back to their proper homes in the Galisteo
Basin, so that they, the original settlers, could regain the *casas reales*.
Vargas wisely temporized.

Each day, the Tewa and Tano inside the ramparts were sending
messengers north and east to call for reinforcements from the far-
flung pueblos. Vargas countered with a bluff, telling José and Bolsas
that 200 soldiers were at that very moment hastening north to join the
governor's force camped north of town.

Meanwhile, the snowbound colonists were genuinely suffering.
Some sort of epidemic had broken out within their squalid camp.
Not only children but a number of priests fell ill. On December 23,
the standard-bearer presented Vargas with a petition on behalf of the
colonists, complaining of the "insufferable winds and freezing weather.
. . . All the children and the rest of the young people could die because
of it, as many already have." What must have been the most dismal
Christmas any of the colonists had ever celebrated came and went
unobserved, at least in Vargas's journal and dispatches.

For once, the resolute governor seemed at a loss for solutions. The
peaceful repossession of Santa Fe now seemed a pipe dream. In the
end, the Puebloans made Vargas's decision for him.

On December 27, scouts for the governor reported unmistakable
signs that the Indians were gearing up for war—even though they
feigned that they were merely arming themselves to go into the hills to
hunt for deer. The next day, a blind Puebloan whom Vargas had enlisted
as a spy recounted that he had overheard José, the governor, declare that
Vargas's claim that 200 soldiers were coming to reinforce the Spaniards
was a lie. José declared himself for war. When others demurred, fearing
that their children might die in a battle, the Puebloan leader angrily
told them "that now was not the time to be looking after their children,
but for fighting to the death and killing us all."

Later on the 28th, Vargas sent his trusted captain, Roque Madrid, to approach the town walls. Madrid returned to report the main gate shut fast, the warriors manning the ramparts "with great shouting, provoking the battle."

Vargas made one last attempt to counter the threat with eloquence rather than arms. In front of the main rampart, he spoke through an interpreter. "If they did not see the harm they were doing to their people," he pleaded, "I regretted it, because they were Christians and most of them my compadres. Everyone would be lost. They should come to their senses and come down; I would pardon them." Antonio Bolsas replied that he would discuss the offer with his people, and come to Vargas's tent later that day to render their decision.

Vargas returned to his camp to wait. Bolsas never came. As night fell, in the distance the Spaniards heard only "furious screaming and war chants."

At dawn on December 29, the Puebloan defenders ranged the tops of the ramparts, shouting down their most contemptuous taunts yet, bragging that their allies from the north were on the point of joining them. "They would kill us without sparing anyone," Vargas paraphrased their vow, "and keep the religious for a time as their slaves, making them carry firewood from the monte, and later they would kill them all, as they did the first time."

The battle began in mid-morning, as the warriors unleashed volleys of "darts, arrows, and many rocks from slings." At last galvanized to action, Vargas cried out to his soldiers, "Santiago, Santiago, kill those rebels!"—Santiago, or Saint James, being the apparition who regularly appeared on horseback to turn the tide of Spanish battles.

One marvels, in retrospect, at the depths of Puebloan fatalism. Bows and arrows, slingshot stones, and even the occasional inexpertly wielded harquebus were no match for Spanish guns and swords and cannons and chain mail. The natives of New Mexico never had won, and never would win, a pitched battle on level ground against the skilled and disciplined Spanish army. The genius of the Puebloans lay in the sudden unexpected attack, the ambush, the chase, as they had proved on August 10, 1680. Yet perhaps fatalism is the wrong word. There may be something noble, after all, in choosing death and defeat in battle as preferable to servitude and vassalage, to the suppression of every last vestige of the religion that had sustained the people for centuries.

Vargas attacked the main gate. Axes could not demolish the heavy wooden door, so the Spaniards set fire to it. By mid-afternoon, they had breached the ramparts and entered the stronghold of Santa Fe. Many Puebloan arrows and stones struck home, but if Vargas is to be believed, not a single soldier was seriously injured. As the Spaniards rampaged through the city, mortars fired from outside tore new holes in the walls. Soon the soldiers held half the town, with their enemy cornered in the other half.

Seeing the Puebloans' allies ranged on nearby hilltops, Vargas sent three squadrons and a horde of Indian auxiliaries to put them to flight. Five of the enemy were killed in that rout, four more inside the villa.

By nightfall, the Spaniards were effectively in control of Santa Fe. The Puebloans trapped inside used darkness to cover their efforts to hide in cubbyholes and kivas. Vargas posted guards through the night, to keep the Puebloans from fleeing.

In the morning, the governor raised a flag of triumph over the smoldering town. Some of the Puebloans surrendered; others were ferreted out like rabbits from their holes. Vargas assembled his prisoners, including Antonio Bolsas, and harangued them through his interpreter. Not only had these wretches "lapsed into their apostasy and risen up against his majesty," but they had committed such unpardonable heresies as "having beaten with macanas [clubs] a very holy image of Our Lady that a settler left in the home of an Indian" and "having thrown stones at the holy cross they had placed in the patio the day of my first entrada, breaking it into pieces." "Overcome by the devil," Vargas ranted on, "they had uttered countless blasphemies, saying that the devil could do more than God and the Virgin."

Gone from Vargas's spirit were the "tenderness and love" he had ceaselessly professed to feel for his "children" all through the previous year. Instead, he ordered the instant execution of every warrior who had fought against the Spaniards. The soldiers led the prisoners out of the plaza. The priests absolved them. Then Roque Madrid commanded the firing squad. In a matter of minutes, seventy Puebloan warriors lay dead in the dirt.

At dawn, the governor, José, had hanged himself with a noose and an iron bar. To the shocked survivors, the hasty executions only proved that Pedro de Tapia's dark prophecy of the previous winter had come true after all. But Vargas's reprisal was not finished. As the women and children huddled outside the ramparts, the governor announced that every one of them would be sentenced to ten years' servitude. He would leave it up to the colonists to distribute the women and children among their new masters.

After an interval of thirteen years, Santa Fe once again belonged to the Spanish. In his official dispatch reporting the victory, Vargas scolded himself for his leniency. In view of the Puebloans' "rebellion and apostasy," Vargas wrote, "this punishment was not what they deserved, which was perpetual slavery."

Each weekday morning, every commuter bombing along State Highway 502 on his way from Santa Fe to Los Alamos comes in sight, just before he crosses the Rio Grande at Otowi bridge, of a handsome butte just two miles away off his right-hand side. If, instead of climbing the Pajarito Plateau toward Los Alamos, he turns north at the junction with Route 30 to head toward Española, he passes less than a mile away from the same butte on the west side.

An extrusion of basalt, the butte stands alone above the fertile plain of the Rio Grande valley. Its level summit, a little less than half a mile long, looms some 400 feet above its base, guarded on most flanks by dark cliffs, though here and there a talus slope wending between the cliffs gives access, not only by foot but on horseback, to the summit plateau.

The butte is called Black Mesa or San Ildefonso Mesa. According to the inhabitants of San Ildefonso Pueblo, which nestles among the cottonwoods on the east bank of the Rio Grande just south of the formation, that mesa had served as a bastion of safety for as long as anyone could remember. But after the taking of Santa Fe and the execution of the seventy warriors on December 29–30, 1693, Black Mesa became the most important refuge in the Tewa world.

To its summit, after Vargas's attack on the former capital of New Mexico, flocked hundreds of men, women, and children from San Ildefonso, Pojoaque, Santa Clara, and Tesuque pueblos, as well as from two pueblos that no longer exist, Cuyamunge and Jacona. Vargas was well aware of the migration. And, weary though he was from a battle he had hoped to avoid, he knew that to complete the pacification of the colony—in short, to accomplish the reconquest he had vainly believed he had achieved without firing a shot in 1692—he must march on Black Mesa and drive the refugees from its summit.

Often, as I drove Routes 502 or 30, I pulled off the shoulder of the highway, got out of my car, and stared at Black Mesa through binoculars. I would have given much to hike to the top of the basalt butte, to stroll across its grassy scree and ponder the events of 1694, but I knew that I would never be allowed to visit the place. One April day, I turned off Highway 502 onto the dirt road that leads into the adobe heart of San Ildefonso. The man behind the desk in the visitor center was helpful and polite. When I mentioned my interest in the Pueblo Revolt, he said, "You might want to write a letter to the governor about that." He wrote the governor's name down in my notebook, and even supplied a fax number.

"I assume nobody's allowed to hike on Black Mesa?" I asked, already knowing the answer.

The man nodded. "It's very sensitive," he said.

It was not until February 26, 1694, that Vargas marched out of Santa Fe toward San Ildefonso. By now, the soldiers were short on corn, horses, and ammunition. The weather of this grim winter continued to dog the Spaniards' efforts: moving north, the troops were hindered by deep snow, and once they were established at the foot of Black Mesa, chilling rainstorms pelted their camp with monotonous regularity. On February 27, the Tewa warriors discovered the Spaniards at the base of the mesa. They uttered their usual "war-cries" and shouted boasts about the imminent arrival of allies from Jemez, Cochiti, other Keres pueblos, and even from Zuni, Hopi, and certain Apache bands. In Vargas's dispirited report, "They spoke shameful words, which led us to fire a few shots at the people, but the heavy snow did not permit beginning the war in the proper manner." Vargas estimated that a thousand refugees ranged the mesa top. (The number is almost certainly too high.)

Rather than launch an immediate attack, Vargas settled in to besiege Black Mesa. There was no spring on the mesa top: surely the soldiers could cut off the paths by which the natives must regularly descend to fill their vessels with stream water. The rainstorms, however, worked in the refugees' favor, and under cover of night and inclement weather, the Puebloans displayed a formidable talent for sneaking down to the water sources undetected. Meanwhile, Vargas sent off scouting parties in search of horses and stores of maize in the abandoned pueblos.

On March 4, Vargas made his one concerted effort to take the mesa top. It began badly, when a soldier fired a mortar only to have the cannon burst into pieces, badly injuring him. Sixty men charged the front of the mesa, while Vargas led fifteen others on a clandestine circuit to the opposite side. It was a strategy he would apply again in attacking butte-top refuges.

For once, however, higher ground gave the Puebloans a real advantage. The slingshot rocks, so ineffective when flung from the Santa Fe ramparts, took their toll from the cliff top. In the skirmish, Vargas estimated that his men killed twelve to fifteen Indians, but at the cost of more than twenty soldiers wounded, two gravely. Vargas ordered a retreat.

Twice more during the following week, Vargas attempted attacks, even employing ladders to try to clamber up the guardian cliffs. Twice he was repulsed by warriors who not only shot arrows and slung rocks, but rolled boulders down upon the vulnerable troops.

Vargas stuck it out until March 18. Recognizing that in nearly three weeks of siege and intermittent attack, he had accomplished little, his ammunition reduced to a half-box of gunpowder and very little lead, he abandoned the siege of Black Mesa. His journal of the campaign does not acknowledge a defeat: instead, the governor obfuscates his setback as he fusses over future logistics. But the entries during those three weeks of failure and cold have a demoralized, frustrated tone otherwise almost absent from Vargas's own record of the reconquest.

The Tewa atop the mesa must have rejoiced as they saw the Spanish plod southward back toward Santa Fe. For yet a while, they had earned the freedom for which their brothers in the capital had paid with their lives.

So commenced the pattern of warfare that would stretch through much of the fateful year of 1694, from late February to mid-September. All over the Pueblo world, the resisters had taken refuge on high, well-defended aeries such as Black Mesa. If Vargas really hoped to subdue the colony he thought he had already won, he must march from one end of New Mexico to the other, and devise a way to take the higher ground from warriors who, however inferior their weapons, were highly skilled at fending off attacks from below.

To comprehend the Pueblo Revolt, it seemed vital for me to visit at least one or two of these "refugee pueblos," as archaeologists designate them. Nearly all of them, however, lie on Puebloan land, and are thus off-limits to Anglo intruders. For a few weeks in the fall of 2003, nonetheless, I had hopes of being allowed to climb to the top of Dowa Yalanne, the proud butte that stands a full thousand feet above present-day Zuni. In 1692, on his pacification tour, Vargas had found virtually all the Zuni in residence on top of the mesa, where they had remained ever since 1680, living in constant fear of Spanish reprisal.

Though wary, the Puebloans had allowed the governor to climb to the summit of Dowa Yalanne that November, where the friars had performed their absolutions and baptisms.

My hopes were buoyed by the fact that in 1989, archaeologist T. J. Ferguson had been allowed—indeed, encouraged by the Zuni tribal council—to make an extensive survey of the mesa top, on which he found the ruins of some 559 rooms that might have housed 1,120 people. Yet in 2003, when I contacted Ferguson, who runs a contract archaeology firm based in Tucson, he told me that just the previous year, when he had thought to hike to the top of Dowa Yalanne to show a colleague the ruins he had surveyed, he had been denied permission.

The spunky guide Lena Tsethlikia, who had used her "grandfather clause" to take me on a tour of Hawikuh, where the Moor Esteban had made his fatal first contact with Puebloans in 1539, thought it might be possible to guide me up Dowa Yalanne. She herself had been to the top only once, and was eager to repeat the trip. We fixed a day for the outing, but at the last minute, someone in the visitor center balked. It would be better if I wrote a letter requesting permission from the Zuni director of tourism, Tom Kennedy. I dutifully wrote such a letter, then, as I expected, heard nothing.

Finally I phoned Tsethlikia. She sounded a bit put out by her own pueblo's recalcitrance. "Just the other day," she told me, "I went to the tribal council to ask for your permission. But Tom Kennedy said we couldn't go. The place was 'culturally sensitive.' He said, 'Why would he want to go, anyway?'

"I said, 'If he's writing a book, he needs to see what the Zuni saw.'"

Kennedy was not convinced. According to Tsethlikia, he admonished, "It's very unsafe up there. People shouldn't even want to go up there."

Two important refugee pueblos, however, lie not on Puebloan land, but in the Santa Fe National Forest. One of them is known as Old Kotyiti. Not only had it served as the refuge for the Cochiti people during the reconquest: it had been an important ancestral pueblo along the route of the people's slow migration, from the fourteenth century onward, south to their present pueblo, which stands on a low plain just west of the Rio Grande.

Virtually all of the thousands of small ruins in Bandelier National Monument, as well as four or five major villages, are ancestral to Cochiti. Exactly why the people moved south over the centuries, at last abandoning the Pajarito Plateau, we do not know. Cochiti men still visit and curate shrines—among them, the astonishing Shrine of the Stone Lions—within the monument. Charles Lummis, that early enthusiast and popularizer of the Southwest, imagined a steady exodus southward from Frijoles Canyon, with its central ruin, Tyuonyi, all the way to present-day Cochiti. Tyuonyi—the tourist cynosure of Bandelier National Monument today—was excavated and stabilized by Lummis's friend, Edgar Hewett, around 1910, but in such a heavy-handed way that all kinds of crucial information have been irretrievably lost.

Lummis, whose flights of celebratory prose are sui generis, sang "The Wanderings of Cochiti," as he titled the essay he published in *The Land of Poco Tiempo* (1893), in all but Homeric strophes. Pausing to ponder the ruins of Yapashi, one of the major pueblos along the route of the slow drift southward, he wondered out loud:

> Here on the grim mesa, amid a wilderness of appalling solitude, they worried out the tufa blocks, and builded their fortress-city, and fended off the prowling Navajo, and fought to water and home again, and slept with an arrow on the string. How many generations of bronze babies frolicked in this lap of danger; and rose to arrowy youth that loved between sieges; and to gray-heads that watched and counselled; and to still clay that cuddled to the long sleep in rooms thenceforth sealed forever, there is no reckoning.

The straightforward sequence from north to south of Cochiti habitation centers that Lummis outlined a century ago, with Old Koty-iti the last stronghold before the people came down from the mesa to live beside the Rio Grande, turns out, in the light of modern archaeology, to be far murkier than the writer guessed. That Old Kotyiti was the last high village occupied along the route of the migration, however, seems borne out by an old tale collected at Cochiti by Ruth Benedict and published in 1931. In "How They Came Down from the Mesa," Benedict's informant tells her,

> Long ago the Cochiti Indians lived on the top of Cochiti Mesa. They had to carry all their water to the top of the mesa, and when they fought the Navaho, they had to come way down where Cochiti is now to have the battle.... They saw that this was too hard work for them, so they thought of moving down off the mesa.

After only two days in the lowlands, however, the Cochiti grew homesick for their high fastness, and returned en masse. During an unspecified length of time, they vacillated, coming down off the mesa, then climbing back on top to rebuild their houses. This period of indecision clearly came after 1598, for according to Benedict's informant, "They said that they were going to put a priest here for them in this place.... All the people were baptized." With the fluidity of oral tradition, the conversions flow seamlessly into the Pueblo Revolt. Having been given a *santu*, an image of the Virgin of Guadalupe, "They went into the church where the santu was and they broke it to bits and chewed it. It was sweet and they ate it all up. After they had done this they all ran back to the mesa."

The tale flows and ebbs in its timeless way. The people are forced by the Spaniards back to the plain beside the Rio Grande. They kill a priest by barricading him inside his house, then throwing chile seeds down the chimney, creating an acrid smoke that suffocates him.

The chronology of the old story is confusing, but its polar values are clear. The lowland pueblo, the site of Cochiti today, is all tied up with the Spanish thrall. The pueblo atop the mesa, Old Kotyiti, means freedom.

Mike Bremer is the Heritage Program manager for the Santa Fe National Forest, and an archaeologist fully conversant with the Pueblo Revolt. On a mild day in April 2003, he guided me through the forest to the mesa top on which stand the ruins of Old Kotyiti. Used to working closely with Cochiti Pueblo, Bremer had left an invitation at the tribal headquarters for any Cochiti who wished to join us, but when we met at the convenience store that serves as an informal rendezvous post, no representatives from the pueblo had showed up.

We drove dirt roads up a series of canyons north of Cochiti, then parked in the driveway of an old ranch, a disused apple farm that now belongs to the University of New Mexico. The orchard through which we walked was snowy with new white apple blossoms. We crossed a rusty barbed wire fence and entered a dark, north-facing stand of piñons, scrub oaks, and junipers. Here and there, hardened cakes of winter snow still clung to matted patches of dead leaves. Bremer picked up a faint, zigzagging trail. I would never have found the path by myself, yet this was one of two routes by which the Cochiti had climbed the mesa for centuries, and still climbed it on the occasional pilgrimage to the ruins that validate their legends.

We switchbacked our way some 600 feet up the inner crook of an elbow of canyon wall, emerging at last on a flat saddle. From there, it was but a ten-minute walk southeast to the near edge of Old Kotyiti.

In the mid-1990s, with the benediction of the pueblo, University of Pennsylvania archaeologist Robert W. Preucel had led an intensive survey of Old Kotyiti. This research project was a tour de force in the "new" archaeology being practiced in such culturally sensitive regions as the Southwest. Without turning a single spadeful of earth, Preucel's teams made an exquisitely subtle and comprehensive study of the architecture as they found it, recording virtually every stone of every tumbled wall where it lay in the grasses. (Here, as I would see, was the antithesis of the kind of gleeful overinterpretation—destruction in the name of restoration—practiced by Hewett at Tyuonyi and by other overconfident excavators shortly after the turn of the twentieth century.) With us, Bremer and I carried photocopies not only of Preucel's report, but of Vargas's published journals.

The ruins of Old Kotyiti are laid out in a symmetrical quadrangle of roomblocks, divided down the middle by yet another roomblock. Each half encloses a plaza, each of which is centered by the depression of a kiva still plainly visible in the earth. With Preucel's map in hand, we could easily identify single rooms, numbered by the survey teams. I was amazed to see some walls still standing as tall as six feet.

"That's what happens when you burn a place," Bremer explained. "Turns it into pottery. This is one giant piece of pottery."

Vargas had first come to Old Kotyiti in October 1692, during his pacification tour of the pueblos. On finding Santo Domingo and Cochiti abandoned, he learned that people from several pueblos were ensconced on the high mesa. With five squadrons, he advanced to the foot of the mesa, then climbed it, probably by the southern trail, on the opposite side from the path Bremer and I had followed. Although he heard war songs being chanted from above, Vargas was greeted on top in peaceable fashion. There was even a large cross erected at the entrance to the pueblo. Father Francisco Corvera baptized 103 Puebloans here. On asking which pueblos were represented on the mesa top, Vargas was told that the people came from Cochiti, San Felipe, and San Marcos. Why had they taken refuge? Vargas was told that these Keresans feared an attack by their enemies, the Tewa and Tano. The governor reassured them that Spanish soldiers would make it safe for the Puebloans to return to their lowland villages.

Yet two years later, Vargas once again found a large horde congregated on top of the ancestral Cochiti mesa. These refugees, he had been told, had made many depredations upon Zia, Santa Ana, and San Felipe, the only three pueblos still loyal to the Spanish when Vargas had returned to New Mexico the previous October. In mid-April 1694, Vargas marched out of Santa Fe, in an angry mood after his failed siege at Black Mesa. He had fifty soldiers, but the key to his eventual success at Old Kotyiti lay in a body of 100 Puebloan auxiliaries. These were warriors from the pueblos of Zia, Santa Ana, and San Felipe, and they knew the mesa well.

In just such a fashion—using one defeated tribe as allies in the attack on the next—Cortés had performed his daring conquest of Mexico in 1521. By the end of the seventeenth century, Cortés had become legend among the Spaniards, his tactics a textbook for latter-day conquerors such as Vargas. In the dark of night early on April 17, Vargas divided his forces into three parties to sneak to the top of the mesa by three different routes.

As we strolled through the ruin, I read Vargas's campaign journal out loud. "The enemy took up arms, resisting and firing on the path up where I was. The captain, officers, and other soldiers courageously responded. . . . Because they were assailed, the people outside could not wait for our men to tear them to pieces and kill them. Therefore, they fled."

The bland smugness of Vargas's diary had Bremer shaking his head. "This guy sounds a lot like George W.," said the archaeologist. It was just weeks after Bush's invasion of Iraq.

With surprising ease, in only a few hours Vargas seized Old Kotyiti. The governor claimed to have captured 342 "noncombatants"—women, children, and old men—whom he sequestered inside a kiva. This was manifestly impossible, in view of the small size of the two kiva depressions we had found. Perhaps the 342 prisoners had been confined in one of the plazas. Only eight Puebloans were killed in the battle. "Thirteen warriors were also captured," I read on. "As soon as one of the two reverend missionary fathers and chaplains who came from the camp had absolved them, I ordered them shot without delay."

"God bless you. Bam!" editorialized Bremer, in disgust.

Vargas also rounded up 900 sheep and goats, as well as seventy horses. Here, as elsewhere in New Mexico, was vivid proof of the failure of the Puebloans, during their twelve years of freedom, to abide by Popé's extremist dictum that the people abjure everything, from wheat to cattle, introduced by the Spaniards.

The conquest of Old Kotyiti, however, proved less simple than Vargas at first believed. In the initial attack, most of the warriors had fled to higher ground. Bremer pointed to the northwest, where a series of cliffs guarded an extension of the mesa, some 200 feet higher than the site of the ruin. "Bob Preucel thinks the warriors were up there, hiding in the trees," said Bremer, "watching Vargas do his thing in the pueblo down here."

On April 21 came the counterattack. "With furious war-cries and a large number of people," according to Vargas, these warriors swarmed into Old Kotyiti and engaged the soldiers in hand-to-hand combat. Though taken by surprise, the Spaniards "bravely went on to offer resistance and succeeded, with everyone fighting courageously." Four Puebloan warriors were killed, but in the pandemonium more than half the 342 captives escaped. To that extent, the Keresan counterattack had succeeded.

Vargas lingered on at Old Kotyiti for three more days. Before climbing down from the mesa, he set fire to the village—preserving its walls, ironically, for Bremer and me to admire 309 years later.

We walked to the south rim of the mesa, sat on the edge of the cliff, and ate lunch. The drought of the previous several years had unleashed a scourge of pine beetles all over the Southwest. Nearly all the piñons here were dead or dying, their brown needles giving a washed-out pallor to the normally verdant forest. With the uneven battle that had raged a hundred yards to the north in our heads, we stared down on the dusty plain more than a thousand feet below. In the distance, we could see the huddle of adobe houses that is Cochiti today. The silence around us seemed to shimmer with the sense of what the Puebloans had lost here in 1694, in the third year of Vargas's bloodless reconquest.

The other refugee pueblo in the national forest is the one to which the people of Jemez had fled after 1692. Long before coming to New Mexico, I had recognized that the confrontation played out on that mesa top in

July 1694 was the pivot point of the whole complicated, tragic reconquest. Before my ill-starred meeting with the Jemez Cultural Committee, I had hoped to ask someone from the pueblo to hike up to the refuge with me. But that Tuesday night in the conference room of the governor's office, once I felt the distrust arrowing toward me from each of the nine Jemez men who were questioning the very propriety of my writing a book about the Revolt, I bit my tongue about the refugee pueblo.

Two months before that meeting, I had had breakfast in Santa Fe with Mike Bremer and his close friend and colleague, Mike Elliott. Resource area archaeologist for the Santa Fe National Forest, Elliott had spent years building a fragile trust at Jemez, managing through tireless consultation to convince at least several members of the pueblo's Department of Resource Protection that archaeology and native tradition need not always be at irreconcilable loggerheads. Elliott would be one of the two forest archaeologists asked to leave the room when I spoke to the Cultural Committee.

At breakfast, both men had impressed on me just how powerful a place for the Jemez was the mesa-top ruin Vargas had attacked on July 24, 1694. I agreed not even to mention the Jemez name of the pueblo in print. Instead, I would call it, as the Spaniards consistently referred to it, "the Pueblo on the Peñol"—"peñol" being an old Spanish word for butte or steep-sided mesa.

"You have to understand," said Bremer. "For the Jemez, that site is like their Gettysburg battlefield—"

"Or their Sistine Chapel," Elliott emended.

"Their Sistine Chapel and their Gettysburg battlefield all rolled into one," Bremer concluded.

In the end, I climbed up to the Pueblo on the Peñol alone. I chose the difficult back-side route, which had proved the key to Vargas's success. Low-angle slopes gave way to a steep, gravelly scree, then to a series of cliffs through which I made a devious scramble. A thousand feet above the valley floor, I crested the rim of the mesa, then walked north to the natural gateway that guarded the back-side approach.

Suddenly, before my feet, I saw something that made my throat catch in sorrow. A pile of smooth, round stones, ranging in hue from gray to brown to reddish orange, spilled toward the gateway. I picked up one of the stones, held it in my palm, and felt, across the span of more than three centuries, the weight of doom.

These stones were the very missiles the defenders of the peñol had used in their slingshots, or simply hurled at the Spaniards as they climbed toward the rim. I turned the round stone, about the size of a baseball, in my hand, as I tried to imagine flinging it off the cliff at a mounted, armored invader. The cliffs and bedrock of the peñol are made of a brown volcanic tuff—too light a rock to serve as an effective weapon. The Jemez had instead gathered hundreds of sandstone river cobbles from the streambeds below, carried them a thousand feet up the mesa, and piled them at the top of the trail that climbs the mesa from the north.

Vargas had approached the Pueblo on the Peñol by way of Zia, Jemez's neighbor pueblo only ten miles to the south. Despite that proximity, the two peoples speak completely different languages (Keresan and Towa, respectively). They had united in 1680 to drive the Spanish out of New Mexico, but Zia and Jemez had a long history of friction and even warfare against each other, exacerbated in 1694 by Zia's having turned loyal to the Spanish. Vargas thus had no trouble recruiting 100 Zia warriors to supplement his mounted soldiers, whose numbers by July had swelled to 120.

The refuge site had been well chosen. Sheer cliffs plunging from the rim defended the triangular mesa on all sides. There were only the two routes to the top: an obvious trail on the south, and the devious, secret path I had followed up the back side. It was the Zia warriors who told Vargas about the latter route.

The governor had approached the Pueblo on the Peñol with the utmost stealth. Under cover of darkness on the night of July 23, he hid his forces behind a low butte beside the Jemez River. At one o'clock in the morning of July 24, the governor sent his captain, Eusebio de Vargas (apparently not a relative), with twenty-five soldiers and the 100

Zia allies, to slink north and attack the peñol from the rear. Vargas himself, with his main army, stayed in hiding until Venus rose in the east, then started up the southern trail on horseback.

From the northern gateway, I rim-walked on the west edge of the peñol toward its southern point. All along the way, wherever the cliffs below the rim were less than sheer and unclimbable, the Jemez had piled up breastworks of tuff stones and boulders, behind which they might hide and fire upon an enemy clambering up the mesa. After I had walked a mile and a half, I arrived at the southern gateway. Here, too, I found a pile of river cobbles, the stones the defenders had not had time to throw or shoot. I climbed fifty yards down the approach trail. There were stones at every hand—the missiles the Puebloans had indeed launched, but which had failed to stem the Spanish onslaught.

I returned to the gateway and stood for a moment, gazing down at the twin streams merging in the middle distance, fringed by cottonwoods just coming into new leaf. Far to the south I saw the blue skyline of Sandía Mountain, Albuquerque's backyard playground. To my east, I heard the whine of a semi gearing down on the highway that spilled from the mountains. At the moment, however, I had the mesa to myself.

On July 24, 1694, it was the same old story—arrows and stones no match for harquebuses, swords, and chain mail. As Vargas wrote in his journal, "Although they hurled some large stones and rocks, as well as shooting many arrows, they were valiantly resisted."

From the southern gateway, I walked a hundred yards north. Along either side of a shallow draw (across which the faint vestiges of check-dams testified to a desperate effort to trap rainwater on the springless mesa top), I saw the collapsed ruins of some 250 rooms, built of squared-off chunks of tuff mortared with mud. Unlike Old Kotyiti, this pueblo looked quickly and haphazardly built.

The twin-pronged attack, with both forces reaching the mesa rim at the same moment, was devastatingly efficient. Now, shortly after daybreak, Vargas's soldiers swarmed through the village, killing as they went. I found one four-foot wall, still standing, that was punctured with a small aperture, through which a crouching Jemez warrior had shot arrows that July day. "From their loopholes," Vargas wrote, "they had wounded and injured many, although not seriously."

The Spaniards enacted a methodical slaughter. Fifty-five men, by Vargas's count, were shot or lanced to death at close quarters. Once the killing was largely finished, Vargas set fire to the pueblo. Four men and a woman were burned alive in the rooms where they tried to hide.

I wandered through the debris of the ruined village back to the south rim. Near the edge, natural hollows in the bedrock had been masoned into subterranean chambers. I clambered through several of these catacomb-like enclosures, finding a few charred roof beams, wondering whether it was here that the five luckless Jemez had been burned to death.

On this perfect day in early April, the mesa seemed a beautiful place. Yet as I stood in the middle of the burned ruin, my heart was heavy with the injustice of colonial history. No single place that I had visited in all my travels across New Mexico, poking among canyons and mesas for traces of the Revolt and its aftermath, had stunned me with the emotional force of the Pueblo on the Peñol. I was glad, after all, to be alone.

I hiked to the east rim and headed north along it. Here, too, piled barricades of tuff boulders and stones still vainly guarded every place on the mesa edge where a nimble attacker might have scrambled through the cliffs to gain the summit. Off this side, Vargas reported, seven fleeing Jemez warriors had jumped to their deaths. Their demise is corroborated by Jemez oral tradition, as recorded by Joe Sando in *Pueblo Nations*. Sando acknowledges the seven suicidal leaps, but then adds, "A likeness of San Diego soon appeared on the cliff. After that, those who jumped landed on their feet, and did not die. The likeness of San Diego is still visible today on the red rock cliffs." Early that morning, I had paused on my drive up the canyon east of the peñol to spy the apparition with binoculars, making out a natural discoloration on the smooth wall that indeed looked like a hooded, cloaked figure. (That a Catholic, Spanish saint should miraculously appear to save Puebloan lives was simply one more evidence of the syncretism, bizarre to my Western way of thinking, that by now seamlessly bridges two apparently irreconcilable faiths.)

The battle of July 24 was over by four in the afternoon. Without the loss of a single Spanish life, the attackers slew eighty-four Jemez men and took another 361 men, women, and children prisoner. Two combatants captured alive were baptized by a Franciscan friar and then shot on the spot.

Vargas was not surprised at his total victory. As he wrote in his journal, as soon as the battle was over, his men "gave thanks to His Divine Majesty and His most holy Mother for having obtained such success, also thanking ... the apostle Santiago, on the eve of his glorious day, on which he doubtless influenced with his sponsorship our most fortunate victory." July 25 is the feast day of Santiago, or Saint James, who once more had appeared on the battlefield to turn the tide in the Spaniards' favor.

In the aftermath of the massacre on the peñol, Vargas offered the captive Jemez men a devil's bargain. He would spare their lives in return for their pledge to fight by the soldiers' sides when they attacked the last remaining refugee pueblo, Black Mesa, to which Vargas had unsuccessfully laid siege the previous March. In the Pueblo Revolt, of course, the Jemez and the Tewa had been the staunchest of allies. Now, however, the demoralized Jemez men took up arms against their fellow Puebloans. The Zia, for their part, were only too glad to make war against the Tewa.

In September, with his vast new army, Vargas returned to Black Mesa. The antagonists fought several skirmishes before the Spanish settled once again into siege mode. This time, it worked. On September 9, the Tewa surrendered. Vargas's *reconquista* was complete.

Or so he thought. Vargas spent the rest of 1694 and all of the following year consolidating the little empire he had made of New Mexico. In April 1695, he founded the second Spanish town in the colony, at

Santa Cruz, thirty miles north of Santa Fe, in the heart of the Tewa country. By March 1696, Vargas could count 276 Spanish families settled in New Mexico, still far short of the 500 he believed necessary to ensure stability in the province.

To the far-flung pueblos, he once again sent Franciscan missionaries to tend to their Indian flocks. One by one, the churches burned in 1680 were rebuilt.

All was not well, however, in the battle-weary colony. The winter of 1695–96 proved as severe as the one two years before, when Vargas's soldiers had slogged through the snow to drive the Tewa and Tano out of Santa Fe and to besiege Black Mesa. With large portions of their stores of maize appropriated to feed the settlers, Puebloans once more began to starve.

Somehow, from Taos to Hopi, messengers carried the tidings of the most recalcitrant leaders and shamans, urging one more union of the pueblos to rise against their despised masters. There was no knotted cord this time, and the imminent revolt was hardly a secret. As early as December 1695, missionaries sent alarming letters to Santa Fe warning of the Puebloan unrest, begging the governor to send soldiers to protect the vulnerable friars. Vargas was slow to act, however. Leery that the approach of mounted troops might itself instigate warfare, he believed instead that he could ride from one pueblo to another and talk the natives back into docile acceptance of Spanish rule.

The inevitable happened. On June 4, 1696, in a coordinated effort, the Puebloans killed five friars and twenty-one settlers across a broad swath of New Mexico. All but five pueblos participated in this last-ditch rebellion, but those five—Zia, Santa Ana, and San Felipe, loyal as ever, but also Pecos and Tesuque—furnished Vargas with invaluable allies in putting down the revolt.

Once more, the Very Rev. James H. Defouri, writing in 1893, employed his omniscient retrospect to witness the lamentable martyrdoms of the friars. At the pueblo of San Cristóbal, on June 4, Fray José de Arvisu and Fray Antonio Carboneli (visiting from Taos) were clubbed to death by Indians who "wished to live a licentious life, and indulge in all the impurities of their devilish rites." Father Arvisu had written to Vargas, warning of the impending uprising, but, according to Defouri, "not the least precaution was taken by the Governor to hinder the shedding of blood. He was too busy at the time . . . in making money for his latter days."

At Nambé, two friars asleep in their convent were killed when the Indians barricaded the windows and doors and set fire to the church. At Jemez, Fray Francisco Casañas de Jesús María was lured to the bedside of a purportedly ill man, but as he crossed the cemetery, he was set upon by Indians lurking in ambush, "and his head was smashed with sticks called *garrotes*." Wandering through the ruins of Giusewa, the missionized Jemez pueblo where Fray Casañas had ministered to his fickle children, Defouri was moved to a Victorian evocation of the place:

> The walls, nine feet in thickness, stand still skyward, the belfrey towers some fifty feet high; the cactus grows inside and outside; some rare birds build their nests there; the little stream, meandering at its base with its cool and clear waters, still murmurs, while the Rio Jemez, at a distance, is heard as it breaks its roaring waves against the bowlders. But in the old church, and its *camposanto*, all is silence! the silence of the tomb! The tourist walks cautiously about, knowing he is walking upon the blood of saints.

Once more, the rebellious Puebloans fled to the mountains. Refuge villages, including Old Kotyiti and the Jemez Pueblo on the Peñol, were reoccupied. For seven months, Vargas rode back and forth across the territory, engaging one enemy after another. The details of this final campaign form such a dreary rehash of the Spanish defeat of the rebels two years earlier, that it would only tire or depress the reader to lay them out in all their one-sided inevitability.

The turning point, however, came early, when Vargas marched out of Santa Cruz to confront a large body of Puebloans, mostly from San Juan and Santa Clara, who were hiding in the hills west of their home villages. Their leader was a brilliant Cochiti tactician named Lucas Naranjo. This warrior had set up an ambush from both rims of a narrow, forested canyon through which he was sure the Spaniards must pass. But the ambush was detected, and in the exchange of fire, a lucky shot by a Spanish soldier pierced Naranjo's neck, entering at the Adam's apple and emerging at the nape, killing him instantly. Another soldier cut off Naranjo's head. At the request of the Pecos auxiliaries, this bloody relic was given to them to carry back to their home pueblo, where it was displayed as a trophy of victory.

By December 1696, Vargas had finally conquered New Mexico for good. Many of the rebel leaders were killed in battle or executed, while yet more of the captives were delivered over as slaves to the colonists.

Vargas did not have long to relish his reconquest. His term as governor had officially ended in early 1696, but it was not until July 1697 that his successor, Rodríguez Cubero, arrived in Santa Fe to replace him. The proud Vargas refused to surrender his office. The Cabildo of Santa Fe, to whom he had given back the capital they had lost in 1680, turned against him. In the end, Cubero arrested the ex-governor, who languished (as Governor Peralta had some eight decades earlier) for three ignominious years in the Santa Fe prison, before he was freed and sent on his way back to Mexico.

The resilient Vargas managed, however, to have himself appointed to a second term as governor of New Mexico in 1703. Still fighting Indians, he fell ill, probably of dysentery or pneumonia, in the midst of a campaign against Apaches who had attacked the newly founded settlement of Bernalillo. His soldiers carried him back to that village, where he died in his bed five days later. He was sixty years old.

Never again would the natives of New Mexico organize a full-scale rebellion. But the story of the Pueblo Revolt does not end with Vargas's final triumph at the end of 1696. Even two years earlier, after his massacre of the Jemez refugees atop the Pueblo on the Peñol, Vargas learned that many warriors had escaped the battle and fled to the north and west. In 1696, this exodus of escapees was repeated many times over.

No aspect of the seventeenth-century history of New Mexico is more shadowy, more difficult to retrieve, than the subsequent fate of these vagabonds. We know the names of almost none of them. We have little idea whether they numbered in the scores, in the hundreds, or even in the thousands. Yet from the Indian point of view, these far-flung refugees are the last heroes of the Revolt, the last free Puebloans who lived beyond the reach of Spanish rule.

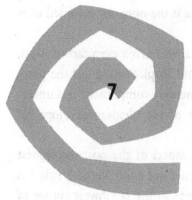

# 7

# DIASPORA

Some of these last refugees made their way to Acoma, which had served throughout the seventeenth century as a hiding place for Puebloan malcontents and rebel leaders. That cliff-top stronghold, the best-defended in the Southwest, had always proved problematic for the Spanish to subdue. As late as August 1696, after having routed the Tewa near Santa Cruz, Vargas marched on Acoma but decided against trying to attack the high pueblo. Instead, he tried to talk the Acomans into coming down to the plain below their millennial village to fight on level ground. Not surprisingly, not a single warrior descended. Vargas halfheartedly besieged Acoma, but after three days gave up and headed back toward Santa Fe. Acoma's eventual capitulation was more a matter of attrition than of conquest, for by December the cause of Puebloan independence had collapsed.

We know that in 1696 there were important men from Cochiti, Santo Domingo, and Jemez, as well as from other pueblos, living at Acoma. Their presence evidently caused tensions within the sky-top village, for in 1697, most of these nonlocal leaders, along with a number of disgruntled Acomans, seceded from the pueblo and established a new one, named Laguna, fourteen miles to the northeast. By 1707, Laguna's population had reached 330, or half that of Acoma. Among all twenty pueblos extant today, Laguna is the only one founded after the Pueblo Revolt.

Other refugees between 1694 and 1696 moved even farther west, taking up residence among the Zuni and Hopi. Sorting out the peregrinations of these wanderers is an immensely complicated and uncertain business—especially the patterns of resettlement at Hopi (of which, more below).

Yet by all odds the most puzzling aspect of the post-reconquest diaspora among the Puebloans who could not abide Vargas's rule has to do with a maze of canyons and mesas in the northwest corner of today's state of New Mexico. This region is known as Dinétah—the legendary homeland of the Navajo.

Dinétah is an area of roughly 2,500 square miles, encompassing a number of tributaries of the San Juan River, principally, from north to south, Los Pinos, La Jara, Frances, Gobernador, Cereza, Largo, and Blanco. The heart of the region lies some forty miles due east of the town of Farmington.

Nomadic tribes such as the Navajo are notoriously difficult to detect archaeologically. Sedentary peoples such as the Puebloans leave behind ruins, rock art, pottery, and other highly visible artifacts. Pre-ceramic nomads leave a tent ring here, the pieces of a woven basket there—in general, the most fugitive and poorly datable of remains.

We know from linguistic analysis that both Navajos and Apaches are Athapaskan peoples—the only Athapaskans, in fact, in the Southwest. As such, they are closely related to tribes that live today in subarctic Canada and Alaska. Virtually all experts believe that both the Navajos and the Apaches arrived from that far northern heartland relatively recently, but by what route and exactly when, the scholars disagree. The two major schools of thought have the Navajo migrating either via the Great Plains, only a few years before Coronado's *entrada* of 1540, or via the valleys and mountain ranges of Colorado, sometime before 1500.

These theories could not be further from the Navajos' own oral tradition. Nearly every elder will tell you that the Diné (as the people call themselves) have lived forever within the quadrangle formed by the four sacred mountains: Sierra Blanca, near Alamosa in southern Colorado; Mount Taylor, northeast of Grants, New Mexico; the San Francisco Peaks, just north of Flagstaff, Arizona; and Hesperus Peak, northwest of Durango, Colorado.

When the Navajo first entered Dinétah is also an unsolved question—at least for Western archaeologists. It is here, however, that the earliest indisputably Navajo remains have been found. These are four traditional dwellings erected near the San Juan River, called forked-stick hogans, dated by tree rings to the last half of the sixteenth century. (A ruined forked-stick hogan looks something like a small teepee reduced to its skeletal framework—the leaning wooden poles that meet in a central apex. The sod and earth that once sealed the dwelling tight have typically been washed away by rain and wind. The doorway almost always faces east.)

Among the Dinétah sites, however, stand some of the most bizarre Native American structures in all the Southwest, which, taken together with other relics and rock art, compose a profound historical conundrum—one that is all tied up with the shadowy Puebloan fugitives from Vargas's vengeance after 1694.

In all my years of wandering across the Southwest, I had never spent time in Dinétah. On several occasions, to be sure, I had driven U.S. Highway 64 between Dulce and Farmington, which bisects the Navajo homeland as it follows Gobernador Canyon almost down to its junction with the San Juan; but at sixty miles an hour, one cannot absorb the nuances of the place. It was not until February 2003 that I turned off the paved highway and started poking, sometimes at only five miles an hour, along the dirt roads that wriggle through Blanco, Largo, Cereza, and other canyons. And I parked my car often to hike up unnamed tributary canyons, my eyes peeled for the hidden wonders that books had taught me to expect.

The mesas here are low, seldom looming more than 500 feet above the winding, sandy arroyos that separate one tabletop from another. The region, though, has an austere beauty of its own. Untouched by tourism, it would be prime wilderness today, were it not for the rich deposit of natural gas beneath the ground. During my time hiking and camping there, I never saw another recreationalist, but the silence was disrupted each day by the wheeze and clank of gas wells, the whine of trucks careening down dirt roads trailing clouds of dust, as their drivers raced hither and yon to monitor the pumping stations. At night, however, the canyons reclaimed their ancestral peace and solitude.

The signature ruins of Dinétah, found virtually nowhere else in the Southwest, are called pueblitos. These are small, intensely defensive, stone-walled outposts characteristically perched atop massive boulders or diminutive buttes. Typically, they occupy every square foot of the surface of the sandstone pedestals on which they are built.

On one of my first days in Dinétah, I found two of the most handsome pueblitos among the more than 100 known to archaeologists. The two stand only about a mile apart, and both are within a mile of a dirt road that comes to a dead end at one of the furiously pumping gas wells atop a prong of a nameless mesa. Yet hidden by the trees, the pueblitos are not easy to find. And because all of Dinétah today is a patchwork of state, Bureau of Land Management, and private land—the latter festooned with locked gates and stern no-trespassing signs hanging from barbed wire fences—I had to make a clever and roundabout circuit on back roads simply to get near these ruins, whose locations I knew only vaguely, from a sketch map published in an old professional journal.

The first of the two pueblitos is a classic boulder-top refuge. The sandstone plug on which it stands has dead-vertical thirty-foot walls on all sides. There is only one weakness: the route by which the inhabitants gained the top after their daily treks to the fields and streams in the valley below. This route would require a rock climb, but for the fact that visitors—ranchers in the first decades of the twentieth century, I guessed—had laid several timbers against the cliff to make a shaky ladder.

On top, I found thirteen rooms masoned out of heavy, shaped stones, divided into two clusters, each with a tiny, plazalike space in the center. Several of the rooms had intact roofs. A hidden tunnel connected the main rooms in the upper cluster. Several still standing room walls stood absolutely flush to the cliff edge. The whole pueblito was like many a small site I had seen elsewhere in New Mexico, with its roomblocks and plazas, except that here the "village" had been squashed by the paucity of bedrock space into a kind of miniature version of a pueblo.

The view from this promontory was magnificent, with a 360-degree panorama overlooking the surrounding valleys. And that was the point: to be able to see the enemy coming, and if he approached, to pull up the ladders and fend him off with stones and arrows. But for the wildest of the thirteenth-century cliff dwellings I had found in southern Utah and northern Arizona—themselves built by Anasazi facing the hardest of times—this was one of the most self-evidently defensive living sites I had visited in the Southwest.

The other pueblito was not nearly so difficult of access: I could walk into it from the mesa shelving toward the cliff to the rim of which it clung. It was a much bigger village than the boulder-top refuge, which stood just out of sight to the south. And it was designed in a fashion utterly unlike anything else I had seen in New Mexico. Two huge stone walls, one wing fully 100 feet long, met in a shallow V. Still standing in places as tall as eight feet, this pair of walls guarded the ruin from potential intruders approaching from the mesa top. Inside this veritable fortress, a complex cluster of about a dozen masoned rooms huddled tight to the cliff edge. But in the open space between the fortress wall and the cluster of rooms, I saw the unmistakable remains of seven forked-stick hogans, six collapsed, one still standing.

Throughout the twentieth century, Dinétah was relatively neglected by archaeologists. Two of the first savants to work here, however, were giants in the field—Alfred Kidder and Earl Morris. (Morris, in fact, had surveyed the two pueblitos I visited that February day, and though he never published his results, his field notes were incorporated in a monograph a University of Colorado colleague brought out in 1965, after Morris's death.)

Marveling over these strange, defensive structures, Kidder and Morris came to what seemed an obvious conclusion. The pueblitos were fortresses against the Spanish built by the Pueblo refugees after 1694. The forked-stick hogans inside the walls of the "fortress" I had visited were, in Morris's view, evidence of later Navajo occupation after the Puebloans had abandoned these sites, or they were proof of a mixed Navajo-Puebloan coexistence in the decades after the late 1690s. This view quickly became accepted as orthodoxy. It would not be until the 1990s that researchers would begin to challenge the explanation.

One must pause here to ponder a glaring question. Ever since they had first reached its periphery, perhaps in the fifteenth century, the nomads who surrounded the Puebloan world—Navajos and Apaches, and to a lesser extent, Comanches and Utes—had been enemies of the sedentary corn growers, raiding at will, transforming their own cultures after the advent of the Spanish with stolen horses and guns. Why, even in extremis, would Puebloans fleeing Vargas after 1694 head straight to the bastion of the Navajo? How could they hope for tolerance, let alone assimilation, among a people against whom they had warred for some two centuries?

The question is important and unsolved. One recalls that, during the seventeenth century, campaigns by Spaniards and Puebloans against the nomads were interspersed with relatively peaceful years when they traded with each other. One remembers also that, during the governorship of Carvajál in the 1640s, twenty-nine Jemez "sorcerers" were hanged on suspicion of collaborating with Apaches and Navajos. And one recalls that, from their refuge pueblos in 1694, the rebels had taunted Vargas with the boast that Apaches and Navajos were coming to join them as reinforcements.

In an influential and controversial 1960 book called *Apache, Navaho, and Spaniard*, historian Jack D. Forbes argued that both before and during the Spanish era, there was far more cooperation and even alliance between Athapaskans and Puebloans than scholars had previously believed. The debate continues today, as witnessed in a shrewdly reasoned 2002 paper by leading New Mexico archaeologist Curtis F. Schaafsma, called "Pueblo and Apachean Alliance Formation in the Seventeenth Century." Vis-à-vis Dinétah in the 1690s, it may be a simple matter that for the most diehard Puebloan refugees, any other Indian peoples were preferable as neighbors to the ruthless Spaniards.

Throughout most of the twentieth century, then, the view of nearly all scholars who pondered the question was that a Puebloan diaspora flooding into the Dinétah had utterly transformed Navajo culture. In the extreme formulation of this hypothesis, the Puebloans not only taught the Navajo how to make dwellings out of stones, roof beams, and adobe, they also taught them to cultivate corn, to make pottery, and to create rock art. In terms of the latter phenomenon, the classic judgment is voiced by Polly Schaafsma, in *Rock Art in New Mexico* (1992), in which she states, "The earliest Navajo rock art is securely associated with the Gobernador Phase (ca. A.D. 1690–1775) in the upper San Juan drainage. . . . Navajo rock art of the Gobernador Phase was the direct outgrowth of the Pueblo/Navajo contact [after the reconquest]."

In that and other works, Schaafsma lucidly demonstrates how, in the earliest petroglyphs and pictographs they carved and painted on the sandstone walls of the canyons of Dinétah, Navajo artists made a masterly appropriation of many Puebloan conventions and designs from the kachina religion to celebrate their own *ye'is* (holy beings that ensure fertility) and gods such as Ghanaskidi (the Humpbacked God) and the War Twins, Monster Slayer and Born-for-Water.

During many days of prowling through Cereza, Largo, Blanco, and other canyons, I never failed to be stunned by the panels of rock art that I stumbled across in the most obscure places. The oldest groups of petroglyphs, often carved high on the walls, were the work of Anasazi artists, centuries before the Navajo arrived. But the most startling panels were mainly Navajo. One of the paradoxes of art history is that sometimes the very first generations of a long cultural tradition produce its finest work. In other parts of the Southwest I had seen Navajo rock art, most of it dating from the late nineteenth and early twentieth centuries. With rare exceptions, these designs struck me as straightforward and representational: two favorite subjects were horses and jalopies. Some of the most recent work, carved probably after 1950, had the crude spontaneity of graffiti.

In the Dinétah, on the other hand, I was transported by the supernatural potency of the images, mingling abstract symbolism with haunting evocations of gods and culture heroes. With the help of Polly Schaafsma's books, I began to learn the shorthand of the art: the bow-and-hourglass emblems that betokened the War Twins; the upraised hands of a *ye'i*; feathered shields and star ceilings; the horned figure seen sideways, holding a downthrust spear, a rainbow bursting from its back, that evokes Ghanaskidi. One amazing panel of red-and-white pictographs, hidden in a short, dead-end bend of an otherwise unimpressive side canyon, marks the very spot (so some experts argue) where the Navajo invented the Night Chant.

Yet at the same time, in the midst of these panels, I kept seeing figures that could have come straight from the Galisteo Basin—the plumed serpents, knife-wing birds, and fierce-toothed masks of the kachina religion. It seemed unarguable that here Navajo artists had learned or at least borrowed much from the Puebloans.

All science is political. As if in reaction to the implied condescension of received theory, which had it that Puebloan refugees had taught the Navajo to build, to plant, to paint, and to make pottery, a generation of younger archaeologists, many based in the Farmington area, has recently set out to prove that the so-called transformation of Navajo life was really an indigenous development. A key manifesto, published by the Farmington office of the Bureau of Land Management in 1991, is Patrick Hogan's "Rethinking Navajo Pueblitos."

Hogan takes umbrage at what he calls "uncritical acceptance of the 'refugee hypothesis'": "The archaeological evidence for a large influx of Pueblo refugees has never been conclusive." Hogan does not deny Puebloan influence on Navajo culture, but argues that similarities in architecture, pottery, and rock art stem from imitation, not from direct tutelage. In their frequent trading missions among the pueblos, the Navajo would have seen plenty of mud-and-adobe rooms, plenty of painted pots; they might have simply gone home and experimented with clay, adobe, and stone to make their own vessels and pueblitos.

It would not be surprising, after all, if the Navajo had transformed their way of life by observing and copying Puebloan productions. Among all the native peoples in the Southwest, the Navajo have long been both damned and praised as the great adapters and imitators. Only a few generations after the Navajo saw their first Spanish sheep and goats, they became the herders par excellence of the Southwest. (After the beautiful black-on-black vases of Maria Martinez and other Tewa potters started to fetch top dollar in art galleries from Santa Fe to Flagstaff in the 1970s and 1980s, certain Navajo craftswomen flooded the market with cheap knockoffs in their own black-on-black style.)

As for the size of the Puebloan diaspora after 1694, Hogan dryly concludes that it numbered "at most, a few hundred individuals." Other experts go even further. Larry Baker, a Bureau of Land Management archaeologist at Salmon Ruins near Bloomfield, told me that he and a close colleague, Farmington BLM archaeologist Jim Copeland, like to tell tour groups and student seminars, only half tongue-in-cheek, "Yeah, there were Puebloan refugees up here—about eight of them."

Meanwhile, in 1996, a pair of Farmington-area scholars made the closest study yet undertaken of Navajo Gobernador Polychrome, proving that the pottery style dates from 1650—almost half a century before the alleged intrusion of Puebloan refugees.

The tour de force of this revisionist understanding of what happened in Dinétah has come in several years of work by Ron Towner, a young scholar working at the Tucson-based Laboratory of Tree-Ring Research. Coring a total of 798 beams from sixty-five pueblitos, Towner came up with dates that consistently clustered in the periods from 1710–14, 1725–29, and the late 1740s. Only two sites clearly dated earlier than 1696. The anomalous early-cutting date found from the odd single beam in an otherwise post-1700 pueblito could be credited to the "old wood problem," the usage of a long-dead tree in constructing a new village.

In *Defending the Dinétah* (2003), Towner draws his conclusions. The pueblitos were built too late to have served Puebloans as refuges against the Spanish. They were built instead almost entirely by Navajos (no doubt to some extent in imitation of Puebloan models), as a defense not against the Spanish, but against Ute raiders. Around 1775, the Navajo abandoned Dinétah en masse, moving west and south to such areas as Canyon de Chelly and the Lukachukai Mountains— driven out perhaps by Ute depredations.

Impressive though Towner's work is, and however much needed the current thrust toward indigenous invention is as a corrective to the old idea of the Navajo learning everything at the knees of their more gifted Puebloan tutors, I had my lingering doubts as I wandered through Dinétah. Was the new emphasis on Navajo origins for Pueblo-looking ruins and rock art just another swing of the eternal academic pendulum?

It is all too tempting, even for the most disinterested scholar, to form an emotional attachment to the achievements of the peoples he spends decades studying. Archaeologists even have a rueful word for this half-unconscious bias: "My-site-itis." I had seen the tendency at work elsewhere in the Southwest: Arizona archaeologists eager to trace the roots of the kachina religion to the Little Colorado River, arguing themselves blue in the face against their New Mexico colleagues who plump for the Galisteo Basin; Four Corners scholars unleashing a mass Anasazi migration just before A.D. 1300 toward their Santa Fe brethren, who say, in effect, thanks, we've got enough folks already down on the Rio Grande by 1300. Had the Farmington group, proud of their understudied backyard Dinétah, perhaps chosen up sides with those perpetual anthropological underdogs, the Navajo?

The work of Towner and friends is far from settling the question. The dean of Navajo studies, David Brugge, has criticized Towner's work for ignoring ethnographic data. The best proof of a substantial exodus of Puebloan refugees into the Dinétah lies, according to Brugge, in the nature and origins of Navajo clans. Brugge cites the pioneering work of Gladys Reichard, who in a 1928 monograph identified seventeen existing Navajo clans that originated with the Puebloans, with two more of probable Puebloan genesis.

For Joe Sando, the Jemez elder and historian, the question is open-and-shut. It was Puebloans who built the pueblitos. "Among the Navajos," Sando told me in his Albuquerque office, "the Coyote Clan, especially, and the Young Corn Clan, still call themselves Pueblo. And lots of Navajos still come to our Jemez feast day every November 12. There are quite a few Navajo words in Jemez.

"When I was a kid, there was a guy [at Jemez] who used to talk Navajo to me all the time. He was just teasing me.

"Our people ran away up there from the Spanish. They built their own houses, and then the Navajo moved in. A good many stayed, and married Navajos."

In any event, Vargas himself believed that a substantial number of refugees, mostly from Jemez, had fled north and west to join the Navajo. From time to time after 1696, he and other New Mexico governors sent punitive raids up into the Dinétah. The most ambitious of these was prosecuted in 1705 by Roque Madrid, who had been Vargas's right hand man in the reconquest. (Mike Bremer on Madrid, as we had read Vargas's journal out loud among the ruins of Old Kotyiti: "I picture a squat little fireplug of a guy.")

In 1996, two excellent New Mexico historians, Rick Hendricks and John P. Wilson, published Roque Madrid's campaign journal of that 1705 raid, after years of using a copy of the manuscript to work out the route of the maestre de campo's rampage through northwestern Nuevo México. Following that campaign by car and on foot in April 2003, with Hendricks and Wilson's book in hand, I managed to find three otherwise obscure corners in this sandstone maze that still bear eloquent testimony to the ravages of Madrid's campaign.

Though at least sixty years old by 1705, when he set out on his ruthless march through Dinétah, Madrid was as tough and unyielding as the most adamantine of conquistadors. The Spaniard had no doubts about the righteousness of his mission. With a typical flourish, he begins his diary thus:

> In this pueblo of San Juan de los Caballeros, on 31 July 1705, I, Maestro de Campo and principal military leader Roque Madrid, by order of the lord governor and captain general, don Francisco Cuervo y Valdés, knight of the Order of Santiago and treasurer and factor of the Royal Treasury office of the city of Guadalajara, go forth to make war by fire and sword on the Apache Navajo enemy nation.

(Navajos were often called "Apaches de Navajo" by the Spanish, who had trouble telling one of the two closely related Athapaskan peoples from the other.)

It took Madrid, however, ten days to find his first Indians. They were a pair of lone women, on the verge of starvation, one with a young boy on her back; one was Navajo, the other Jemez. Madrid promptly had the women tortured until they revealed the whereabouts of the rest of their people.

On August 10, Madrid at last made contact with "the enemy," who fled before his advance, the soldiers killing a few stragglers. It was not until two days later that the first true battle was waged. Forewarned, the Indians had taken refuge atop a butte south of Gobernador Canyon. Armed with Hendricks and Wilson, I located this stark plug of sandstone, which even today is seldom visited, though it stands visible for miles around and commands a lordly panorama of distant horizons. The butte caps a steep, 350-foot-tall cone of calcified mud, which requires a nasty scramble to surmount. The summit of the butte is guarded on all sides by vertical walls ranging from sixty feet tall to over 100. There is but a single weakness, a series of ledges separated by short cliffs on the northwest side of the formation.

Madrid camped beneath the butte on the night of August 11. The Indians on top screamed curses and taunts. Wrote Madrid, "Though we called them through the Indian interpreter to come down and fight, they did not want to. They told me that when the sun came up we would fight, that the people were united to have done with us." At dawn, the Navajo and Jemez launched an attack from ambush. Madrid drove them back up to the summit of the butte. The Indians had placed a ladder against the final cliff, but, Madrid reported, "As they blocked each other's way up, some misstepped and fell, dying before their people's eyes; they saw them dragged away and scalped [by the Spaniards' Puebloan allies]."

Madrid and his soldiers forced their way to the foot of the ladder, but could not succeed in scaling it: the enemy "concentrated their force there, throwing and rolling rocks down." After having two soldiers and three Indian allies wounded, Madrid called off the attack. For the first and only time in Dinétah, the natives repulsed the invaders.

Two hundred and ninety-eight years later, I started up the cliff where the ladder had once stood. With no rope, climbing gear, or belayer, I almost backed off: the pitch was about 5.4 in difficulty, its hardest move just below the top. Pulling myself onto the summit, I felt a burst of gratification. I spent the next hour exploring the refuge, which was waterless, only three quarters of an acre in extent.

None of the local Bureau of Land Management archaeologists I talked to had ever been on top of this butte, because of the difficulty of the climb. I found a profusion of potsherds scattered everywhere. Some time before, historian John Wilson (one of the two editors of Madrid's journal) had gained the summit, adducing with his trained eye that the pottery was both Navajo and Puebloan. (This seemed to me a strong argument for the Jemez presence among the warriors.) I found also a number of stone rings, which Wilson had recognized as the bases for Navajo hogans. Most vivid were the piles of big rocks still stacked on the rim above the ascent route—the very ammunition that the besieged warriors had flung down upon the Spaniards trying to clamber up the ladder.

I sat for a while, gazing at distant vistas. Not even the faint rumble of a natural gas truck miles to the south marred the tranquillity of this eyrie. Yet my head was full of the desperate battle of 1705. I imagined that, even as they nursed their wounded and sank into the relief of temporary reprieve, the Navajo and Jemez who had here repulsed Roque Madrid stared down at the retreating army and envisioned the doom about to befall their cousins to the west.

It took me a while to find Tapacito Ruin: though it stands only a stone's throw from a meandering dirt road, on a bench above a 200-foot cliff, it is hidden from all three logical approach routes. Four well-preserved, square rooms, made of stones mortared with mud, constitute the ruin. Two of the rooms incorporate a feature—a curved stick masoned into one corner, two feet off the ground, called a "hooded fireplace"—that the Puebloans adapted from the Spanish.

At Tapacito, Ron Towner, the tree ring virtuoso, got a date of 1694, one of only two sites among the sixty-five pueblitos he studied that clearly predated the reconquest. Towner brought two Navajos to Tapacito, who swore that the ruin had not been built by their people. Despite his summary argument that the pueblitos were almost solely a Navajo phenomenon, Towner nonetheless conceded that Tapacito "may be the only genuine Pueblo refugee structure in the Dinétah."

Two days after his repulse at the sheer-cliffed butte, Madrid led his army down Tapacito Creek to its mouth. At its junction with Largo Canyon, on the bench above the streams where the ruin stands, he found a considerable number of the enemy amassed. "Immediately after I arrived," wrote Madrid, "the Apaches [Navajo] began to shout, saying that they wanted to do us no harm, that they wanted peace, and that for this reason we should talk at length." The maestre de campo feigned agreement with the Indians, meanwhile devising a ruse to "give them the punishment they so deserved." Through his interpreter, Madrid kept up the parley for more than two hours. All the while, a flanking party was sneaking up to the mesa top and circling behind the Navajos on the Tapacito bench.

With lances and guns, the flanking party attacked. The defenders were routed. "Of the more than thirty that were there," Madrid dryly noted, "no more than five escaped, not counting two who in a great fury threw themselves over the edge." One of these suicides was tied to a rope held by a Puebloan ally of the Spanish, who, neglecting to let go, was likewise pulled off the cliff. At last Madrid withdrew his troops, "thanking God that in the whole battle only one of my men was lost, and he was an Indian."

Though he fought no more pitched battles in Dinétah, as he completed his long loop through the Navajo country Madrid burned every cornfield he could find. He was back in Zia Pueblo by August 20, smug in the conviction that it was "impossible to punish [the Navajo] more than we have done." In early 1706, a delegation of Navajo men arrived in Santa Fe to sue for peace. Madrid lived on in New Mexico to a ripe old age, retiring from his military career only after reaching seventy.

So far as I know, no ethnographer has ever recorded the oral traditions kept by the Navajo about the devastating campaign of Roque Madrid, who was the first Spaniard ever to explore Dinétah. But one day in Largo Canyon, I found an intensely vivid memorial of that incursion. At the mouth of Largo's tributary, Cuervo Canyon, on a south-facing sandstone cliff, stands an astoundingly rich panel of Navajo—and perhaps also Puebloan—petroglyphs. Corn plants with ripe ears sprouting from them, the life-giving *ye'is*, horned supernatural beings redolent of kachinas, the bow-and-hourglass designs emblematic of the Warrior Twins, and a masterly portrait of Ghanaskidi, the Humpbacked God, sprawl across the orange stone. Some of these faces seem to be caught in frozen screams of agony.

In the middle of the panel, moving from left to right, ride two Spaniards on horseback. Their left hands hold the reins tight, their right hands clutch upraised swords, ready to smite. Even the skeptical Bureau of Land Management archaeologists in Farmington agree that this ominous tableau surely records the scorched-earth passage of Roque Madrid through Dinétah.

The final mystery of the Puebloan diaspora unfurls, however, not in Dinétah, but on the Hopi mesas of Arizona. From the very start of my inquiry into the Pueblo Revolt, I had puzzled over Hopi's role in the uprising. To the Spanish, from Coronado forward, those western villages lay so far from the heart of the Pueblo world that conquistadors and governors alike tended to ignore Hopi for years at a time. Yet three of the priests killed on August 10, 1680, were ministers to the Hopi, one at Awatovi, two at Oraibi. (A puzzle within the puzzle: Hopi lies some 250 miles as the crow flies from Tesuque. How could even the swiftest of runners have carried the knotted cords across such a distance in time for the killings to be carried out—as all sources insist happened—on the same day as the Puebloans slew the other eighteen Franciscans in New Mexico?)

James Defouri, the Victorian panegyrist of the priest-martyrs, offers an alternative (and most likely apocryphal) story of Fray José de Espeleta's fate at Oraibi: "There are authors who say he was not put to death, but was kept by the people of Oraibi as a slave in the Pueblo, the beast of burden of those cowards; that he lived for years in the vilest conceivable servitude, the laughing object of every one, old and young.... Be that as it may, if Father Espeleta was kept a slave by the Moquis [Hopi], it was only a long torturing martyrdom, a lingering death."

If Hopi remained marginal to the Spanish colony of Nuevo México throughout the eighty-two years after Oñate's conquest, it would become central to the story after Vargas had completed his reconquest. Yet my efforts to plumb the role Hopi had played as refuge for the Puebloan diaspora after 1696 were frustrated at every hand.

As many observers have noted, no indigenous peoples anywhere in the world have been more intensely studied than the Hopi. And no Native American tribe has been the object of more sentimental clap-trap on the part of well-meaning Anglos than the Hopi. The cult of the Hopi as mystics in tune with the universe, as peaceful philosophers liv-ing in harmony with the earth, reached its zenith in Frank Waters's 1963 best-seller, *The Book of the Hopi*. And though that work has long since been denounced at Hopi as both invasive and just plain wrong, hippies from all over the world still show up almost daily on the Hopi mesas, tattered copies of Waters's tome in hand, expecting to find gurus to set them on the path to spiritual enlightenment.

During the last ten or fifteen years, as I had discovered to my dis-may over and over again, the pueblos in general have turned steadily more suspicious of outsiders. Nowhere is this shift more pronounced than at Hopi. As I had researched my earlier book about the Anasazi in the early 1990s, I had gained much insight from my consultations with Leigh Kuwanwisiwma, cultural preservation officer for the tribe, who in those days called himself Leigh Jenkins. With his blessing, I had been guided to the highly sensitive ruins of Kawaika'a and Awatovi.

In 2003, I had no hope of visiting those or any other Hopi ruins. And although I made eight or ten phone calls to Kuwanwisiwma, and three times stopped by his office, I was never able to exchange a word with the man in charge of preserving Hopi's legacy.

In Winslow, Arizona, I visited archaeologists Kurt and Cindy Don-goske, who had long worked at Hopi. A 2002 paper they had jointly published, about Franciscan conversions as reflected in rock art panels on the Hopi reservation, had me aflame with curiosity. One panel, sketched in a diagram in the paper, appeared to depict, among a crowd of figures and symbols, two lines of small humans, shown in profile moving from right to left, their arms raised high to support massive logs held on or above their heads. The Dongoskes believe these petro-glyphs may portray "the forced labor of the Hopi in transporting logs from the San Francisco Mountains for the construction of the mis-sions." If so, these etchings represent a vivid tableau of oppression, carved by the oppressed—a circumstance virtually unique in the rock art of the Southwest.

"I think I'm the only person who knows where this rock art is," said Cindy Dongoske. But there was no chance that she could guide me to the panels below Antelope Mesa. Within the previous year, under strained circumstances, both Dongoskes had terminated their associations with Hopi, Kurt after twelve years as Leigh Kuwan-wisiwma's assistant in the cultural preservation office. Anglos working for other pueblos have sometimes been accused of disseminating culturally sensitive information to a larger public. During his time at Hopi, Kurt had sat in on many meetings of the Cultural Resource Advisory Team. "I understand that some information is sensitive," Kurt told me in frustrated tones. "But in twelve years, they never told me anything they didn't want me to know. I didn't hear anything that hadn't already been published." (It was Kurt who had personally guided me to the ruins of Kawaika'a and Awatovi in 1994.)

The most striking manifestation of Hopi as a refuge for Puebloans after the reconquest persists today in the village of Hano, on First Mesa. It was founded in the year 1700 by a group of Tano emigrants from the Galisteo Basin, invited to relocate en masse to a site less than a stone's throw away from the existing pueblo of Sichomovi. Today, the three villages on First Mesa—from east to west, Hano, Sichomovi, and ancient Walpi—blend into each other like the seamlessly conjoined suburbs of Boston or Washington, D.C. Yet, remarkably enough, the denizens of Hano still speak Tewa, a language their neighbors in Sichomovi and Walpi have never bothered to learn, even though the Hano men and women have become fluent in the Uto-Aztecan tongue of Hopi. (Hano today is the last surviving pocket of spoken Southern Tewa, once the lingua franca of the Galisteo Basin. According to one expert, "The Hopi-Tewa [i.e., Hano] and Rio Grande Tewa can understand each other's speech, but only with some difficulty and after a short period of adjustment.")

The Tano, from such villages as San Lázaro, San Cristóbal, and Galisteo, were among the ringleaders in the Pueblo Revolt and in the

attempt to hold Santa Fe against Vargas in late 1693. Their reputation as great warriors lives on in the beguiling fact that at Hopi, most of the tribal police officers come from the village of Hano. It would have been fascinating to talk at length with some Hano elder about his people's story of the journey from the Rio Grande, to hear him explicate their proud autonomy within the otherwise alien culture of Hopi, but all my efforts to locate such a person were to no avail.

Unable to meet with or even talk to Leigh Kuwanwisiwma, I stumbled quite by accident upon an informant who would give me some unexpected insights into the various riddles of Hopi. In a gift shop on Second Mesa, I met Gary Tso, an enthusiastic thirty-five-year-old who ekes out a meager living leading tourists around the Hopi Reservation. Gary's business card promises "Private Cultural & Archeological Tours Deep into Hopiland." He calls his business "Left-Handed Hunter Tour Company." When I asked him what that meant, he breezily explained, "I like hunting, and I'm a lefty. That's not necessarily a good thing. People say we're thieves. People will come up to me and say, 'What you goin' to steal today?'"

I was immediately drawn to this likable young guide with a sense of humor. We drove back roads in his pickup, then spent most of a warm, milky-skied October day at a place called Dawaki, or "House of the Sun"—off-limits to Anglos except under the aegis of a Hopi escort. At first blush, Dawaki looked like an unremarkable low sandstone cirque facing south across a badlands of stubble and dirt. I had never read or heard of the place, but Dawaki proved to be one of the most astonishing open-air museums of rock art I had seen anywhere in the Southwest. "The cultural preservation office estimates there's 15,000 petroglyphs here," Gary told me.

In the course of our slow meander beneath the cliff, I learned about Gary's background. His father was a Navajo from Grand Falls, a small settlement just inside the border of the Navajo Reservation, a mere thirty miles from Flagstaff; his mother, a Hopi from Shungopavi on the Second Mesa. "My first language was Navajo," Gary told me,

"my second was Hopi. English was my third language." He had served as a marine in the Far East from 1986 to 1990.

The sheer abundance and variety of the rock art at Dawaki, carved over a span of several millennia, had me murmuring out loud. Tribal regulations forbade my photographing or even sketching these petroglyphs, so I simply stared. There were scores of familiar Anasazi designs—spirals and shield symbols, duck-headed humans, bighorn sheep in profile, flute players—but also scores of designs I had seen nowhere else. These included what Gary called "starblowers"—flute players out of whose instruments sprayed minor constellations of stars; lizard-men with plumes protruding from their backs; a kachina mask so stylized it was reduced to a pair of circles for eyes, a pair of horizontal slabs for the mouth (and all the more haunting for its Picasso-like simplicity). I even spotted a row of four triangle-bodied humanoids who seemed to be carrying aloft a huge timber. Was this another record of the forced harvesting of roof beams for the Spanish missions, like the petroglyphs Cindy Dongoske had found below Antelope Mesa?

Among several hundred trips to this site, Gary had visited on the dates of both equinoxes and both solstices. He was convinced Dawaki was an archaeo-astronomical observatory, and now he scrambled up fissures and slabs in the cliff to demonstrate how sun "daggers," formed by prongs and narrow gaps between them, caused either sharp shadows or needles of light to point exactly at etched whorls and spirals in the stone, at sunrise, sunset, or noon on those four pivotal days of the yearly calendar.

We sat down in the shade of a leaning slab to eat lunch. I asked Gary how he had first learned about the Pueblo Revolt. He frowned. "When I was seven or eight years old, I heard my first stories," he said. "The tone was hush-hush. In the Hopi language, it's so much more ominous. It was just people talking about it, not really telling a story, but the tone was almost a whisper. Like it was something to be scared of."

I asked further about refugees from the Rio Grande pueblos after the reconquest. Gary told me about a ruin on Second Mesa known as Piyüfki or Payupki. The site had been offered by the Hopi to refugees

from Sandía Pueblo, who had built a village there in which they had lived for several decades in the early eighteenth century, before returning to their home pueblo. Gary had sometimes guided tourists to Payupki, but now it was too late. A few months earlier, another Hopi guide had discovered human remains coming out of the ground. "She told Leigh about it," said Gary. "The cultural preservation office closed the site. Leigh said, 'You can go cover up those bodies, or I'll do it.'"

On the side of Gary's family that is Navajo, whose avoidance of places of the dead is legendary, his uncles were shocked by his chosen profession. "They ask me, 'How can you walk around there by yourself?' But I don't have bad intentions, so I think I'll be all right.

"I identify more as Hopi than as Navajo. I'm of the Sun Forehead Clan—one of the very last to arrive at Hopi. We came from Homolovi [a large ruined pueblo just north of Winslow]. And before that, from somewhere farther south."

Farther south than Homolovi? According to archaeologists, that would put Gary's ancestors in the Mogollon country—generally thought to be an entirely separate people from the Anasazi who became the Puebloans. The mysteries of the diaspora, I thought, were fathomless.

We rose to leave. "We're lucky I could still take you here," said Gary. "The folks in Hotevilla"—the nearest village to Dawaki—"want to close this place down."

In the end, I would gain my best understanding of Hopi's role in the diaspora not in the Southwest, but in New York City. At the American Museum of Natural History, I met Peter Whiteley, an English-born anthropologist who has spent decades working at Hopi. His 1988 book, *Bacavi: Journey to Reed Springs*, about a village formed in 1909 as a result of the famous schism at Oraibi (and, coincidentally, Leigh Kuwanwisiwma's hometown), has become a classic of popular ethnography.

"After the reconquest," Whiteley told me, "there were refugees at Hopi not only from Sandía and the southern Tewa who founded Hano, but also from Isleta, Quarai, Alameda, and other pueblos. There

were a lot of folks from Jemez. In general, there was a great deal of population movement all over the Pueblo world after the Revolt— more than is usually recognized."

The Isleta refugees intrigued me. Most history books baldly assert that Isleta did not participate in the Revolt because of Popé's distrust of the pueblo, and that its inhabitants, loyal to the Spanish, joined Otermín's caravan trudging southward toward El Paso in late August 1680. But now Whiteley remarked, "Not all of Isleta was sympathetic to the Spanish and took off to the south. Some of the refugees stayed at Hopi for a good twenty years. I've met folks at Isleta who spoke a little Hopi."

Whiteley also offered an interesting footnote to my difficulties finding Puebloans who would talk about the oral tradition of the Revolt. With a wry smile, he said, "Puebloans don't want to talk to outsiders about *anything* historical. The possibility of good relations with Hispanos and Anglos today depends on suppressing some of the past."

Inevitably, our conversation turned to what happened at Awatovi in the fall of 1700. In all the post-contact history of the Puebloan world, no event is more shocking—and despite more than a century's worth of "explanations" by anthropologists who heard Hopi stories about Awatovi, no episode remains more baffling or fundamentally ambiguous.

On the edge of Antelope Mesa, the southeasternmost of the Hopi villages, Awatovi was the first visited by Coronado in 1540. For the Spanish, the pueblo became a gateway to the rest of Hopi. The first mission church among the Hopi was built here in 1629, and though it was burned to the ground in 1680, and its priest stoned to death, Awatovi became the focus of new missionary efforts among the Hopi after 1696. The oldest and simplest story of what happened at Awatovi focuses on this supposed fact: the pueblo accepted the return of the Franciscan priests, and so earned its doom.

Thus one of the earliest Spanish documents about Awatovi, written by Fray José Narváez Valverde in 1732, claims that after the reconquest, "These Moquis remained on their height in primitive freedom,

subject to one Indian among them called Francisco de Espeleta because of his having been brought up and taught to read and write by a religious whose name was Espeleta." (The "religious" was Fray José de Espeleta, put to death at Oraibi in the Pueblo Revolt, or, if Defouri is right, kept there after 1680 as a slave in "the vilest conceivable servitude.") To Hopi in 1700, "carried away by zeal," hastened a pair of priests named Juan de Garicochea and Antonio Miranda. "They reached the first pueblo, called Aguatubi," writes Valverde, "where they reduced all the natives and baptized many."

This aroused the wrath of Francisco de Espeleta, who arrived at Awatovi with more than 800 warriors. "The Indians entered the pueblo, where the religious labored more than six hours, preaching to the said Don Francisco de Espeleta and those of his chiefs who were acquainted with the Castilian language." Yet these Hopi leaders went away "indifferent and obstinate."

The overconfident missionaries, believing they had succeeded in re-Christianizing Awatovi, set out for Santa Fe to report to the governor. Meanwhile, the rest of the Hopi, "infuriated because the Indians of the pueblo of Aguatubi had been reduced to our holy faith and the obedience of the king," returned to the village on Antelope Mesa. With a hundred picked warriors, Espeleta entered Awatovi, "killed all the braves, and carried off the women, leaving the pueblo to this day desolate and unpeopled." Governor Cubero (Vargas's successor) came to Hopi on a punitive mission, "killed some Indians and captured others, but not being very well prepared to face the multitudes of the enemy, he withdrew and returned without being able to reduce them." After 1700, in fact, uniquely among the pueblos, Hopi would never again submit to the reinstallation of Franciscan priests and their churches.

Don Francisco de Espeleta remains a problematic character. He is known only from the Spanish records, not in Hopi accounts told to ethnographers after the 1880s. It would not have been likely that a single individual in 1700 could have been the "chief" of all the Hopi; each village would have had its own headman and principal shamans. Yet in a fasci-

nating 2002 paper, called "Re-imagining Awat'ovi," Peter Whiteley credits Espeleta's existence, identifying him tentatively as an Oraibi *cacique* (or headman) of the Badger Clan—an affiliation that might prove significant in understanding Hopi stories of what happened at Awatovi.

In the 160 years since the Spanish had first entered the Southwest, they had become aware that pueblos occasionally made war against one another. Nothing like Awatovi had ever happened, however—the wholesale destruction of a pueblo by its own people from neighboring villages. And in the 304 years since the massacre at Awatovi, nothing like it has occurred again in the Puebloan world.

Over the decades, a series of historians and anthropologists culled stories from Hopi informants—at times convergent with each other, at others strikingly divergent—of what had taken place at Awatovi. They include John G. Bourke (later to aid General George Crook in the final campaign against Geronimo's Apaches in southern Arizona) in 1881; the pioneering archaeologist Jesse Fewkes in 1893; the Mennonite missionary and self-taught ethnographer Henry R. Voth in 1905; the great photographer of Indian life Edward S. Curtis in 1922; and a number of others in more recent years.

By all odds the most "inside" account of the destruction of Awatovi, as well as by far the most confusing for the non-Hopi reader, was published in 1993 by Ekkehart Malotki, in a landmark but controversial book called *Hopi Ruin Legends*. Malotki is an oddity among Southwestern scholars. German-born, a professor of German and Latin at Northern Arizona University in Flagstaff, never formally trained as an anthropologist, Malotki is a gifted linguist who, most observers agree, is the single non-Hopi who has best mastered the immensely complicated Hopi language. To compile *Hopi Ruin Legends*, Malotki tape-recorded and transcribed the words of three Hopi elders whom he calls "story rememberers," as they told old tales pertaining to the ruins of seven ancestral pueblos, including Awatovi. (The book presents both Hopi and English texts on facing pages.) The controversy over this and other

of Malotki's Hopi works hinges on whether he published sensitive information that no non-Hopi should ever be allowed to learn.

Malotki's informant for the Awatovi story was a Third Mesa man named Michael Lomatuway'ma, since deceased. The tale, which covers a full fifty-five pages of tightly printed text, follows the rigorous conventions of what Malotki calls Hopi "mytho-historical" narrative. A long preamble, set in an unspecified and fluid time frame, details the supernatural characters and events that coalesce in the founding and development of Awatovi. The second half, more clearly historical, recounts the destruction of the village in 1700.

What is most curious about Lomatuway'ma's digressive but vivid tale is that it makes only a very glancing allusion to Catholic priests or conversions—although Malotki believes that the Franciscan disturbance can be read between the lines. The preamble deals with such eerie figures as a "moisture deity" called Pavayoykyasi, an evil tempter of women called Icicle Boy, and a protectress named Old Spider Woman. It is impossible to correlate this part of the story with any history recorded by the Spanish. Yet the key assertion Lomatuway'ma makes in this preamble is that sometime before Awatovi's destruction, the village had lapsed into a state of *koyaanisqatsi*, which Malotki glosses as a "social disease of turmoil and corruption." Lomatuway'ma's particulars are hair-raising:

> People began to change in their ways. There was no mutual respect any more. . . . A woman would be taking piki [bread] somewhere, only to have others snatch it away from her. . . . Men and boys would reach under the dresses of women and girls and rape them. . . . They got worse and worse. For example, if children encountered an old person relieving himself, they would smear excrement all over him. . . .
>
> Once in a while they actually committed murder. Prime targets were women, of course. When they encountered a single woman, they ripped off her clothes and raped her one after the other.

Adding to the Awatovi misery was a prolonged drought. For two whole years, no rain fell. "By the fifth year no one had anything left. People would go out in search of cactus and plants of that sort. That's all they were eating." The people blamed their own state of *koyaanisqatsi* for this punishment by the gods.

With the introduction of Ta'palo, the headman of Awatovi, the tale shifts into recognizably historical mode. Ta'palo suffers three personal setbacks. In the middle of a spirited rabbit hunt, his beautiful daughter is accidentally run over and killed by a man on horseback. A gambling game called Sosotukwpi degenerates into a promiscuous sexual orgy, disgusting and shaming the headman. And in a dance inside a kiva, Ta'palo observes his wife flirting outrageously with her partner; the headman follows the pair out into the night, where he watches them make love in the corner of a house.

For the Hopi, *koyaanisqatsi* is the work of witches, or *popwaqt*. (Even today, the Hopi live in constant fear of being accused of witchcraft.) In a deep funk, Ta'palo decides that the only remedy is the annihilation of Awatovi, even if it means that he himself must die in the carnage. He goes to the leaders of Walpi and Shungopavi to plead for them to attack Awatovi. They demur. The Walpi chief says, "We would be fighting against Hopis there, and that is not right." Finally, at Oraibi, he gains a sympathetic ear. (It is Peter Whiteley's identification of this leader as Francisco de Espeleta, based on a speculative cofraternity between him and Ta'palo as members of allied clans, Badger and Tobacco, respectively, that tries to reconcile Spanish accounts with oral tradition.)

In the lament that Ta'palo pours out to the Oraibi leader lies the one allusion to the Spaniards' role in Awatovi's corruption. "My children over in Awat'ovi are out of control," complains Ta'palo. "The elders are nothing to them. They are ravishing the women and girls. Our shrines and ceremonies are in shambles. They don't mean anything. These Spaniards, nothing but sorcerers and witches, are hoping to settle here for good. That's why they came."

The fateful attack is launched at dawn on a signal from Ta'palo.

The attackers swarm through Awatovi, pulling the ladders out of the kivas to trap the sleeping men inside. They set fire to the village, throwing chile peppers into the kivas to suffocate their victims. "There was crying, screaming, and coughing," Lomatuway'ma recounts. "Finally, the screams died down and it became still. Eventually the roofs caved in on the dead, burying them."

In the massacre, not even old men and women are spared. Villagers attempting to flee are shot or hurled off cliffs. A band of captive women and girls is marched toward Walpi, to be distributed as spoils among the attackers. But when the victors start quarreling over rights to the women, they end up slaughtering most of them out of spite.

"Thus the village leader Ta'palo sacrificed his own children to get rid of this life of evil, craziness, and chaos," Lomatuway'ma concludes. "In getting his wish fulfilled he lost his own life. He succeeded in eradicating Awat'ovi, for the village is no more. Only a few remnants of its walls are left. And here the story ends."

Though it raises more questions than it answers, Lomatuway'ma's hallucinatory narrative would seem to stand as some kind of last word on Awatovi. Yet in his 2002 paper, "Re-imagining Awat'ovi," Peter Whiteley comes up with a wholly novel hypothesis. A stray remark made to the anthropologist some twenty years before by a Hopi man had nagged at him ever since. "You know," the man had said, "the real trouble at Awat'ovi was peyote."

Whiteley had dismissed the remark because, as he puts it in the paper, "There are no mentions at all that I know in the body of Hopi ethnography about peyote use." The nearest source of peyote mushrooms is far-off southwest Texas, and in general, the hallucinogen seems to have played little or no part in Puebloan life. Then, in 1998, as he pored over some obscure handwritten Spanish documents about population movements after the Revolt, Whiteley was startled to find an allusion to the use of peyote at Taos, "in which one's strength and capacities are deprived; one sees in the imagination fantasies that are taken for experiences."

A cautious scholar, Whiteley warns himself and his readers that "one archival swallow does not make a summer of interpretation," but then he goes on to build a convincing case that peyote might have served as the fuel for a revivalist movement among the *Wuwtsim* society at Hopi, a secret manhood cult all but extinct today. The leader of this movement might well have been "a charismatic, conjunctural figure like Espeleta." And first on the agenda of the revivalists must have been the eradication of the *popwaqt* whose sorcery had turned Awatovi into a sink of corruption and crime. It is here, at last, that the oral traditions may be dovetailed with the Spanish record. As Whiteley told me in his office, from the Hopi point of view, "The real *popwaqt* were the Hopi who supported the church at Awatovi."

All this is maddeningly speculative. Yet the massacre of Awatovi is no legend: it remains the terrible last chapter in the dramatic story of twenty critical years in the Southwest, from the brilliant stroke of the Pueblo Revolt to the collapse of Puebloan unity in the years thereafter, from Vargas's far from bloodless reconquest to the diaspora of refugees it sent fleeing to the north and west.

In his office, Whiteley summed up our modern ignorance: "I think there was a lot more going on at Awatovi than we'll ever know."

Which leaves all those who have pondered long and hard about the massacre to draw their own conclusions. As Kurt Dongoske had told me, "This is just my own theory. There's no concrete evidence. But I think Awatovi was chosen by the Spanish [for missionization] because it was the most prestigious Hopi village. It was the gateway to Hopi, and it controlled the distribution of trade products. It was a strong ceremonial center. I think this created jealousy among the other villages. Given the chance to knock Awatovi on its ass, they said, 'Let's do it.' They just used the idea of eliminating the Spanish presence as a pretext."

Gary Tso, left-handed hunter and rock art guide, took the opposite view, one that startled me in its directness. "The old people say, oh, Awatovi, that was a terrible thing," he told me as we ate lunch at Dawaki. "But I just think it was our most glorious day. We could have ended up like them."

From the very start of my research on the Pueblo Revolt, I had been tantalized again and again by the inaccessible, by understandings that floated just beyond my grasp—from the stories Puebloans were not willing to tell me, to the lacunae in the Spanish records, to the mute ambiguity of ruins and rock art that I hiked miles into the back-country to behold. It would be left for Peter Whiteley to tantalize me one last time. "You know," he said in his office at the American Museum of Natural History, "the holy grail of Awatovi studies is in Adolph Bandelier's *Final Report*." I knew well the impressive mono-graph that the Swiss-born pioneer of Southwestern research had pub-lished between 1890 and 1892, summarizing five years of work in the field and among the archives. "Bandelier writes about a 1713 inventory of documents he had found in Santa Fe. The inventory includes first-hand testimonials taken in 1702 from Puebloan witnesses to the destruction of Awatovi."

Whiteley paused for effect. I raised my eyebrows, dreading the scholar's next words.

"It's lost. Nobody can find the inventory. It's gone forever."

# EPILOGUE

"**W**e don't know a lot about this site," said Mike Elliott, "because it's never been professionally excavated." The tall, soft-spoken archaeologist for the Santa Fe National Forest was surrounded by a group of fifteen listeners. As part of New Mexico's Historic Preservation Month, Elliott had sacrificed a Saturday off to lead a tour of Sayshukwa, a little-known ruin high on a mesa north of Jemez. The fifteen of us included tourists who had seen the notice advertising the outing at Walatowa, the Jemez visitor center on State Highway 4, just north of the pueblo. But our group also included two men from Jemez: Tom Lucero, of the Department of Resource Protection, and Joseph Tsosie, chief ranger for the pueblo. Just a couple of weeks before, it had been Lucero who, at the beginning of my meeting with the Jemez Cultural Committee, had asked Elliott and his colleague to leave the room.

It was a chilly, windy day in early May. We were high in the forest, almost 8,000 feet above sea level. Around us, the crowns of Ponderosa pines swayed in the breeze, while the occasional cone dropped softly to the needle-covered ground.

"Sayshukwa," Elliott pronounced. "The name means 'Eagle Dwelling Place.'" A dirt road, winding up the hills north of the hamlet of Ponderosa, goes right by the ruin. The fifteen of us had driven to the site in our own cars, parking within a hundred yards of Sayshukwa. Yet no sign announces the ancestral Jemez ruin, and nearly all the passersby—college kids on balmy summer nights, heading for their campouts, hunters in November avid to bring down their elk for the season—speed by the place without suspecting that anyone ever lived there.

Now Elliott walked us from north to south through the elongated ruin, pointing out earthen ridges that hid rows of roomblocks. The less archaeologically savvy members of our group were having trouble—as I myself had, on my first trips to mesa-top ruins such as this—seeing much of anything except those earthen ridges, even though potsherds lay all about us. "The whole site's 330 meters long," Elliott coaxed. "There were more than a thousand rooms here. It was as tall as three stories." The archaeologist climbed to the top of a ridge, then addressed a woman in the group: "Look at this. My feet are higher than your head. So think how tall this roomblock stood.

"Think of this as a church," Elliott went on. "Because it is one. People lived here, died here. People are buried here."

It had been more than a year since Elliott had visited Sayshukwa, but the place was special for him: as one of his first jobs for the Forest Service, decades before, he had refilled some eighty depressions in the ruin, the holes left by illegal pothunters seeking treasure. "I don't know how many times I've been here," he mused, gazing over one of his favorite places in the forest. "I've cross-country skied into here in the middle of winter, with several feet of snow on the ground."

We came to a room that had recently been dug by pothunters. A wall had partially collapsed under the ravages of the shovel. "Would you even rebuild that?" an older man in the group asked.

"I don't think we could. It wouldn't be natural. It would be our own idea of what it looked like. And besides, I don't think the pueblo would support rebuilding it." Tom Lucero nodded his head in agreement.

"The site wants to relax and go back to the earth," Elliott added.

The sad truth is that Sayshukwa, and many other ancestral Jemez ruins, are still being regularly pothunted. There is no way a handful of rangers can police the huge upland spread of the Santa Fe National Forest, and unless a ranger catches a vandal redhanded, it is virtually impossible to prosecute him for violating the Antiquities Act. "We did nab a pair of pothunters here not so long ago," Elliott went on. "They were a schoolteacher and a scientist from Los Alamos. They were just out to have some fun. They pled ignorance, but they were convicted." Elliott's next words came as close to cynicism as this gentle optimist allowed himself: "They got a fine and some hours of community service.

"The two of them had disturbed seven burials in the plaza here." Elliott waved his hand toward the open space before us. "We refilled the holes, and a man from Jemez performed a ceremony of reinterment."

We came to a handsome two-foot-high wall of masoned stones, still standing in place. Several people in our group murmured in admiration, while Elliott withheld his revelation for a few moments. "Five years ago," he said at last, "this wall was eight feet tall." He pulled out a photo taken before the collapse. We passed it around.

"What happened?" a man asked.

"People pushed it over. Maybe gang members, because they tagged the site with spray paint."

I waited until I could ask Elliott my question out of earshot of the others. "Not Jemez kids, I hope?" I queried.

"Nope," Elliott whispered. "We know who did it." I backed off, sensing the archaeologist's discomfort.

We strolled slowly south through the ruin. Suddenly Elliott turned in his tracks. "Oh, man," he groaned. "The big pondo's dead!" We all stared at the towering Ponderosa, its needles a sickly brown—another victim of drought and the pine beetle. "That's the tallest tree in the site," Elliott continued, his voice full of loss. "That tree's a couple of hundred years old."

After a few moments, Elliott recovered his tour guide composure. Gathered around him in the middle of the ruin, we listened to his dissertation on Sayshukwa. "We're at 7,920 feet here. A lot of people say you can't grow corn at this altitude. But if you save the best corn from each harvest, it can adapt to altitude. It's genetically mutable. But nowhere else in New Mexico was corn ever grown this high."

Elliott pointed east, where the mesa shelved off. "The nearest water's way down there, in the side canyons. So perhaps aesthetics played a role in choosing the site. There's magnificent views from here.

"Sayshukwa wasn't built until the 1500s. The last tree ring date we got here is 1609. We think the Spanish probably never came to the site. But there are references to 'the great pueblo of the Jemez.' They must have looked at the mesa and wondered, 'Who lives up there?'

"The history we know and read wasn't written by the Jemez. It was written by an invading army. There's a lot we don't know. I think that's sort of cool. There should be some mystery."

Tom Lucero spoke up. "I think what Mike's saying is that not all that you read of history is the facts. The only true history is the oral history."

I reflected. Lucero's formula wasn't really what Elliott was saying at all. Archaeology and oral tradition, I remained convinced, were ultimately irreconcilable. But in that moment, I also realized that in all my months in New Mexico, I had seen no more promising bridge between Puebloans and Western scholars than I was witnessing here, as we walked through Sayshukwa. It depended on Elliott's years of patient consultation at Jemez, as well as on the openness of Puebloans such as Lucero to what tree ring dates and pottery classification could tell him about his people's past. And it depended on the two men's common love for this landscape—for the land itself.

Lucero had told me that he, like Elliott, had been to Sayshukwa many times. I asked Joseph Tsosie, the Jemez ranger, who so far had not said a word. "I came here as a kid with my father," he said almost sheepishly. "But that was a long time ago."

Lucero overheard our conversation. "We have to keep an eye on what's ours," he said.

As we walked back to our cars, I turned Lucero's comment over in my mind, like a well-worn stone. It seemed loaded with contradictory meanings. Was there the faintest hint of his scolding Joseph Tsosie in it—and by extension, all the other Jemez folks who never took the time to visit their ancestral ruins on the mesas?

I knew that the fact that so many of those ruins—including the fatal Pueblo on the Peñol, which I had visited alone in April—lay on federal land was an unending grievance for the Jemez. The Santa Fe National Forest was established in 1905 by Teddy Roosevelt—"without," as Joe Sando complains in *Nee Hemish*, "consulting the owners." For decades, the Jemez have lobbied to have these mesas returned to the people, but by 2003 there seemed no hope whatsoever that the National Forest Service would willingly cede thousands of acres of prime wilderness, with all its recreational potential, to a band of Native Americans numbering only 3,400 souls.

Thus, for Tom Lucero, the best that could be done was what he had just done, in the company of the gangly archaeologist who had become his friend. For his people, and in the conviction that a handful of sympathetic government employees such as Elliott really had the best interests of the Jemez at heart, Lucero had come back to Sayshukwa, to keep an eye on what was his, and theirs.

When I had first set out to investigate the Pueblo Revolt, I had regarded it as a tragic failure, in view of the ease with which the Spanish achieved the *reconquista*. By now, however, I had formulated a different conclusion.

In one cardinal sense, the Revolt was a profound success. Having resumed control of New Mexico in 1696, the Spanish recognized that they must make major compromises to prevent another such uprising. Gone for good were the hated *encomienda* and *repartimiento*. The pueblos were allowed to self-govern, electing their own officials, in a democratic structure that persists to this day. (There is more than a little irony in the fact that the chief official in each pueblo is called its "governor.") Most important, the Puebloans were finally allowed to practice their kachina religion. The syncretic faith that steeps the villages today is not so much a matter of dogma imposed by the Franciscans as of the natives picking and choosing which aspects of Catholicism were compatible with their traditional beliefs.

As a result, the Puebloans never lost their languages, their dances, the tales that conjure up their history. No Native American peoples anywhere in the United States have kept their cultures more intact than the twenty pueblos in New Mexico and Arizona.

In 1975, Herman Agoyo, the San Juan spokesman, had been one of forty Native Americans invited to participate in the nation's Bicentennial the following year. "Before we got to Washington," Agoyo told me, "we said to ourselves, why do we want to take part in this? The treatment of the Indians by the U.S. government was terrible. After we'd thought about it a while, we decided to dedicate our participation to Popé."

Agoyo smiled. "When I got to Washington, the coordinator from the Hopi delegation—a white guy—said to me, 'You know, five years from now will be the tricentennial of the Pueblo Revolt.' I said, 'You're right.'"

In that moment was born the planning for a celebration of the Revolt among the pueblos, which eventually spread through several weeks in the summer of 1980. A symposium of experts, both Anglo and Puebloan, convened to debate such questions as the roots of the Revolt and the dynamics of Popé's leadership. Alfonso Ortiz, the San Juan–born anthropologist, concluded his essay on a triumphant note: "Because of a desperate, despair-born gamble on the part of the Pueblo people of 1680, their descendants have lived to find that their well-being and continued cultural integrity is regarded as essential to the well-being of all of New Mexico and of the Southwest. A successful revolution, it seems to me, can have no greater legacy than this."

In July 1980, San Juan hosted a two-day festival and parade that brought participants from many other pueblos. And in August, relay runners reenacted the deed of the 1680 messengers with the knotted cords, covering 300 miles from Taos to Hopi. Thanks to the writing and teaching of such Puebloan scholars as Ortiz, Agoyo, Tessie Naranjo, and Joe Sando, Puebloan children have only now begun to grow up with an awareness of the great rebellion their ancestors perpetrated more than three centuries ago. Despite the people's premium on secrecy and sacred knowledge, some of the Puebloan lore surrounding the Revolt is at last being committed to print.

During the course of his own self-education in the Pueblo Revolt, Herman Agoyo became aware that there was a vacancy in Washington, D.C., waiting to be filled. A long-standing federal program called the Capitol Project had granted to each state the right to have the statues of two distinguished figures mounted in the National Statuary Hall of the Capitol building. By the 1980s, New Mexico had only one statue in Washington—that of Dennis Chávez, who had served in the U.S. Senate from 1935 until his death in 1962. (His statue was installed in 1966.)

Agoyo began to campaign for a second statue to celebrate Popé. "It took six years to get it through the state legislature," Agoyo told me. "There was opposition from the residents of Española. There was lots of negative stuff. The bill was finally signed in 1997."

Clifford Fragua, a sculptor from Jemez, was chosen to craft the statue. In May 2002, he made a ceremonial tap of hammer on chisel as he chipped loose the first piece of a seven-ton block of marble. Fragua, who is still at work on the sculpture, has a tricky task, for no one today has any idea what Popé looked like. It was Fragua who chose the pinkish-brown marble block, shipped to his studio from a quarry in Tennessee. "I have chosen the stone because it spoke to me," he told the *Albuquerque Journal*. "It has the color of Earth. It has the color of Indian people."

From Sayshukwa, I drove farther north into the national forest, winding my way on increasingly vestigial dirt roads to an obscure clearing among the Ponderosas. An hour before sunset, I parked and set up camp. The unseasonal cold of early May still gripped the upland forest, but as the sun went down, the wind died.

The temperature plunged to 15 degrees Fahrenheit, and the water froze solid in my drinking bottles. I huddled before a campfire of sticks, trying to get warm. The stars seemed to glitter preternaturally. In the middle of the night, snug in my sleeping bag, I half wakened to the distant howl of coyotes.

The next morning, in chilly sunlight, I hiked south through the trailless forest, paying close attention to the invisible contour lines in my head. The wind picked up again. I passed by a big tuff boulder, engraved with a huge kachina face that glared blankly back at me. At last I came to another clearing. Swales of cholla-covered earth billowed into the distance. For the next several hours, I slowly walked the site, reading its buried architecture.

I had made my way to the largest of all the ancestral Jemez ruins, a pueblo where some 1,850 rooms once enclosed five plazas, sheltering fourteen kivas. The true meaning of the Jemez name of the site has been lost even to elders such as Joe Sando. The village was occupied long before the time of Coronado, and for at least a century afterward. It is barely possible that Oñate spent a single day here in 1598, but only if his vaguely defined "great pueblo" requiring a steep ascent can be correlated with this distant village. On the other hand, writing in 1982, Joe Sando insisted that this pueblo "was obviously never visited by the Spaniards, since it has never been mentioned in print before."

At 7,880 feet above sea level, the massive settlement stands only forty feet lower than Sayshukwa. Exactly how, during the fourteenth and fifteenth centuries, the Jemez mastered a highland style of life as no other Puebloans ever did, remains a cultural and archaeological mystery. Scattered through the Santa Fe National Forest are the ruins of no fewer than two dozen high mesa-top villages, each of them com-

Among them, I would single out historians Carroll L. Riley, John L. Kessell, and Marc Simmons. Other students of the field whom I communicated with only by telephone or by e-mail, but who, every one of them, gave unstintingly of their expertise, include historians and editors Rick Hendricks and John P. Wilson, Zuni experts Keith Kintigh and T. J. Ferguson, linguist and Hopi specialist Ekkehart Malotki, founders of the Cíbola Project Barbara De Marco and Jerry Craddock, University of Pennsylvania archaeologists Robert W. Preucel and Matthew J. Liebmann, tree ring virtuoso Ron Towner, and Farmington Bureau of Land Management archaeologist Jim Copeland.

A bevy of other scholars dropped their more serious duties to invite me into their offices, where I spent magical hours learning arcana and incunabula I would never have otherwise guessed—as well as steeping myself in the accumulated wisdom of their professional journeys. They include ace-of-all-trades generalists Stephen Lekson and Eric Blinman; Dinétah scholars Larry Baker and Richard Wilshusen; Hopi experts Peter Whiteley and Kurt and Cindy Dongoske; Santa Fe history aficionada Cordelia Snow; Polly Schaafsma, the leading expert on Southwestern rock art, and her iconoclast husband, Curtis Schaafsma; David Hurst Thomas, a "big-picture" guy if there ever was one; and advisers-at-large David Grant Noble, John Roney, and Kurt Anschuetz (who had written a screenplay about the Pueblo Revolt that reached important Hollywood eyes). Rudy Fernández, head of the Santa Fe Fiesta Council, willingly shared the traditional Hispanic view of the great conflict, even as he suspected that I strongly disagreed with it. Finally, I must tip my cap to Bill Whatley, then archaeologist for Jemez Pueblo, who one frosty morning a decade ago first set the mysteries of the Revolt buzzing in my brain.

Several other scholars and enthusiasts not only tolerated my invasion of their offices, but laced up their boots to guide me to well-hidden sites in the field. It's hard to call hiking in New Mexico "research," but I retain vivid memories, suffused with gratitude, of my outing at Old Kotyiti with Santa Fe National Forest archaeologist Mike Bremer; of our tour of Sayshukwa, high in the Ponderosas, with Bremer's colleague Mike Elliott; of a day rambling through Bandelier backwaters with park archaeologist Rory Gauthier; of Katherine Wells's private tour of the rock art wonders on her own land; and of project volunteer Bill Baxter's patient tour, on one of the coldest and nastiest days of spring 2003, of the San Marcos ruins and the Cerrillos turquoise mines.

Despite the habitual secrecy, sometimes approaching a (well-earned) xenophobia, that obtains among the pueblos today, I gained irreplaceable insights from a number of savvy Puebloans. Without my consultations with Herman Agoyo at San Juan, Jemez historian Joe Sando at the Indian Pueblo Cultural Center, Tessie Naranjo from Santa Clara, Peter Pino at Zia, and Brian Vallo at Acoma, my understanding of the Pueblo legacy of the Revolt would have been infinitely poorer. Two Puebloan guides—Gary Tso at Hopi and Lena Tsethlikia at Zuni—led me on memorable private tours of sites that would otherwise have been off-limits to me. (Joseph and Janice Day, who run the Tsakurshovi trading post on Hopi's Second Mesa, gave me a warm welcome and introduced me to Gary Tso.) Leo Patricio, tour guide at Acoma, delivered a passionate recitation of syncretic wisdom that still has me scratching my head a year later. And I will confess a grudging gratitude to the Jemez Cultural Committee for agreeing to meet with me at all, regardless of how discouraging that meeting turned out to be—as well as an ungrudging gratitude to Mehrdad Khatibi and Tom Lucero of the Jemez Department of Resource Protection for making that meeting happen.

Most of my forays into the New Mexico backcountry were undertaken alone, but several companions shared blissful hiking days with me as I hunted down the half-lost pivot points of the Revolt. They are Sharon Roberts, Susan Robertson, Tom and Elise Noble, and Inna Livitz. Each of these companions deepened my appreciation of what an ambiguous landscape might signify, and Inna also performed invaluable work locating source materials both in Cambridge and in Santa Fe.

Not all my so-called research, alas, was prosecuted among the piñon-juniper mesas of New Mexico. I spent many an hour in libraries and archives, where my searches often yielded pleasures of a subtler kind than stumbling upon ruins and rock art. By far the most valuable such institution was the Laboratory of Anthropology of the Museum of Indian Arts and Culture in Santa Fe, where I spent weeks poring through obscure articles, typescripts, and site reports. Librarian Mara Yarbrough served as my sure-footed guide to that priceless but labyrinthine collection, which she seemed to know her way through in the dark; by the end, we had become good friends as well. Assistant librarian Minnie Murray skillfully leapt into the breach whenever Mara wasn't available.

Other Santa Fe repositories that aided my quest were the School of American Research, the Chavez Historical Library at the Palace of the Governors, and the New Mexico State Records Center and Archives. In Albuquerque, I benefited from the Center for Southwest Research at the University of New Mexico and from the Indian Pueblo Cultural Center. Elsewhere in New Mexico, the Salmon Ruins Bureau of Land Management headquarters and the Santa Fe National Forest office proved helpful. In Cambridge, where I live, I would have ground to a halt early on without the incomparable resources of the Widener and Tozzer libraries at Harvard, upon which I depended weekly when I was not on truant sabbatical in New Mexico. The Harvard Map Collection kindly reproduced for me the 1657 map printed on page 125.

My agent, Stuart Krichevsky, guided my project from start to finish with diligence and support, all the while ensuring—who would have thought it possible?—that I might actually get paid to write a book. His tireless aides in this sleight-of-hand, Shana Cohen and Liz Coen, dotted all the "i"s, crossed all the "t"s, and still seemed glad to see me when I dropped by the office.

At Simon & Schuster, Johanna Li, Gypsy da Silva, and Frederick Chase performed their often thankless chores with their usual perspicacity and their usual enthusiasm, for which I continue to be lastingly grateful. As for my editor, Bob Bender, I am tempted to write, "Please see encomiums in my previous seven books." There comes a point when effusions of acknowledgment run the risk of verging on the fulsome, and Bob Bender is the sort of modest fellow who is easily embarrassed by praise. But, darn it all, Bob, you've done it again—made me happy beyond words (a dangerous state for a writer) to work with the finest editor I've ever known or ever heard about.

# ANNOTATED BIBLIOGRAPHY

## PRIMARY SOURCES

De Marco, Barbara, and Jerry R. Craddock. "Letter to the Viceroy, dated 19 June 1693, from the Franciscan Procurador General, Fray Francisco de Ayeta." Unpublished ms.

▪ This and the following two publications represent some of the first fruits of the Cíbola Project, an ambitious enterprise that is retranslating hundreds of Spanish colonial documents from the original autographs (Hackett and Shelby worked from transcribed copies), as well as publishing many documents for the first time.

De Marco, Barbara. "Voices from the Archives, Part 1: Testimony of the Pueblo Indians in the 1680 Pueblo Revolt." *Romance Philology*, vol. 53, no. 2, Spring 2000, pp. 375–448.

▪ Full, authoritative Spanish texts, with English summaries, of the crucial testimonies of the nine Puebloans captured by Otermín during his failed attempt to reconquer New Mexico in 1681.

De Marco, Barbara. "Voices from the Archives, Part 2: Ayeta's 1693 Letter to the Viceroy." *Romance Philology*, vol. 53, no. 2, Spring 2000, pp. 449–508.

▪ Authoritative Spanish text of Ayeta's important summary of the Revolt, published here for the first time. "Letter to the Viceroy," above, is a rough-draft English translation.

Escalante, Fray Silvestre Vélez de. *Letter of the Father Fray Silvestre Vélez de Escalante Written on the 2d of April, in the Year 1778*. Ramona, California: 1983.
■ A tantalizing document, because Escalante summarizes materials that have since vanished.

Espinosa, J. Manuel. *The Pueblo Indian Revolt of 1696 and the Franciscan Missions in New Mexico*. Norman, Oklahoma: 1988.
■ Documentary record of primary sources, translated into English, for the last, failed revolt of 1696. In part superseded by Kessell, Hendricks, and Dodge, *Blood on the Boulders* (q.v.).

Hackett, Charles Wilson, editor. *Historical Documents Relating to New Mexico, Nueva Viscaya, and Approaches Thereto to 1773* (three volumes). Washington, D.C.: 1923–37.
■ An ambitious compilation of English translations of primary colonial texts originally collected by Adolph F. A. and Fanny R. Bandelier in the 1880s. Volume 3 is especially valuable for New Mexico.

Hackett, Charles Wilson, and Charmion Clair Shelby, editors. *Revolt of the Pueblo Indians of New Mexico, and Otermín's Attempted Reconquest, 1680–1682* (two volumes). Albuquerque: 1942.
■ The monumental collection, in English translation, of scores of original Spanish documents pertaining to the Revolt. But see also Barbara De Marco, above.

Hammond, George P., editor. *Don Juan de Oñate and the Founding of New Mexico*. Santa Fe: 1927.
■ Equally monumental compilation of primary sources, in English translation, for Oñate's conquest of New Mexico in 1598–99. See also Hammond and Rey, *Don Juan de Oñate: Colonizer of New Mexico*, below.

Hammond, George P., editor. *The Rediscovery of New Mexico, 1580–1594*. Albuquerque: 1966.
■ Collection of primary documents for the five Spanish expeditions of exploration and attempted conquest between Coronado and Oñate.

Hammond, George P., and Agapito Rey, editors. *Don Juan de Oñate: Colonizer of New Mexico, 1595–1628* (two volumes). Albuquerque: 1953.

■  Updated and fuller version of *Don Juan de Oñate and the Founding of New Mexico*, above.

Hammond, George P., and Agapito Rey, editors. *Narratives of the Coronado Expedition, 1540–1542*. Albuquerque: 1940.
■  The canonical collection of texts for what we know from firsthand sources of Coronado's colossal yet still mysterious exploration of the Southwest from 1540 to 1542.

Hendricks, Rick, and John P. Wilson, editors. *The Navajos in 1705: Roque Madrid's Campaign Journal*. Albuquerque: 1996.
■  Recently published for the first time in English, Roque Madrid's vivid diary of his punitive raid through the Dinétah in 1705.

Kessell, John L., and Rick Hendricks, editors. *By Force of Arms: The Journals of Don Diego de Vargas, New Mexico, 1691–93*. Albuquerque: 1992.
■  This and the following two entries—four of the six magisterial volumes devoted to Vargas's diaries, personal letters, and reports—give an exquisitely detailed account of the bitter and complex campaign of reconquest from 1692 to 1696. See also Espinosa, The Pueblo Indian Revolt of 1696.

Kessell, John L., Rick Hendricks, and Meredith D. Dodge, editors. *To the Royal Crown Restored: The Journals of Don Diego de Vargas, New Mexico, 1692–94*. Albuquerque: 1995.

Kessell, John L., Rick Hendricks, and Meredith D. Dodge, editors. *Blood on the Boulders: The Journals of Don Diego de Vargas, New Mexico, 1694–97* (two volumes). Albuquerque: 1998.

Malotki, Ekkehart, editor. Michael Lomatuway'ma, Lorena Lomatuway'ma, and Sidney Namingha, Jr., narrators. *Hopi Ruin Legends: Kiqötutuwutsi*. Lincoln, Nebraska: 1993.
■  Contains the most complete and at the same time puzzling account ever gleaned from oral tradition of the destruction of the Hopi pueblo of Awatovi by other Hopis in 1700.

Morrow, Baker H., editor. *A Harvest of Reluctant Souls: The Memorial of Fray Alonso de Benavides, 1630*. Boulder, Colorado: 1996.
■  New translation of the important *Memorial* by the first head of the Inquisition in New Mexico, in some sense the first ethnography of the territory ever written.

Pupo-Walker, Enrique, editor. *Castaways: The Narrative of Alvar Núñez Cabeza de Vaca.* Berkeley: 1993.
■ One of many translations of Cabeza de Vaca's narrative of the astounding journey of the first Europeans ever to enter the Southwest.

Sariñana y Cuenca, Dr. Ysidro. *The Franciscan Martyrs of 1680: Funeral Oration over the Twenty-one Franciscan Missionaries Killed by the Pueblo Indians, August 10, 1680.* Santa Fe: 1906.

Villagrá, Gaspar de. Translated by Gilberto Espinosa. *Historia de la Nueva México.* Los Angeles: 1933.
■ Prose translation of the clumsy and florid epic poem written by one of Oñate's lieutenants, which nonetheless has considerable value as a firsthand account of the conquest.


## SECONDARY SOURCES

Adams, E. Charles. *The Origin and Development of the Pueblo Katsina Cult.* Tucson: 1991.
■ With Polly Schaafsma, *Kachinas in the Pueblo World* (q.v.), the most penetrating analysis yet published of the evolution of the kachina phenomenon, which transformed Puebloan culture after A.D. 1325.

Agoyo, Herman, editor. *When Cultures Meet: Remembering San Gabriel del Yunge Oweenge.* Santa Fe: 1987.
■ Papers from a 1984 conference dealing with the short-lived first Spanish capital of New Mexico.

Anschuetz, Kurt. "The Significance of Popé's Summoning of Caudi, Tilini, and Telume at Blue Lake." Unpublished ms.

Anschuetz, Kurt F., et al. *"That Place People Talk About": The Petroglyph National Monument Ethnographic Landscape Report.* Albuquerque: 2002.
■ A provocative gathering of the testimonies of living Puebloans as to the meaning and sacredness of a body of prehistoric rock art that is seriously threatened by the expansion of Albuquerque's suburbs.

Ball, Jane Anne. "Contradiction and Compliance in a New Mexico Pueblo." Unpublished Ph.D. dissertation, University of Minnesota, 1990.
■ A testament to scholarly frustration: Ball's account of her fifteen-month

attempt to study factionalism at Jemez. Useful for its keen insights into how secrecy functions today among the pueblos.

Bandelier, Adolph F. A. *Final Report of Investigations Among the Indians of the Southwestern United States Carried on Mainly in the Years from 1880 to 1885* (two volumes). Cambridge, Massachusetts: 1890 and 1892.

■ The first great archaeological and ethnographic report from the heart of the Pueblo world.

Barrett, Elinore M. *Conquest and Catastrophe: Changing Rio Grande Settlement Patterns in the Sixteenth and Seventeenth Centuries.* Albuquerque: 2002.

■ The best attempt yet published at sorting out the identities, locations, and histories of the scores of variously named pueblos reported by early Spanish explorers in New Mexico.

Benedict, Ruth. *Tales of the Cochiti Indians.* Washington, D.C.: 1931.

■ Contains an interesting early oral story of the last stages of the migration of the Cochiti people from the Pajarito Plateau to the north.

Beninato, Stephanie. "Popé, Pose-yemu, and Naranjo: A New Look at the Leadership in the Pueblo Revolt of 1680." *New Mexico Historical Review,* vol. 65, no. 4, October 1990, pp. 417–35.

Bloom, Lansing B., and Lynn B. Mitchell. "The Chapter Elections in 1672." *New Mexico Historical Review,* vol. 13, 1938, pp. 85–119.

■ A key early piece of research on Jemez during the seventeenth century.

Bolton, Hubert E. *Coronado, Knight of Pueblos and Plains.* Albuquerque: 1949.

Brandt, Elizabeth A. "On Secrecy and Control of Knowledge: Taos Pueblo," in Tefft, *Secrecy: A Cross-Cultural Perspective.*

■ A compelling argument, based in part on fieldwork at Taos, that Puebloan secrecy, far more than simply a response to Spanish oppression, is intrinsic to the culture.

Brugge, David M. "Navajo Archaeology: A Promising Past," in Towner, *The Archaeology of Navajo Origins.*

■ Contra Towner, *Defending the Dinétah,* Brugge argues for a thorough intermixing of Navajo and Puebloan peoples in the Dinétah.

Carlson, R. L. *Eighteenth Century Navajo Fortresses of the Gobernador District.* Boulder, Colorado: 1965.

■ Carlson used Earl Morris's field notes on pueblito ruins in the Dinétah as the basis for this article, the locus classicus for the argument that the pueblitos were of Puebloan, not Navajo, design.

Chávez, Fray Angelico. "Pohé-yemo's Representative and the Pueblo Revolt of 1680." *New Mexico Historical Review,* vol. 42, no. 2, April 1967, pp. 85–126.
■ An intriguing if far-fetched thesis about the ringleaders of the Revolt, seriously compromised, however, by Chávez's condescension toward Puebloans.

Cordell, Linda S. *Archaeology of the Southwest.* San Diego: 1997.
■ The classic general survey of Southwestern prehistory.

Defouri, Very Rev. James H. *The Martyrs of New Mexico: A Brief Account of the Lives and Deaths of the Earliest Missionaries in the Territory.* Las Vegas, New Mexico: 1893.
■ A quirky, quasi-omniscient early account of the lamentable deaths of Franciscan priests at the hands of "savage" Indians.

Dongoske, Kurt E., and Cindy K. Dongoske. "History in Stone: Evaluating Spanish Conversion Efforts through Hopi Rock Art," in Preucel, *Archaeologies of the Pueblo Revolt,* pp. 114–31.
■ Definitive analysis of little-known rock art panels below Antelope Mesa.

Dougherty, Julia D. *Refugee Pueblos on the Santa Fe National Forest.* Santa Fe: 1980.
■ Preliminary survey of some of the ruins of the refugee pueblos attacked by Vargas in 1694.

Dozier, Edward P. *The Pueblo Indians of North America.* New York: 1970.
■ Excellent survey of Puebloan history and culture by a Puebloan from Santa Clara. Contains a possibly biased explanation of why the Puebloans exercised restraint instead of attacking Otermín's caravan as it moved down the Rio Grande in 1680.

Elliott, Michael L. *Large Pueblo Sites Near Jemez Springs, New Mexico.* Santa Fe: 1982.
■ This and *Archaeological Investigations at Small Sites* (q.v.) are the definitive field surveys of ancestral Jemez sites in the Santa Fe National Forest.

Elliott, Michael L. "Mission and Mesa: Some Thoughts on the Archaeology of the Pueblo Revolt Era Sites in the Jemez Region, New Mexico," in Preucel, *Archaeologies of the Pueblo Revolt,* pp. 45–60.

■ A shrewd attempt at sorting out the identities and histories of the various seventeenth-century missions among the Jemez.

Elliott, Michael L., Sandra L. Marshall, and J. Andrew Darling. *Archaeological Investigations at Small Sites in the Jemez Mountains, New Mexico.* Santa Fe: 1988.
■ See Elliott, *Large Pueblo Sites,* above.

Ferguson, T. J. "Dowa Yalanne: The Architecture of Zuni Resistance and Social Change during the Pueblo Revolt," in Preucel, *Archaeologies of the Pueblo Revolt,* pp. 33–44.
■ Deft use of architectural survey to reconstruct the history of the Zuni refugee pueblo from 1680 to 1692.

Flint, Richard, and Shirley Cushing Flint, editors. *The Coronado Expedition to Tierra Nueva.* Boulder, Colorado: 1997.
■ Collection of papers representing the latest research on Coronado. Includes Edmund J. Ladd's "Zuni on the Day the Men in Metal Arrived."

Folsom, Franklin. *Red Power on the Rio Grande: The Native American Revolution of 1680.* Chicago: 1973.
■ A novel that, despite its title, retells the story of the Revolt from a thoroughly pro-Puebloan point of view. Quite readable, but cannot be taken seriously as history.

Forbes, Jack D. *Apache, Navaho, and Spaniard.* Norman, Oklahoma: 1960.
■ A controversial manifesto, written by a Native American, arguing for much greater cooperation and interaction between Puebloans and Athapaskans in the sixteenth and seventeenth centuries than other scholars have believed took place. See also Curtis F. Schaafsma, "Pueblo and Apachean Alliance Formation in the Seventeenth Century."

Ford, Richard I., Albert Schroeder, and Stewart L. Peckham. "Three Perspectives on Puebloan Prehistory," in Ortiz, *New Perspectives on the Pueblos.*
■ A rigorous attempt to trace pre-contact migrations and movements among the various Puebloan peoples.

Garcia-Mason, Velma. "Acoma Pueblo," in Ortiz, *Handbook of North American Indians, Volume 9: Southwest,* pp. 450–66.

Gibson, Daniel. *Pueblos of the Rio Grande: A Visitor's Guide.* Tucson: 2001.
■ Useful guidebook for tourists visiting today's pueblos.

Givens, Douglas R. *Alfred Vincent Kidder and the Development of Americanist Archaeology.* Albuquerque: 1992.

Gunn, John M. *Schat-chen: History, Traditions and Narratives of the Queres Indians of Laguna and Acoma.* Albuquerque: 1917.
- The first ethnographic work published about Acoma.

Gutiérrez, Ramón A. *When Jesus Came, the Corn Mothers Went Away: Marriage, Sexuality, and Power in New Mexico, 1500–1846.* Stanford, California: 1991.
- Highly controversial and original analysis of colonial New Mexico history in terms of marriage and sexuality. Gutiérrez has been accused of a strong anti-Franciscan bias.

Harbert, Nancy. "A Land Left Behind." *American Archaeology,* vol. 3, no. 3, Fall 1999, pp. 18–25.
- Popular account of Galisteo Basin pueblos.

Harrington, John P. *The Ethnogeography of the Tewa Indians.* Washington, D.C.: 1916.
- Brilliant but controversial early work linking oral traditions with sites located on the ground (Harrington's maps are extraordinary). The book is considered offensive today by many Tewa people.

Hendricks, Rick. "Pueblo-Spanish Warfare in Seventeenth-Century New Mexico: The Battles of Black Mesa, Kotyiti, and Astialakwa," in Preucel, *Archaeologies of the Pueblo Revolt,* pp. 181–97.
- Superb résumé of the three pivotal battles Vargas fought against refugee pueblos in 1694.

Hewett, Edgar L. *Pajarito Plateau and Its Ancient People.* Albuquerque: 1938.
- A charming memoir distilling decades of work in and around Bandelier National Monument.

Hibben, Frank C. *Kiva Art of the Anasazi at Pottery Mound.* Las Vegas, Nevada: 1975.
- The only record of the most astounding set of kiva murals ever found in the Southwest—layer upon layer of polychrome paintings destroyed forever by the team that excavated them in the 1950s. See also Lister, *Behind Painted Walls.*

Hickerson, Nancy Parrott. *The Jumanos: Hunters and Traders of the South Plains.* Austin, Texas: 1994.

■ Diligent attempt to fix the identity of a shadowy people who, forming a buffer group to the pueblos on the southeast, may have been partly Puebloan themselves.

Hoebel, E. Adamson. "Zia Pueblo," in Ortiz, *Handbook of North American Indians, Volume 9: Southwest*, pp. 407–17.

Hogan, Patrick. "Navajo-Pueblo Interaction During the Gobernador Phase: A Reassessment of the Evidence," in Marshall and Hogan, *Rethinking Navajo Pueblitos*.
■ One of the strongest arguments that the pueblitos in Dinétah were built almost solely by Navajos rather than Puebloans.

John, Elizabeth A. H. *Storms Brewed in Other Men's Worlds: The Confrontation of Indians, Spanish, and French in the Southwest, 1540–1795*. Norman, Oklahoma: 1975.
■ Vast, ambitious survey of many campaigns by Europeans against Indians all over the Southwest during the sixteenth, seventeenth, and eighteenth centuries.

Kessell, John L. *Kiva, Cross, and Crown: The Pecos Indians and New Mexico, 1540–1840*. Tucson: 1987.
■ Definitive history of Pecos Pueblo.

Knaut, Andrew L. *The Pueblo Revolt of 1680*. Norman, Oklahoma: 1995.
■ A dry, conservative scholarly account of the Revolt, which oddly minimizes the Puebloan achievement.

Ladd, Edmund J. "Zuni on the Day the Men in Metal Arrived," in Flint and Flint, *The Coronado Expedition to Tierra Nueva*, pp. 225–33.
■ Transcription of an informal lecture in which the Zuni-born scholar whimsically imagines the arrivals of Esteban and Coronado at Hawikuh.

Lambert, Marjorie F. *Paa-ko: Archaeological Chronicle of an Indian Village in North Central New Mexico*. Albuquerque: 1954.

Lang, Richard W. "Archaeological Survey of the Upper San Cristóbal Arroyo Drainage, Galisteo Basin, Santa Fe County, New Mexico." Unpublished ms. (1977).

Lange, Charles H., and Carroll Riley, editors. *The Southwestern Journals of Adolph F. Bandelier, 1880–1882*. Santa Fe: 1966.

Lee, Morgan. "Movement Pushes Dialogue on Popé." *Albuquerque Journal*, February 26, 2001.
■ Newspaper account of the controversy over Popé's nomination for second New Mexico figure to have a commemorative statue erected in the U.S. Capitol building.

Lentz, Andrew. "Bronze Oñate Receives New Foot." *Rio Grande Sun* (Española), January 22, 1998.
■ This and the following article are newspaper accounts of the "amputation" of the foot of Oñate's statue on the 400th anniversary of the conquest.

Lentz, Andrew. "Who Has Oñate's Missing Foot?" *Rio Grande Sun* (Española), January 15, 1998.

Liebmann, Matthew J. "Signs of Power and Resistance: The (Re)Creation of Christian Imagery and Identities in the Pueblo Revolt Era," in Preucel, *Archaeologies of the Pueblo Revolt*, pp. 132–44.
■ Clever and convincing analysis of a single figure carved inside a cavate dwelling at Bandelier National Monument, arguing for the assimilation by Puebloan artists of kachina imagery with European traditions of painting saints and the Virgin.

Linthicum, Leslie. "Rebel on a Pedestal." *Albuquerque Journal*, May 11, 2002.
■ Newspaper account of commencement of work by Jemez sculptor Clifford Fragua on Popé's statue.

Lister, Florence C. *Behind Painted Walls: Incidents in Southwestern Archaeology*. Albuquerque: 2000.
■ Contains a no-holds-barred account of the desecration of Pottery Mound. See also Hibben, *Kiva Art of the Anasazi at Pottery Mound*.

Lummis, Charles F. *Some Strange Corners of Our Country*. New York: 1906.
■ Contains "The Stone Autograph-Album," Lummis's prescient paean to El Morro, or Inscription Rock.

Lummis, Charles F. *The Land of Poco Tiempo*. New York: 1893.
■ A classic hymn of praise to New Mexico, containing "The Wanderings of Cochiti," a lyrical if now somewhat discredited reimagining of the migration of the Cochiti people from Frijoles Canyon to their present pueblo.

Marshall, Michael P., and Patrick Hogan. *Rethinking Navajo Pueblitos*. Farmington, New Mexico: 1991.

■ One of the first and most important reassessments of pueblitos, claiming they are almost exclusively of Navajo, rather than Puebloan, origin. See also Towner, *Defending the Dinétah*.

May, Glenn. "Walking in the Footsteps of History." *Rio Grande Sun* (Española), January 8, 1998.
■ Newspaper account of Hispanic hiker's attempt to retrace Oñate's route on foot during the 400th anniversary of the conquest.

Mednick, Christina Singleton. *San Cristóbal: Voices and Visions of the Galisteo Basin*. Santa Fe: 1996.
■ Lavish picture book about Galisteo Basin.

Miller, Jay. "Ashes to the Moon, Oñate's Missing Foot Provide Fun." *Rio Grande Sun* (Española), January 22, 1998.
■ Ironic editorial about the theft of the Oñate statue's foot. See also Lentz, "Bronze Oñate Receives New Foot" and "Who Has Oñate's Missing Foot?"

Minge, Ward Alan. *Acoma: Pueblo in the Sky*. Albuquerque: 1991.
■ Definitive history and account of modern Acoma, the only book of its kind approved by the pueblo.

Naranjo, Tessie. "Thoughts on Two World Views." *Federal Archaeology*, vol. 7, no. 3, Fall/Winter 1995, pp. 16–17.

Nelson, N. C. *Pueblo Ruins of the Galisteo Basin, New Mexico*. New York: 1914.
■ The pioneering excavator's report on his digs in Galisteo Basin, including Pueblo Blanco.

Ortiz, Alfonso, editor. *Handbook of North American Indians, Volume 9: Southwest*. Washington, D.C.: 1979.
■ The landmark scholarly compendium, part of a multivolume Smithsonian series covering all the Native Americans on the continent. Somewhat dated, but still invaluable.

Ortiz, Alfonso, editor. *New Perspectives on the Pueblos*. Albuquerque: 1972.
■ Collection of papers on recent Pueblo research. Contains Ford, Schroeder, and Peckham, "Three Perspectives on Puebloan Prehistory."

Ortiz, Alfonso. "Popay's Leadership: A Pueblo Perspective," in Simmons et al., "The Great Pueblo Revolt," pp. 18–22.

■ The San Juan Pueblo scholar's effort to ferret out the significance of otherwise arcane details about Popé.

Ortiz, Alfonso. "Some Concerns Central to the Writing of 'Indian' History." *The Indian Historian*, vol. 10, no. 1, Winter 1977, pp. 17–22.

Ortiz, Alfonso. *The Tewa World: Space, Time, Being, and Becoming in a Pueblo Society*. Chicago: 1969.
■ A classic intellectual analysis of the beliefs and worldview of the Tewa, based largely on Ortiz's experience at his home pueblo, San Juan.

Parmentier, Richard J. "The Pueblo Mythological Triangle: Poseyumu, Montezuma, and Jesus in the Pueblos," in Ortiz, *Handbook of North American Indians, Volume 9: Southwest*, pp. 609–22.

Parsons, Elsie Clews. *Pueblo Indian Religion* (two volumes). Chicago: 1939.
■ Sprawling, comprehensive anthology of origin, migration, and other myths among all the pueblos. Dated today, but includes much information no ethnographer could now gain access to. See also Tyler, *Pueblo Gods and Myths*.

Parsons, Elsie Clews. *The Pueblo of Jemez*. New Haven, Connecticut: 1925.
■ Classic ethnography of Jemez, containing much information the Jemez people feel should never have been shared with outsiders.

"Popé Played Key Historical Role." *Albuquerque Journal*, February 28, 2001.
■ Newspaper editorial in favor of Popé statue.

Preucel, Robert W., editor. *Archaeologies of the Pueblo Revolt: Identity, Meaning, and Renewal in the Pueblo World*. Albuquerque: 2002.
■ Papers from a Society for American Archaeology conference: the most important recent work on the Pueblo Revolt. See also listings of individual chapters by K. and C. Dongoske, Elliott, Ferguson, Hendricks, Liebmann, C. Schaafsma, Suina, and Whiteley.

Preucel, Robert W. "Living on the Mesa: Hanat Kotyiti, A Post-Revolt Cochiti Community in Northern New Mexico." *Expedition*, vol. 42, no. 1, 2000, pp. 8–17.
■ Popular account of survey of Old Kotyiti refugee pueblo.

Preucel, Robert W., et al. *The Kotyiti Research Project: Report of the 1996 Field Season*. Santa Fe: 1998.
■ Field report of same.

Reed, Eric K. "The Southern Tewa Pueblos in the Historic Period." *El Palacio*, vol. 50, no. 11, November 1943, pp. 254–64, 276–89.

Reff, Daniel T. "The 'Predicament of Culture' and Spanish Missionary Accounts of the Tepehuan and Pueblo Revolts." *Ethnohistory*, vol. 42, no. 1, Winter 1995, pp. 63–90.

Reiter, Paul. *The Jemez Pueblo of Unshagi, New Mexico.* Santa Fe: 1938.

Riley, Carroll L. "Puaray and Coronado's Tiguex." *Archaeological Society of New Mexico Anthropological Papers*, vol. 6, 1981, pp. 197–213.
■  Attempt to identify the pueblo villages devastated by Coronado in 1541.

Riley, Carroll L. *Río del Norte: People of the Upper Rio Grande from Earliest Times to the Pueblo Revolt.* Salt Lake City: 1995.
■  Readable and well-informed history of colonial New Mexico, partly superseded by *The Kachina and the Cross.*

Riley, Carroll L. *The Kachina and the Cross: Indians and Spaniards in the Early Southwest.* Salt Lake City: 1999.
■  The best modern history of colonial New Mexico.

Roberts, David. *In Search of the Old Ones: Exploring the Anasazi World of the Southwest.* New York: 1996.

Sando, Joe S. "Jemez Pueblo," in Ortiz, *Handbook of North American Indians, Volume 9: Southwest*, pp. 418–29.

Sando, Joe S. *Nee Hemish: A History of Jemez Pueblo.* Albuquerque: 1982.
■  The Jemez-born scholar's fascinating history of his home pueblo, often condemned by conservative Jemez elders.

Sando, Joe S. "Popé and the Pueblo Revolt" and "Aftermath of the Revolt," in *Pueblo Profiles: Cultural Identity Through Centuries of Change.* Santa Fe: 1998.
■  Sando's reconstruction of the movements and the very speeches of the architects of the Revolt.

Sando, Joe S. *Pueblo Nations: Eight Centuries of Pueblo Indian History.* Santa Fe: 1992.
■  The history of Spanish-Puebloan conflict in New Mexico, from the Puebloan point of view.

Sando, Joe S. "The Pueblo Revolt," in Ortiz, *Handbook of North American Indians, Volume 9: Southwest,* pp. 194–97.

Schaafsma, Curtis F. *Apaches de Navajo: Seventeenth-Century Navajos in the Chama Valley of New Mexico.* Salt Lake City: 2002.

■ Controversial new thesis attempting to prove that many ruins in the Chama district were those of Navajo peoples before they moved to the Dinétah, rather than those of Tewa, as commonly believed.

Schaafsma, Curtis F. "Pueblo and Apachean Alliance Formation in the Seventeenth Century," in Preucel, *Archaeologies of the Pueblo Revolt,* pp. 198–211.

■ Argument for greater Apache-Pueblo cooperation than is usually believed. See also Forbes, *Apache, Navaho, and Spaniard.*

Schaafsma, Curtis F. "The Tiguex Province Revisited: The Rio Medio Survey." *Collected Papers of the Archaeological Society of New Mexico,* vol. 13, 1987, pp. 6–13.

Schaafsma, Polly, editor. *Kachinas in the Pueblo World.* Albuquerque: 1994.

■ A collection of papers from a 1991 symposium. With Adams, *The Origin and Development of the Pueblo Katsina Cult* (q.v.), the most penetrating analysis yet published of the evolution of the kachina phenomenon, which transformed Puebloan culture after A.D. 1325.

Schaafsma, Polly. *Indian Rock Art of the Southwest.* Santa Fe: 1980.

■ Definitive work on the pictographs and petroglyphs of the greater Southwest.

Schaafsma, Polly. *Rock Art in New Mexico.* Santa Fe: 1992.

■ The locus classicus for the argument that Puebloan refugees in the Dinétah taught the Navajo how to make rock art.

Schaafsma, Polly. "War Imagery and Magic: Petroglyphs at Comanche Gap, Galisteo Basin, New Mexico." Unpublished ms. (1990).

Schaafsma, Polly. *Warrior, Shield, and Star: Imagery and Ideology of Pueblo Warfare.* Santa Fe: 2000.

■ With previous article, a brilliant analysis of one section of Galisteo Basin rock art as a war shrine for Puebloans during the centuries before the coming of the Spanish.

Towner, Ronald H. *Defending the Dinétah: Pueblitos in the Ancestral Navajo Heartland.* Salt Lake City: 2003.
- A tour de force of tree ring analysis aimed at establishing that the pueblitos were almost entirely built by Navajos as defense against Utes, not by Puebloans as defense against the Spanish. But see Brugge, "Navajo Archaeology: A Promising Past."

Towner, Ronald H., editor. *The Archaeology of Navajo Origins.* Salt Lake City: 1996.
- Contains David Brugge's "Navajo Archaeology: A Promising Past."

Tyler, Hamilton A. *Pueblo Gods and Myths.* Norman, Oklahoma: 1964.
- Supplements and to some extent corrects Parsons, *Pueblo Indian Religion.*

Weber, David J., editor. *What Caused the Pueblo Revolt of 1680?* Boston: 1999.
- Aimed at undergraduate classrooms, a slender collection of extracts from scholars of the Revolt. A good introduction to the subject..

White, Leslie A. *The Acoma Indians.* Washington, D.C.: 1932.
- The first in-depth ethnography of Acoma. Like Parsons on Jemez and Stevenson on Zia, much regretted by today's Puebloans.

Whiteley, Peter. *Bacavi: Journey to Reed Springs.* Flagstaff, Arizona: 1988.

Whiteley, Peter. "Re-imagining Awat'ovi," in Preucel, *Archaeologies of the Pueblo Revolt,* pp. 147–66.
- Probes the rumor heard at Hopi by the anthropologist that peyote was the ultimate cause of the destruction of Awatovi.

Wilshusen, Richard H., Timothy H. Hovezak, and Leslie M. Sesler. *Frances Mesa Alternative Treatment Project, Volume 1.* Dolores, Colorado: 2000.
- Field report of northern Dinétah area. Supports the thesis of very little Puebloan influence on Navajo culture in the area.

Wilson, John P. "Before the Pueblo Revolt: Population Trends, Apache Relations and Pueblo Abandonments in Seventeenth Century New Mexico," in Nancy Fox, editor, *Prehistory and History in the Southwest: Collected Papers in Honor of Alden C. Hayes.* Santa Fe: 1985.

# INDEX